Transforming Lives

Transforming Lives

Analyst and Patient View the Power of Psychoanalytic Treatment

EDITED BY
JOSEPH SCHACHTER

JASON ARONSON
Lanham • Boulder • New York • Toronto • Oxford

Published in the United States of America
by Jason Aronson
An imprint of Rowman & Littlefield Publishers, Inc.

A wholly owned subsidiary of
The Rowman & Littlefield Publishing Group, Inc.
4501 Forbes Boulevard, Suite 200, Lanham, Maryland 20706
www.rowmanlittlefield.com

PO Box 317
Oxford
OX2 9RU, UK

British Library Cataloguing in Publication Information Available

Library of Congress Cataloging-in-Publication Data

Transforming lives : analyst and patient view the power of psychoanalytic treatment / edited by Joseph Schachter.
    p. cm.
  Includes bibliographical references and index.
  ISBN 0-7657-0118-9 (cloth : alk. paper)
  1. Psychotherapy. 2. Psychoanalysis. 3. Therapist and patient. I. Schachter, Joseph, M.D.
  RC480.T675 2005
  616.89'17—dc22   2004023147

Printed in the United States of America

∞™ The paper used in this publication meets the minimum requirements of American National Standard for Information Sciences—Permanence of Paper for Printed Library Materials, ANSI/NISO Z39.48-1992.

Contents

Acknowledgments

I would like to acknowledge the help of several persons who facilitated the writing of this book. The first is my wife, Judith S. Schachter, M.D., who helped me select the seven analyst/authors and who reviewed each of my chapters (and this acknowledgment as well) and made valuable suggestions regarding both content and style. Next, I'd like to express my appreciation to our editor, Eve Golden, M.D., who skillfully and sensitively helped the authors make sure their writing and their tone would be interesting and accessible to our intended audience. Her perspective and talent consolidated the separate elements into a book. Finally, I'd like to commend the four anonymous patients who contributed commentaries about their analyses. Their willingness to tackle and complete a complex and challenging task provides this book with its most unique attribute—the patients' points of view.

Introduction

Joseph Schachter

I have seen people's lives dramatically transformed by psychoanalysis. Yet the decision to undertake this enterprise can seem so formidable that many people deny themselves an extraordinary experience. With this book, my coauthors and I hope to make that decision—admittedly a complex one—better informed, clearer, and easier.

People who are considering psychoanalysis usually struggle with three questions: What does it do? Can I afford it? and What is it like? I will address the first of these questions in this introduction and the second in chapter 10; the answer to the third comprises the body of this book.

Psychoanalysis is a process by which the patient, or *analysand*, learns to recognize and understand the characteristic workings of his or her own mind and the way that hidden feelings and expectations shape our reactions to other people and to our life experiences. These new perspectives allow the patient to make better choices and to pursue more freely desires that are personally meaningful and constructive. Since its introduction more than a century ago, the theory of psychoanalysis has been profoundly influential, both as an approach to healing emotional pain and as a way of looking at the world in general.

Recently, however, psychoanalysis has fallen from grace—at least in the opinion of some—and a furor of social, political, medical, and financial change has obscured its life-transforming potential. There are many reasons for this. In the 1950s and 1960s, psychoanalysis basked in the glow of the psychiatric and psychotherapeutic successes of World War II and thrived in an economically expansive society. At that time, it was the only game in town, and people with emotional problems turned naturally to psychoanalysts, who were in great demand. In the 1970s, other psychotherapies became available. Some of these derived from psychoanalysis, while others—the behavioral therapies, for example—were totally unrelated. In addition, drugs that could (in some

1

cases) directly remediate emotional disturbances became available, and the prospect arose of achieving symptom relief inexpensively and quickly. Costs of medical care were rising, and insurance companies looked for reasons to withdraw coverage of treatments from which they did not profit; psychoanalysis was one of these. The growth of alternative psychotherapies was continuing its exponential rise, while sociopolitical changes (such as the rise of feminism and other revisions of traditional views of gender) raised questions about psychoanalytic theory itself.

Psychoanalysis has been vulnerable to these dynamics in part because its effectiveness has never been empirically established. It has been vulnerable to severe criticism for the same reason. Yet the very nature of psychoanalysis makes any controlled study of treatment outcomes practically impossible. An ideal study requires that a large number of patients be assigned randomly to three groups. One group would then receive psychoanalytic treatment, one some other form of psychotherapy, and one no treatment at all over a period of several years. Yet most people in emotional distress are not willing to leave treatment to that kind of chance; such a patient population would be very hard to find. Because all patient–analyst psychoanalytic pairs are unique, testable generalizations are not easy to establish—another challenge. Finally, improvement in psychoanalysis is a subjective matter that does not lend itself to objective assessment. Changes in clearly defined symptoms may be relatively easy to monitor, but people often undertake analysis for reasons having nothing to do with identifiable behaviors or thoughts. How do we quantify a sense of comfort and satisfaction, the deepening of a marriage, or greater success as a parent? Ways of studying psychoanalytic effectiveness are much sought after (and to a limited extent have been found; these will be discussed in chapter 10), but difficulties such as these have precluded large-scale empirical study of psychoanalytic effectiveness in the past and will remain obstacles to such study in the future.

So how can a troubled person seeking relief decide whether psychoanalysis is worth the substantial investment of effort, time, and money that it requires? Despite the expense and complications, few hesitate to undergo coronary bypass surgery when it is likely to extend life. But the decision to undertake psychoanalytic treatment must be pondered—and made—without empirical guidance or "scientific" support. We're talking about three, four, or even five sessions per week for several years. Insurance companies reimburse rarely (and incompletely) for psychoanalysis, so costs add up unless there is a psychoanalytic institute nearby to provide low-fee clinic treatment. Yet people who have learned from experience that psychoanalysis can be life transforming consider that their time, money, and effort were well spent. What is a transformed life worth?

What Is Psychoanalysis?

Psychoanalysis differs from other psychotherapies in its goals and in its process: how the analyst works with the patient. The degree to which psycho-analysis can be distinguished from other forms of psychotherapy (psychoana-lytic psychotherapy in particular) remains controversial. Such formal charac-teristics as three to five sessions per week or the use of a couch on which the patient lies do not in themselves make a psychoanalysis, nor does their absence preclude one. Some analysts do feel that more frequent sessions result in a process that is qualitatively different from that of the other psychotherapies; other analysts disagree, seeing the two modalities as essentially, qualitatively, the same.

The essential qualitative characteristics of psychoanalysis are the attention paid to the ways that conscious and unconscious feelings and fantasies of both analyst and patient influence the interactions between them. As the analytic part-ners examine these interactions, the patient begins to understand how feelings and expectations of which he or she may not be aware can shape reactions—to the analyst and to other persons as well. The patient learns something about how these feelings and expectations developed earlier in life, the purposes they served then, and what (possibly less useful) purposes they serve now. In exploring the past, the patient develops a meaningful personal narrative that helps explicate the specific ways that he or she has been shaped by past experiences and feelings. Fi-nally, and of great importance, as the work progresses, the patient engages in a series of broadening new experiences with the analyst that he or she may never have had before and that enhance the fluidity of his or her interactions with other persons. We will endeavor to illustrate this process so clearly in these pages that readers will be able to imagine exactly how such enhanced freedom in rela-tionships can indeed transform a life.

Psychoanalysts come to their work from many professions (mainly but not necessarily psychiatry, psychology, and social work). Their long and intensive training includes years of classes and seminars and practice conducting psycho-analytic treatment under the supervision of experienced clinicians. In psychoan-alytic institutes associated with the American Psychoanalytic Association, the oldest and most traditional analytic organization in the United States, psycho-analytic training typically takes eight to ten years. Furthermore, all analysts in training are required to undertake an extensive personal psychoanalysis. This is considered the most important element in analytic training. It ensures that ana-lytic candidates have firsthand experience of being an analytic patient and a good understanding of what the analytic process feels like. It helps them deal more ef-fectively with personal issues that might otherwise interfere with their work with their patients. And it fosters the improved access analysts need to their unconscious feelings and fantasies so that their influence on the psychoanalytic work can be monitored and so that they are optimally useful to that work when necessary. How analysts monitor and use their own feelings and fantasies in the service of an analysis will be amply illustrated in this book.

In this book, we will be dealing with psychoanalysis proper. Generally, psychotherapy is appropriate for limited or specific emotional problems or symptoms, while psychoanalysis is the treatment of choice for people who seek more extensive changes in their fundamental feelings about themselves and in how they relate to others. Since the mechanisms of change in psychotherapy and psychoanalysis are closely related, if not identical, this book may be of interest to those considering psychotherapy as well as those considering psychoanalysis.

In support of my conviction that psychoanalysis can enable great changes, I've collected in this book detailed case reports of seven psychoanalyses in which the patients' lives—in their own judgments—were transformed. My coauthors and I have worked hard to make these studies easy to read and free from technical jargon. Our goal is to give our readers the opportunity to develop an informed opinion about the cause of the dramatic improvements described here. Was it the experience of analysis that accounted for the changes in these seven people's lives? Or was it something else—a chance event, a new relationship, a spontaneous remission of symptoms? I think you may conclude, as I do, that the psychoanalytic treatment was indeed the probable cause of the change and transformation.

To demonstrate the applicability of psychoanalysis to a variety of people and problems, I've chosen case reports of seven quite different patients for your review. Furthermore, no two patients or analysts are alike, and individual patients may work more comfortably with some kinds of analysts than others. This choice is wider now than it once was, as the theory of psychoanalysis is more diverse and encompasses more diverse views of psychoanalytic technique—that is, of how exactly one should conduct a psychoanalysis. Consequently, I have also selected a variety of analysts whose styles range widely from traditional through various nontraditional ways of working. All, however, focus on the examination of unconscious feelings and fantasies that is characteristic of and unique to psychoanalysis.

Evidence suggests that the analyst's personal qualities and values as well as his or her technique may influence the treatment. (These two variables—theory of technique and the analyst's personal qualities and values—may be related since any psychoanalyst is likely to adopt the particular technique that feels most congenial to his or her personality and value system.) Similarly, a patient will probably feel more comfortable with some analysts' personalities and working styles than with others'. This is another reason that I tried to select psychoanalysts with a wide range of explicit personal qualities. The group of seven analysts includes men and women, training analysts and nontraining analysts, Americans and Europeans, heterosexuals and homosexuals, Democrats and Republicans, and, last but not least, people who vacation in the mountains and people who vacation by the sea.

However, my preeminent criterion in selecting the contributors to this book was the excellence of their work. I went not by professional position, publication record, or even general reputation but by my own familiarity with their psychoanalytic work and my confidence in their clinical competence. I considered only analysts to whom I can refer patients confidently and comfortably.

Confidentiality

Of course, whenever psychoanalytic case material is presented, questions of confidentiality arise. This is a matter of utmost seriousness in psychoanalysis. Decades of work have gone into establishing effective ways of sharing certain kinds of clinical material with colleagues (which is necessary to increase knowledge and skill within the field, as it is in medicine and in law) without compromising the identity or secrets of the individuals involved. We have made use of all these ways here. The seven participating analysts are identified by name and by professional biography so that you may satisfy yourselves about their credentials, but they are not identified as the authors of individual case reports. This way, information about the treating psychoanalyst—locale, professional associations, and such other clues—cannot be used to identify the patient. Only the gender of the treating psychoanalyst and of the patient is disclosed. Beyond that, it was left to the seven analysts to decide what disguises to use in their write-ups. Six analysts obtained the patient's permission to publish their reports; the seventh felt that it was not in the patient's best interest to ask permission and relied instead on extensive disguise to protect the patient's privacy.

At best, any effort to document the life-transforming capacity of psychoanalysis will include the patient's view of the experience as well as the analyst's. While this may seem self-evident to laypersons, asking a patient to provide such a view is controversial among analysts for reasons that will be discussed in chapter 9. Certainly analysts' theoretical convictions influence their decisions about whether to make such a request; however, the overriding consideration is the well-being of the patient. In some cases, asking a patient to share aspects of his or her experience may be neutral or even helpful; in others, it may not be. For every patient, the analyst has to decide afresh whether it is appropriate to raise the subject. If the request is made, the patient then will make his or her own decision about whether to contribute. Five of our seven analysts asked their patients if they would like to submit their own views of the analytic experience, to be published alongside of the analyst's report. Four of the five patients took the opportunity, and the inclusion of their impressions is a unique attribute of this book. One patient chose not to contribute, and in two cases the analysts felt that it would not be in the patient's best interest to raise the subject.

The past hundred years have brought to psychoanalysis changes that have increased its effectiveness. To illustrate these changes, I have written a short review of Freud's most successful and still very puzzling case—the patient he codenamed the "Rat Man." In that context, I have discussed some of the ways that this 1907 analysis would likely be quite different if it were to take place today.

Just as Freud and the Rat Man were a unique pair, so are the other seven patient–analyst pairs in this book. Very early in its history, psychoanalysis moved away from a focus on symptoms to a concern for the well-being of the whole person. Individual patients' problems are peculiar to themselves, and so are individual analysts' ways of working. Their personalities, histories, and values are different too, so it is easy to see that each patient–analyst pair must be unique. (This is another part of why it is so extremely difficult to conduct a comparative empirical study of psychoanalytic efficacy. How on earth do you select a matched control group?)

The case reports in this book illustrate just how diverse successful psychoanalytic therapies can be. Sarah's, for example, was conducted in the atmosphere of secure neutrality that is characteristic of traditional analytic treatment; the analyst's carefully maintained anonymity kept Sarah's disorganizing anxiety to a minimum, enabling her to begin for the first time to organize her thoughts, feelings, and behavior. Andrew's analyst worked very differently, using his own life experience to illustrate his view of the world and providing suggestions and guidance that enabled Andrew to make radical changes in his personal and professional relationships. Underneath these differences, however, lay the common factors that seem to be responsible for much of the success of all analyses. Each analyst had a passionate belief in his or her own way of working, was confident in his or her ability to help the patient, and was able to communicate this confidence to the patient. All the analysts were genuinely concerned about their patients, developed fond feelings for them, and transmitted these feelings to them (usually nonverbally). On the patients' side, all seven were committed, persevering, and capable of trust, although several struggled at times with serious doubts. All were able to learn to handle strong feelings.

It is not hard to imagine how an analytic ambience like this could enhance a person's sense of self. To feel lovable and loving, worthwhile and competent, and free to experience and express love and anger in an intimate relationship—which analysis certainly is—can radically alter the way a person lives. On the other hand, there is no indication in these reports of other elements—relationships, events, remissions, and so on—that explain equally plausibly the transformations delineated here.

My own conclusion, therefore, is that psychoanalytic treatment was the effective element of change in these seven patients' lives. I do not mean to imply that psychoanalysis always or even usually achieves such dramatic improvement. But I do want to establish that in some instances it does yield transformative results. We hope that these case studies will prove intriguing in their own right and that they will help our readers think knowledgeably about psychoanalysis and assess its potential as a life-changing enterprise.

CHAPTER 1

An Early Psychoanalytic Success: Freud's Treatment of the "Rat Man"

Joseph Schachter

When Freud was first trying to build his medical practice, his friend and mentor Josef Breuer referred neurotic patients to him. In 1888, Freud, aged thirty-two, tried Breuer's cathartic method with his neurotic patients, by which the patient was asked to report whatever thoughts came to mind while meeting with the doctor. This was a radical innovation at a time when physicians were interested only in the patient's symptoms and their history.

In 1892, Freud hypothesized that the symptoms of two women patients suffering from hysteria were caused by *repression*, that is, by their exclusion from consciousness of memories and feelings about a current sexual trauma. In the case of Lucy R, he hypothesized that her symptoms of depression, fatigue, and subjective sensations of smell were caused by unrequited love for her employer. Elisabeth von R had suffered for more than two of her twenty-four years from pains in her legs and difficulty walking. She developed a pain in her right thigh, Freud hypothesized, when "she succeeded in sparing herself the painful conviction that she loved her sister's husband by inducing pains in herself instead" (Breuer and Freud, 1893–1895, 157).

Freud's understanding of the symptom formation in these two patients in 1892 represented the beginning of his *fundamental discovery of the power and influence on behavior of unconscious thoughts and feelings*. This discovery revolutionized the treatment of the mentally ill, and its many implications had a dramatic impact on Western society.

By 1896, Freud was asserting that neurotic symptoms were caused by retention of an unconscious memory of "*a precocious experience of sexual relations with actual excitement of the genitals, resulting from sexual abuse committed by another person . . . [in] earliest youth*—the years up to the age of eight to ten, before the child has reached sexual maturity" (152).

Eleven years later, Freud treated a twenty-nine-year-old lawyer who became famous as the "Rat Man." The patient came to analysis tormented by an obsession that had begun five years before on his sudden realization that the first of his state law examinations was a month away. His obsessions intensified over the following years as the higher-level examinations came and went and consisted chiefly of fears that a dreadful torture involving rats would be inflicted on two people of whom he was very fond—a "lady" he admired and his father, who had died several years previously. He had a history of obsessional concerns dating back to his childhood, and he also experienced compulsive impulses—for instance, to cut his throat with a razor.

Why review this case of Freud's from a hundred years ago? Just as knowledge of the Model T Ford can enhance one's appreciation of the complexity, sophistication, and power of modern cars, so having some knowledge of early psychoanalytic treatment can illuminate the contemporary psychoanalytic transformations that we describe in this book.

Freud's account of the Rat Man is the longest and most detailed report that we have of his clinical work and the only write-up that includes the notes he made on the day of each session. He continued to practice analysis for another thirty years, but the Rat Man was his most successful reported treatment. He reported few, however. In his twenty-three-volume oeuvre, he described only a half dozen cases at any length. This is probably because, as he once candidly admitted, "I am not basically interested in therapy and I usually find that I am engaged—in any particular case—with the theoretical problems with which I happen to be interested at the time. . . . I am also too patriarchal to be a good analyst" (Kardiner 1957, 52). Today, analysts who do clinical work *are* basically interested in therapy, and that is one of the important differences between the analytic attitudes of our day and Freud's.

The duration of the analysis is in some dispute. Mahony (1986) determined that the Rat Man's treatment lasted less than nine and a half months in all and that the period of frequent and regular sessions didn't exceed several months. A contemporary analysis lasts several years; the increased duration is probably a function of efforts to increase the therapeutic effectiveness of analytic treatment and to treat a broader spectrum of patients.

After obtaining permission from his mother, who controlled his money, Dr. Paul Lorenz, the Rat Man, began his analysis on October 1, 1907. Even at the very beginning, we can see here a difference between the way Freud worked and how a contemporary psychoanalyst would think and intervene. While Freud made no mention in his notes of any discussion of this arrangement, a contemporary analyst would wonder about the significance of a twenty-nine-year-old professional being completely dependent on his mother financially and needing her acquiescence to start psychotherapy. A contemporary analyst would almost certainly have inquired what Dr. Lorenz's feelings were about his mother's control of his finances. And such an intervention would have shaped the course of treatment substantially because it would have signaled to the patient that the subject of his relationship with his mother was important and warranted exploration.

An intervention like that would also likely have introduced the theme of how Dr. Lorenz regulated and dealt with anger and whether anger was a source of concern or difficulty to him. There is no evidence that Freud discussed the patient's relationship with his mother or his feelings about anger at any time during the treatment. This is understandable in the light of Freud's early exclusive focus on explicit sexuality as the cause of neurotic symptoms. He had not yet come to appreciate how difficulties with anger regulation can cause symptoms and distress. We now believe that obsessions are one of the symptoms that develop when a person's ability to regulate anger threatens to break down. A modern analyst might hypothesize that something was making Dr. Lorenz angrier than he could handle. Perhaps it was being forced to take the state exam; perhaps the exam reaction was cloaking a more dangerous anger—at the controlling mother who was pressuring him to marry a wealthy woman relative.

(In fact, I believe that Freud became engaged in the Rat Man's treatment because he saw it as an opportunity to develop his theory of the cause of obsessional neurosis. Freud thought that a cure of the Rat Man would validate his theory, although we now know that the success of any therapeutic method does not constitute proof of the correctness of the theory on which the therapeutic technique was based [Marmor 1986]).

Freud introduced Dr. Lorenz to psychoanalytic treatment by explaining that the only condition was that the patient "say everything that came into his head, even if it was *unpleasant* to him, or seemed *unimportant* or *irrelevant* or *senseless*" (Freud 1909, 159), instructions that many analysts still give to their new patients. Dr. Lorenz tried to abide by Freud's instruction to *free associate*, as the attempt at uncensored speech is called, and went from topic to topic, often without any transition. Many of his thoughts were about sexual matters. When Freud asked him what made him put such stress on his sexual life, he replied that his reading of Freud's theories made him think that this was expected—an understandable conclusion given the early papers he had read. That Dr. Lorenz had looked for and found Freud's papers suggests that he was a resourceful person. It also indicates that even before his first session, suggestion had influenced what he discussed with Freud.

Furthermore, from reading Freud's theories, the Rat Man had developed a perception of him as a source of knowledge and power. This was reinforced in the ninth session, when Freud explained to his patient that it would be pointless to reassure him regarding his obsessions since the feelings that underlay the obsessions would eventually return. In stating what he knew would *not* be helpful, Freud implied that he knew what *would* be helpful to Dr. Lorenz. Thus, the *suggestion* that Freud had the power to help him was multiply reinforced. Suggestion in its various guises is unavoidable in psychoanalysis, now as then. Certainly there are few adults today who consult a therapist without having first been influenced by cartoons, movies, or friends who talk about what analysts are "after." These expectations and their significance are considered "grist for the mill," material that will be explored and analyzed.

In his second session, Dr. Lorenz spoke of the notably bizarre fantasy involving rats that gave him the name under which his case became famous. A Captain Novak, a man obviously fond of cruelty, had described to him a "punishment" in which "'the criminal was tied up . . . a pot was turned upside down on his buttocks . . . some rats were put into it . . . and they . . .'—he had again got up and was showing every sign of horror and resistance—'. . . bored their way in . . .'—Into his anus, I helped him out" (Freud 1909, 166).

Freud describes many interpretations that he made while he and the patient worked with this material—not all of which were accepted by his patient. Kris (1951) has labeled some of these "intellectual indoctrination," and they may represent Freud's attempts to find support for his theories. Consider, for example, his comment in the eighth session: "I could not restrain myself from constructing the material at our disposal into an event: how before the age of six he had been in the habit of masturbating and how his father had forbidden it, [and used] as a threat the phrase 'it would be the death of you,' and [Freud added] perhaps also threatening to cut off his penis" (263).

Freud assumed that the patient's memory was a valid one and specific to the father; he did not consider the possibility that it might have been unconsciously constructed to reflect Dr. Lorenz's current sense that *Freud* was critical of his *present* sexual impulses. Freud's making up the father's threat to cut off his son's penis illustrates how explicitly theory driven Freud's work was.

Freud's *interpretations*—his explanations to Dr. Lorenz of what the unconscious meaning of his thoughts and feelings might be—were inconsistent. He assigned the same dates and the identical effect (Dr. Lorenz's inability to work) to two different events: an aunt's death and the mother's plan that her son should marry one of her wealthy relatives (Mahony 1986, 32)—though how Dr. Lorenz felt about either of these was never discussed. And neither the aunt's death nor the mother's pressure was a childhood experience, although Freud's hypothesis was that childhood experiences were the cause of obsessional neurosis in adults. In focusing on current circumstances, therefore, Freud is closer to the modern use of *"here-and-now" interpretations*—that is, explanations of how *current* experiences and relationships influence thoughts and feelings—than to his own theory, which postulates that *childhood* feelings and experiences are the causative agents. "In short, Freud's description of the Rat Man's adult life was incoherent" (Mahony 1986, 35).

"Incoherent" seems a little harsh; Freud was searching, trying to find his way without a road map, and Mahony's judgment is based on our current, advantaged understanding of treatment. Freud's fumblings gave psychoanalysis its first map, making later journeys much easier.

Freud, whom Mahony (1986) characterized as a "befriending educator," made many *supportive interventions*—comments designed to make Dr. Lorenz feel better about himself—in addition to the *interpretations* that were intended to make conscious thoughts and feelings of which the patient was unaware. In the fifth session, for example, when Dr. Lorenz expressed doubts about his ability to modify obsessions of such long duration, Freud told him that "his youth was very much in his favor as well as the intactness of his personality. In this connection I said a word or two upon the good opinion I had formed of him, and this gave him visible pleasure" (Mahony 1986, 178). Contemporary analysts would give real weight to this intervention. Dr. Lorenz was concerned about his masturbation and his repugnant feelings and fantasies. To learn that Freud's positive feelings about him could persist despite these was very reassuring and hopeful.

Some of Freud's actions with Dr. Lorenz are not readily classified either as interpretations or as supportive efforts; Lipton (1977) considers them to be outside the sphere of analytic technique altogether. On one occasion, Freud offered Dr. Lorenz some herring. (Anna Freud told Beigler [2002] that it was quite common at that time for an analyst to provide food to a patient.) Similarly, Freud asked Dr. Lorenz to bring in a picture of the "lady," whom he had been reluctant to describe, and he sent Dr. Lorenz a postcard from a vacation trip. This was not unusual either. But in the latter case it is noteworthy that the patient was irritated with Freud about what he considered an inappropriately intimate form of closing—Freud had signed his postcard, "Cordially."

This anger, which I consider the only anger directly expressed to Freud during the treatment, was apparently not discussed, and other reported expressions of "anger" appear more sham than genuine. For example, Freud (1909) noted, "Things soon reached a point at which, in his dreams, his waking phantasies and his associations, he began heaping the grossest and filthiest abuse upon me and my family, though in his deliberate actions he never treated me with anything but the greatest respect" (209).

Freud behaved in similar ways with other patients with whom he developed personal relationships. We now recognize that such actions may foster positive feelings toward the analyst, thereby enhancing the sense that patient and analyst are working together on the patient's behalf. This attitude, which is now called the *therapeutic alliance*, clearly developed between Freud and Dr. Lorenz.

It is now regarded as the single best predictor of positive therapeutic outcome (Luborsky 2000).

There were other occasions when Freud's consulting-room behavior departed from "prescribed" technique. Much of the later rigidification of analytic technique—the insistence that the analyst remain anonymous, for example, and not "gratify" or reassure the patient—has been ascribed to later followers of Freud who for a variety of reasons felt it necessary to become more Catholic than the pope. One day Dr. Lorenz reluctantly admitted that he had mistrusted Freud even before coming to see him because he had heard that Freud's brother had been convicted of murder. Freud laughed. Although this reaction has been characterized as "unanalytic" and an expression of some personal difficulty of Freud's (Gottlieb 1989), a more parsimonious explanation, and one consistent with Freud's personal relationship with Dr. Lorenz, is simply that Dr. Lorenz's mistaken belief was so far from reality that it struck Freud as ludicrous. He naturally and spontaneously laughed, a response that might well have released the tension and been reassuring to Dr. Lorenz.

Mahony (1986) summarizes Freud's technique as "frequently intrusive, reassuring and seemingly more drawn to genetic interpretations [of the patient's history] and to reconstruction of past events than to the current interplay [between patient and analyst] in the clinical situation" (90). Given the very early stage of Freud's analytic development, this seems hardly surprising. Nonetheless, the Rat Man's treatment, incoherent or not, was successful. After a little more than three months of work, Freud presented the patient with an interpretation of his obsession with the rat punishment. "When we reached the solution that has been described above," he tells us, "the patient's rat delirium (obsession) disappeared" (1909, 220). It is not easy to determine from Freud's notes exactly which interpretation he presented at that time. But after seven months of treatment, Dr. Lorenz was able to accept work in his profession. Approximately one year after termination, Freud reported that Dr. Lorenz's engagement to his lady had been announced in the newspapers and that he was "facing life with courage and ability" (McGuire 1974). Dr. Lorenz married his lady in 1910, thus foiling his mother's attempt to choose his spouse.

Did Dr. Lorenz's obsession disappear after only three months through the effect of some specific interpretation? Through the authoritarian Freud's own conviction that the interpretation had the power to remove the symptom? Through Freud's concern about, positive feelings for, and support for Dr. Lorenz? How can anyone determine which or which combination was mutative? Dr. Lorenz's positive identification with a benign, charismatic, and powerful figure has been emphasized by numerous analysts; Beigler (1975) considered that Freud and Dr. Lorenz loved each other and that Dr. Lorenz figured prominently in fashioning Freud's new science by elucidating the purported cause of obsessional neurosis.

Today we have detailed tape recordings of analyses of much longer duration than Dr. Lorenz's, but as yet no agreement has been reached about the *mutative factors* that contribute to patient improvement. We can hardly expect consensus about the mutative factors in a treatment that took place one hundred years ago. It isn't possible to rule out any of the possible factors—interpretation, suggestion, support, personal relationship, adventitious experiences—individually or in combination. Every analytic pair is unique, and its dynamics involve conscious and unconscious intersubjective factors (personal values, feelings, and fantasies) in both patient and analyst that are difficult to assess. The particular mutative factors may well vary with the individuals. We have to settle for uncertainty about the mutative factors in past as well as in current analytic treatments, although this is not fully satisfying for any of us—patient, analyst, or reader. But the uncertainty does not change the fact that treatment can produce a dramatic, positive transformation in a patient's life, as it did in the Rat Man's.

Freud reported later that the one point that still gave him trouble (father complex and transference) had shown up clearly in his conversations with this intelligent and grateful man. Presumably, this reflects some communication that occurred after treatment had terminated; Freud presents no other details. We know little more about the course of Dr. Lorenz's life, as, unfortunately, he perished in World War I.

It is striking that despite the notable absence during the analysis of any explicit discussion of his relationship with his mother, Dr. Lorenz did escape from her control. He took work as an attorney and married his lady. Had the powerful, authoritarian Freud, who clearly controlled the treatment, been viewed by Dr. Lorenz as a substitute controlling maternal figure? Was the anger at Freud about the postcard *displaced* (shifted) from his anger at his mother, who also intruded on him in "too intimate" ways? Did the successful risk of being angry at Freud without deleterious consequences reassure Dr. Lorenz about his ability to regulate and safely discharge his anger at controlling and authoritarian individuals? We can only speculate, but in a contemporary treatment these questions would have been explored openly and at length.

Freud, struggling to develop and establish a new discipline, was intensely theory driven in his work with patients. His preoccupation with theory probably interfered with his capacity to discover additional therapeutic issues that we now know to be relevant. Contemporary analysts are interested in developing analytic theory, but they have come to believe that the route to theory formulation about technique of treatment is through effecting the patient's therapeutic improvement As a result, treatment is now patient centered and therapy focused in comparison with Freud's early work rather than theory driven. Today's patients can be certain that clinical analysts are interested in treatment for its own sake—in relieving the patient's distress and fostering personal development.

CHAPTER 2

George: Transformation Viewed from a Thirty-Year Follow-Up

George's psychoanalysis is one which I am fortunate enough to have an unusually long perspective, as he was my first psychoanalytic patient. In the thirty years that have passed since we did our work together, I have had many opportunities to watch how he used the insights from his psychoanalysis to establish a successful career and a satisfying intimate family life with his wife and children. I will describe how George came to see me, the course of our analytic work together and its complications, and how my psychoanalytic training both compromised and aided the course of the analysis. I will also discuss the outcome. Back then, psychoanalytic theory prescribed that the analyst should make no arrangements to keep in touch with a former patient or to keep informed of his progress. But in George's case I did come to know about the continued unfolding of his life, and I will recount why and how.

George had had some brief psychotherapy in college and in graduate school for symptoms connected with competition and relationships with women. He was very successful in his work and had many friends, but he was anxious about besting his colleagues and fearful of hurting the women with whom he became involved. He had also tried a number of practical ways of dealing with his discomforts about competition. Following a grueling graduate program at an outstanding university, he had taken a less challenging junior faculty position at a university in a distant city. He had made this move in the hope that in a less pressured environment he could get away from his competitive strivings and develop the capacity to relax more. On the other hand, he knew that he sometimes shied away from situations where he *should* be competitive and had tried taking boxing lessons as a way of developing greater ease in competitive situations. But after a few months at the new university, he realized that he was feeling the same way he had during his graduate studies. His performance was outstanding, but he felt guilty about his successes. He felt uncomfortable under his mentors' guidance and also when competing with his peers. At the same time he felt smarter than his colleagues and angry that he had to submit to his professors.

He was also still disturbed about his relationships with women. He noticed a pattern: he would be attracted to a woman and date her, but when he anticipated the possibility of having sex, he became frightened that he would hurt her physically or emotionally. This fear was so intense that he had not permitted himself to have sexual intercourse. When these problems recurred at his new university, he decided on the recommendation of his previous therapist to apply for a low-cost analysis. (Psychoanalytic institutes offer low-cost analyses in which trainees—analytic candidates—see at reduced cost the patients they need to fulfill their training requirements. The candidates' work is supervised by a senior analyst. George understood this arrangement when he applied for a low-cost analysis to the institute where I was in training, but of course this didn't mean that his feelings about it wouldn't make an appearance in his analysis.)

Like all candidates, I was eager for solid cases for my training. I needed to have at least three patients in psychoanalysis and to complete the treatment of one of them. So I was pleased to have George referred to me. He was in his mid-twenties at the time and a successful professional, but he nevertheless had serious conflicts. I felt confident that his previous capacity for and experience of success would enable him to withstand the rigorous self-examination that psychoanalysis demands.

In the first months of analysis, George seemed comfortable with little guidance from me. He was surprised that I was young, he said. He hoped that didn't mean I wasn't experienced enough to help him. But he dove in, proceeding to describe events in his upbringing that he thought might be the cause of his difficulties, weaving his family background into explanations for his symptoms in the intellectual way he thought was expected of an analytic patient. Sometimes he expressed the fear that he was usurping my role as analyst, but he seemed confident about his explanations and didn't appear to want any corroboration from me.

George recounted that his father, who commuted a long distance to his work, returned home late in the evenings. He seemed to have little patience with George's mother, who appeared easily wounded by his criticisms. George thought that perhaps his father stayed at work late so as to avoid the mother's complaints and having to take care of the children. He had missed not doing sports with his father, who seemed too tired or preoccupied on weekends. Although both mother and father seemed to love George and his younger sister, his father seemed to him too harsh and his mother too vulnerable. George's sister admired him and followed him around. He remembered when his mother first brought her home from the hospital. While looking at her he "patted" the crown of her head and noticed how soft her skull was. As a young adolescent, he noted that she wasn't doing nearly as well as he in school and conceived the worry that patting her that way might have injured her brain and impaired her intelligence. Although she had gone on to become a lawyer, George still wondered if his act had compromised her intellectual ability.

His mother had usually indulged him, usually giving him free reign in his activities, but she occasionally accused him of being selfish and not appreciating her. George felt that her chronic complaints about his behavior led him later to inhibit his free expression of feelings with girlfriends. He equated the thought that he had injured his sister as an infant with the feeling that he could easily hurt a woman with sexual activity. He felt anxious about surpassing his father and others with his intellect. Outside of work, he preferred the company of his colleagues and many male friends to that of women. At work, however, he was very competitive with his peers and also feared depreciating his mentors once he learned what they knew. He linked these feelings with his fear of surpassing his father.

As this pattern of George's independent theorizing persisted over the early months of analysis, we both began to get anxious. He increasingly worried that he had taken over my job because he was smarter than I. Despite my pleasure in having him as my patient, I felt intimidated by the way he seemed able to proceed without me and wondered if he was in fact so smart and confident that I was superfluous. Could I continue to conduct analysis with him if I felt this way? I sought the reassurance of my supervisor, who reminded me that no matter what our respective IQs might be, George's attitude was a reflection not of intelligence but of transference, that is, that he was bringing his feelings about being smarter than his father (or teachers or colleagues) into the psychoanalytic situation and experiencing them in his relationship with me. George had feelings like that toward just about all the men he dealt with—his father, his mentors, his peers. His wish to be smarter than everybody else made him uneasy. The idea pleased him, but he also feared that it might evoke retaliation. That is, George felt conflicted about it. The fact of transference (that people bring their habitual feelings into analysis and experience them with the analyst) brings such feelings into the therapy in a very alive way. It allows them to be studied by both parties in vivo and in all their intensity rather than in the abstract way that George had been pursuing. If he could experience those wishes and fears and learn to understand them in a meaningful way in the analysis with me, he would give himself the opportunity to explore them and eventually find it possible to sustain his own ideas without fear of retribution or that he was hurting the other person. As uncomfortable as that was for me, my part was to be able to let George transfer these feelings onto me. If I could tolerate them, I would eventually be able to help him tolerate them too.

George's belief that he was smarter than I was alternated with a conviction that he was too frightened to accomplish anything without me. He criticized himself for thinking that he was so smart. He put himself down further with the thought that being in psychoanalytic treatment proved that he was weak and that there was no way for him to get better without my "expert" help. Then he would turn from these humiliating thoughts to a renewed and more aggressive questioning of *my* abilities. He knew that I was in psychoanalytic training and at first had not thought that it wouldn't matter, that he could obtain excellent treatment from me. But as time went on and he acquired more comfort with his competitive strivings, he began to entertain serious questions about whether I was doing anything for him. I pointed out how the intensity of these alternating feelings with me was similar to the ones that he experienced with colleagues and professors. (Although what I said was undoubtedly true, I probably also used that statement to reassure myself. I think that I had to get away from the feeling that George didn't need me. I believe that most analysts have strong feelings about their patients that are often difficult to modulate.)

As George experienced stronger feelings toward me in the transference, he gradually became more comfortable with me in our analytic work. He became more confident about his competitive feelings in general and less anxious about work. What happened in our work to cause this change? Did it have to do with his endless elaboration of his competitive experiences with the father of his childhood? Maybe—but more likely it was connected with our growing comfort with one another and our growing realization that the situation was tolerable. I could continue to function as his analyst, and he could stand negative feelings toward me as we continued to work together. His competitiveness did me no harm, and I did him none in return.

With his new confidence, George decided to pursue a relationship with a young graduate student to whom he was attracted. For the first time in his life he had a successful sexual relationship, and he was proud of himself. But this young woman wanted a more casual relationship than he did, and his intensity and seriousness led her to reject him after a few months. At first George blamed himself for not being relaxed enough, but then he shifted to blaming me for letting him get sexually involved before he was emotionally ready. He also began to blame me for his bad moods.

He expressed his reservations about me clearly in a dream he had at the beginning of the second year of the analysis. He was beginning to wonder if he was getting any better and wondered if I knew what I was doing. In the dream, he was inside a room at the Psychoanalytic Institute. He had been invited by my teachers to sit in on a discussion of how I was progressing in my training. The consensus was that I was doing only marginal work. My teachers thought they might have to interrupt my psychoanalytic education. They asked George his opinion of my work with him. He hesitated but then said that despite my mediocre performance, I should be given more time to see if I could improve.

In describing his feelings about the dream, George emphasized the sadness associated with his disappointment in me. I linked this disappointment to some earlier feelings about his father and his discoveries that several of his professors weren't as smart as he had first thought. What seemed to help most, however, was letting George focus on his disappointment in me. Because it was happening right then, on the spot, it was more intense than his old experiences with his father and more accessible to exploration. The wishes, fears, and fantasies connected with his disappointment in me gave us a window onto related feelings about others, and as we clarified them, George began to apply what he learned to earlier disappointments, looking at them differently and eventually resolving them. There was another potential meaning of this dream—that George felt that *he* was making slow progress and was pleading for more time to improve. Dreams can often be understood in more than one direction. But I didn't think of this reversal at the time. I felt challenged and asked for more support from my supervisor, who didn't think of it then either. As most candidates are, I was anxious about my performance, and I felt intimidated by the judgment implied in George's dream. My supervisor had to keep reassuring me that George's feelings were based on transference, and in fact it was the intensity of George's transference, and particularly my reaction to it, that plagued me as the analysis continued.

For instance, he would often recount several dreams in a single hour, expecting me to interpret them. When I did, however, he discounted my interpretations with remarks like "Thanks, I know that already" or "Can't you do any better than that?" or "I can't believe an analyst would say something so inane. What would a *real* analyst say?" He had another complaint too, and this became a regular refrain: "How come you encouraged me to get sexually involved? Someone with experience wouldn't have let me do that!" Although intellectually I knew that a lot of George's criticisms were part of the transference, it was hard for me not to feel justifiably blamed and to believe that if I were smarter and more experienced, he would indeed be more satisfied with me as an analyst. In our weekly supervision sessions, my supervisor kept reassuring me, "It's only transference." And I would return to George and point out yet again that these were feelings that he had (with contextual variations, of course) about all the men in his life.

Another troubling thought for George was that he might be latently homosexual. When I explored this idea with him, we found that it was directly connected with his alternating wishes to dominate and then to submit to the colleagues or professors he was competing with. It appeared that he didn't feel sexual desire for men, but he assumed that the men with whom he was struggling would want to submit to or dominate him in sexual ways. As I interpreted his homosexual thoughts as related to problems that he had around dominating or submitting, I probably aggravated his conflict occasionally by needing to dominate him myself with my "correct" interpretations. Sometimes after I had made a forceful interpretation that I felt was particularly timely, George would respond, "I know this already, but it doesn't seem to help me"—thus neatly putting me in my place.

During this period, while George was trying to describe why he felt the way he did, memories came up. As a young boy, he occasionally noticed his mother naked. When she saw him looking at her, she put her finger to her lips, as if they should keep this secret from his father. George felt that his mother was overprotective of him out of fear that he would be injured. He knew his father hated homosexuals and that his mother mocked his father for that. As George talked about these memories of his father and mother, he could gradually take some distance from his thoughts about homosexuality and began to discuss more specific and more emotional instances of his fear of dominance and submission with his colleagues, his professors, and me.

Over the next two years, George gradually improved. He had sexual relationships that were satisfying, and he became less anxious about his relationships with his colleagues. He permitted himself to be more competitive, asking boldly for and getting a large pay raise and promotion. He no longer felt so guilty toward his peers when he surpassed them.

In the third year of the analysis, a striking change occurred in his behavior toward his sessions and me. Until that point, George had behaved as a busy professional who was trying to squeeze analysis into his life. He was preoccupied with a great deal of work, and he had a long commute to my office. He would rush into the office a few minutes late and leave hurriedly at the end of the hour for important appointments elsewhere. Now he would arrive an hour and a half before his appointment and leisurely read magazines or newspapers in my waiting room. Analytic hours consisted of a relaxed description of his day, in which the scheduling conflicts of yore were apparently absent. He would talk about how he had spent the previous evening at a local bar watching a basketball game on TV with some friends. He remained comfortably silent for long periods during the hour, noticing the birds singing outside my office window. He'd talk about maybe dating a woman he knew casually but wouldn't get around to calling her. In the past he would have accused himself of being lazy and not being able to face his fears, but now there was no urgency.

I was puzzled by this behavior, and my attempt to interpret it as an avoidance of his conflicts failed to produce anything new. I was also uncomfortable with the role George seemed to want me to play: a quiet listener who enjoyed his relaxation and had no desire for him to tackle his issues. Gradually both of us began to understand that this relaxing with me was a way of making up for the relative absence of his father during his childhood. George couldn't remember any significant playful periods with him. This relatively quiet period lasted about four months. George then became more pressured with work and scheduling again but noticeably less so than early in the analysis. He was also less challenging of my statements.

That July, two and a half years into the analysis, I took a long summer break of two months. I was concerned that this would upset George, but as far as I could tell, he didn't mind. He planned to use the extra time to catch up on academic projects. On my return, he began to talk about how much he had improved and about wanting to make plans to take a prominent academic position near the university where he had done his graduate work. He felt thankful that he had made academic gains, and he attributed this in part to his analytic work with me. He regretted that he still hadn't found a woman he loved enough to marry and have children with. He had hoped that he would be able to accomplish this during the analysis but was confident, he said, that it would happen later.

In November, he announced that he would definitely be leaving by the end of the following summer. After returning from a winter break, he reported the following dream: He began to have intercourse with a woman he was infatuated with. In the middle of intercourse, she changed into me. Without discussing the dream, he announced a date about six months thence for ending the analysis. This was at the end of May, about four months before he had previously talked about leaving the area.

I wondered with George why he had to leave the analysis that early. I also asked about how he understood his dream. He responded rationally to my questions: He felt that he should have a few months to organize himself without analysis, and he saw the dream as possibly meaning that he was uncomfortable with my intruding too much into his life. I said that the dream might also represent his fear of attachment to me and his wish to get away from that feeling. George agreed. He wished he could stay longer, he said, but he felt that the analysis was interfering with his career goals.

As we came closer to the date that he had chosen for leaving, George talked about feeling guilty that he was rejecting me. He remembered how he had earlier accused me of incompetence. His feeling that he was rejecting me reminded him of his first girlfriend's rejection of him. I said that maybe he was not only feeling guilty about leaving; perhaps he was also trying to avoid rejection from me by leaving me first. George now agreed that he would stay longer and agreed to work a little longer. He was certain that he would leave by the end of the summer. It wasn't clear why he decided to remain, but I thought that he recognized that he had been unwittingly anxious to avoid strong feelings about me but that once he became aware of this avoidance he could make the decision to challenge it.

Now new memories appeared, this time attached to stronger emotions than George had permitted in the past. He hadn't felt paid attention to by his mother at age three when his sister was born, and he wondered now if that led him to imagine injuring her by patting her head—if he got rid of her, he could have his mother to himself. He recalled the despair he felt when his father left on an extended plane trip when George he was six. He linked that with feelings about my long vacation the previous summer. We continued to work on these connections, and I emphasized that he might be trying to leave early, to turn around earlier feelings of having been left by me or ignored by his parents. George, however, was resolute in his plans to leave by the end of the summer. He had made all the final arrangements: He had been accepted for a prestigious post at a distant university, and he had signed a lease on an apartment. In my supervision hours at this time, I admitted to a great deal of anxiety about the prospect of George leaving. Clearly he was doing better, but had we really completed his analysis? This question was complicated by my own need to complete a case to fulfill my last analytic training requirements. Would my institute consider my work with George good enough and comprehensive enough to count it toward my graduation? Even leaving training considerations aside, most analysts at that time would have judged George's wish to leave at the end of the summer as premature.

Then and even now, there are differences of opinion in analytic circles about whether a patient should make important life changes in the context of an incomplete analysis. This is because the issues aroused in analysis are complex and multilayered, and before they are completely explored they may present a confusing or misleading face. It is agreed, however, that patient and the analyst must examine these issues thoroughly to come to the best mutual understanding possible about why an analysis should continue, be interrupted, or end. Did George now sufficiently understand his conflicts to be able to find and marry an appropriate woman? Was it possible that silent dissatisfaction in my analytic capacity had made him want to leave prematurely? Did he feel that he should leave before he could reveal his feelings of disappointment in my analytic capacities and me? My wish for George to complete his treatment for my training requirements complicated this discussion further. My supervisor was puzzled by George's decision and felt, based on my reporting, that George seemed attached to me. He thought George might change his mind at the last minute. I was less convinced. Even though I trusted my supervisor's judgment, I couldn't count on George staying. I was very attached to George and wanted to continue to work with him. I finally decided to make a personal plea. In an hour when George was reciting his plans to leave and describing how happy he would be in the new university setting the following fall, I said, "I really think you're making a big mistake to leave me at this time. I think you should stay until our work is finished."

George was moved and surprised. He wondered why I hadn't said this before. I wondered with him whether he had been ready to hear that before now. Within a few days, George had completely altered his plans to leave and decided to work with me for another year. The university was disappointed but understanding and invited George to come to them at some future time.

Why did my personal statement enable George to continue? Maybe he needed to know that I was personally involved. Maybe my plea reassured him that he *could* go deeper into his dependent and competitive feelings toward me. I believe that from the beginning he had worried that I wasn't good enough or personally involved enough for him to put all his trust in me. George was an intellectually gifted man. Early in the analysis he had understood the process to be a cognitive one in which he did the thinking and I merely listened. In this last year of our work, however, the atmosphere had become more emotional. My two-month vacation the year before had made him question my commitment to him—a frightening idea as his feelings in the analysis became ever more intense. My forceful emotional plea for him to stay encouraged him about the strength of my involvement.

The work in the subsequent year was much deeper and centered on the ways that George protected himself from rejection. At the end of it, George decided that it was time to leave. We had worked together for four years and three months, and he felt that I had been very helpful to him. He had for a while become involved with a young woman who was studying to be a professional in a related field, and even though the affair with her broke off, he felt more relaxed about relationships. George felt that he had made considerable gains, although he hadn't yet achieved the lasting relationship that would lead to marriage. I recommended that we continue for a while longer to accomplish this, but this time George remained adamant about leaving. In a plaintive way he said, "I feel grown up, but I will never know for sure unless I leave." We both realized that he had improved considerably and thought of our work as a qualified success.

In the year after George left, I finished my formal psychoanalytic training. My work with George had been considered complete for the purposes of my graduation. Nevertheless, I felt that more could have been done. After all, George had felt he had to leave in order not to feel childish about giving into his wish to stay. Certainly, I thought, in a "complete" analysis he would no longer be driven by feelings like that.

In the second year after his departure, he came back to the university in my city again, and the return of old symptoms of anxiety and guilt led him to resume his psychoanalytic work with me for another year. At first he spoke with great despair about his inability to be independent. I made few remarks except to speak again of his discomfort with his feelings of competitiveness and to identify as the cause for his despair his fear that he would hurt his colleagues or his girlfriend. I believe that it was the power of our earlier analytic relationship that helped George return to his usual high level of functioning within a few weeks.

George rapidly revived the relationship with the woman he had met the summer before he left analysis. They shared many career interests, and this time they made plans to live together while she pursued her graduate studies. For the first time he experienced a relaxed feeling in his intimacy with her, and this persisted; he no longer felt pressured to stay at work in order to get away from "childish" intimate feelings toward her. Initial worries that he wasn't sufficiently potent or excited gave way to an un-self-conscious sexual involvement.

Now George's feelings toward me alternated between gratitude for my help, wondering whether he could have achieved these newfound pleasures by himself and fearing that I wanted to take the credit for what he himself had done. A previously cool relationship with his father now blossomed into a more intimate one. He no longer felt guilty about his previous difficulties with his mother and sister, and now was able to keep in touch with them more easily. In our years of work, George had explored and resolved many of his earlier conflicts about closeness and autonomy. He could be both closer and more challenging with me without feeling guilty about either. This experience led him to reexamine his feelings toward his family and to find that he could be more relaxed with them. When guilt-provoking situations arose now, he could successfully use sardonic humor to resolve negative feelings. Mostly he felt closer to them without reservations.

George now planned once again to return to the high-powered university where he had done his graduate studies, this time as a professor. That winter, he and his girlfriend made plans for a June marriage. George wanted the analysis over before then, and he ended it on his own initiative, three months before the wedding day. Although I didn't say it, I felt that George had to stop the analysis when he did to prove to himself he was on his own, that he was marrying without help from me. In the final months, he was confident about his future, and in the final hours he expressed deep gratitude and feelings of warmth toward me. Characteristic of George, these feelings alternated with thoughts that he had done most of it himself but that he had to give me some credit to placate me.

One might ask, How could George's analysis have been complete if George still needed to keep his distance by not giving me credit for his improvement? As much as some of us might wish it otherwise, analysis does not erase people's personalities and provide them with completely new and rational ones. George still had his same old issues. But he had a different attitude toward them now, and his behavior belied his harsh words. He was playful and humorous about these feelings, whereas when we started he had been stiff and deadly serious about them. He was much more comfortable with his competitive feelings toward me. As we went back over this familiar terrain, it was as if we were playfully sparring with one another; it was no longer a battle. This more relaxed attitude extended to the rest of his life. Closeness was easier for him now in all his relationships.

Thirty years ago, analyst and patient did not make any arrangements to contact one another after ending an analysis. The belief at that time was that any such arrangement would leave the analysis incomplete since the patient would still have the promise of future support from his former analyst and so did not have to deal analytically with his feelings about separation, independence, and loss. For this reason, I never raised with George the idea that we should stay in touch. I was very curious about how he was doing, though, and wondered particularly if he had maintained the gains he had made during the analysis.

After two years, George wrote me an informative letter letting me know that things were going reasonably well. He mentioned that he would be returning to my area to give some lectures and that he would like to stop by to visit. I was pleased to see him again but felt constrained in my behavior. Should I continue to behave as his analyst, still looking for unresolved conflicts and the motivation for his visit? In the end I decided to follow George's lead—he seemed to be motivated to report to me as if I were a chronicler of his life. After he spoke for most of the hour, he asked how things were going for me. At that time I didn't know how to respond other than "as an analyst."

That may sound odd, but the feelings between analysts and their former patients are complicated, and they have developed under very unusual conditions. How do they fare when you transplant them out of the stylized and formal analytic greenhouse into the field of everyday relationships? Can analyst and patient become friends? Should the old roles be maintained? What is comfortable for the patient? Should the option be kept open for future psychotherapeutic work? If so, does more personal knowledge of the analyst interfere with or help the patient in that process? As I will report, in my brief contacts with George, he seemed to prefer that I remain relatively anonymous. Other patients may desire to know and benefit from knowing the "real" personality of the analyst when they see him after the end of the analysis. Indeed, the current belief is that, in general, analysis is not compromised if patient and analyst meet or develop a different relationship some time after the analysis is over.

But thirty years ago, things were different. Neither of us explored the abstract nature of our relationship at this first meeting or at the subsequent ones that occurred at irregular intervals two or three times over the next several years. On all those occasions, George invited me to pay him a reciprocal visit him if I should ever be in his area, but I never seriously considered doing this until many years later. At that time I was invited to give a talk near George's university, and I thought it would not interfere with our long-ago analytic relationship if I were to accept his invitation. This was eighteen years after the end of the analysis, and much had changed in psychoanalytic theory since then. But even so, I had a qualm or two about initiating the visit. Perhaps my desire to see George was more personal than psychoanalytic. I was curious about what happened to him, the same way I would have been about a friend I hadn't seen for many years.

I visited George at his office at the university, as he had willingly agreed. He seemed tense but talked about his professional successes and his happiness with his family. With more directness he asked how my life was going. This time I responded by telling him about some major life changes. George appeared stunned, and I immediately realized that he did not want to know anything "real" about my life. We changed the subject back immediately to his current situation. Around the recent death of his father he had developed some anxiety symptoms and nightmares and had entered psychotherapy with a local psychiatrist. I wished him well in this treatment as we parted.

As I thought about my response to George's question, I realized that I had told him more than he wanted to hear and that he wanted me to keep my analytic role. Although an analyst can be deeply involved with a patient, as I was with George, the analytic relationship is different from a relationship with a friend. A certain professional distance is maintained to give both parties some room to handle the intensity of the feelings that arise. George apparently did not want to relinquish that space. It is well known that patients may sometimes feel frustrated by the analytic distance, but it is equally true that analysts who have enjoyed working with certain patients may feel frustrated when we can't change our former patients into friends. Analysis requires discipline and self-control on both people's parts. So although I felt disappointed when George was uncomfortable with my personal response, I quickly reverted to my analytic role. Was *I* afraid that if he knew about my real life, he would lose me as his former analyst?

I still hear from George every few years, most recently around his turning sixty. He said explicitly that he saw his motivation for writing as the desire to chronicle his life. He had successfully finished the therapy around his father's death years before, but now he had reentered treatment with the same psychiatrist because of anxiety symptoms associated with his mother's failing health. In all correspondence with me he always ends with, "I hope things go well with you." In my correspondence with George, however, I never mentioned anything more about myself than some generalizations about my professional life; after the university visit it seemed clear that George preferred that I maintain my former analytic role.

This year, when I wrote George to ask his permission to write this chapter, I also asked if he would write about his impressions of the analysis and its results. He didn't respond immediately. When he did, he readily gave me permission to write about him, although he did not agree to write about his own views of the analysis. "I am not certain I want to read how you saw our work," he wrote, "but I understand that I should do it in any case." I imagine that he did not necessarily want to have to review what *I* thought as opposed to what he had been able to resolve on his own—not necessarily out of unwillingness to give me credit for helping him but rather out of a wish to keep his thoughts to himself. Later he did read the draft of the manuscript, however, and he approved of it except for a few details. He remembered his fear of hurting his sister by "patting" her head at birth; I had mistakenly remembered it as having come up years later when I thought he reported her having hurt her head in their rough-and-tumble play. He also thought that I exaggerated his academic performance. He felt that he was a good teacher and writer but that his technical skills weren't that strong. How can we evaluate this difference in our opinion of George's performance? I don't think there is a resolution since both of our evaluations are subjective.

Our subjective judgments do coincide, however, over George's satisfaction with his family life. We both agree that he has an excellent relationship with his wife and children. What is most convincing is how much closer he and his children are than he and his parents were able to be. He has been very involved in his wife's career, helping her with many professional decisions and enjoying the relationship between their two fields of study. He also mentioned in a recent letter that he has successfully completed his most recent treatment and continues to be living both a productive and a pleasurable life.

Discussion

I would like to focus on two aspects of George's analysis as I review my work with him. The first has to do with his conflicts and what I said to help him resolve them. When George and I began working together, he was a young adult who was troubled by his competitiveness with men in his work and his fear of hurting women in a sexual relationship. His ambitious strivings, which he feared were hurtful toward others, alternated with submissive feelings that were tinged in his mind with homosexuality. Conversely, his sexual feelings toward women were complicated by the feeling that he might be exploiting them or hurting them. What happened in the analysis was that he discovered that these ideas about sexuality, competition, dominance, and submission had roots in his relationships with his father, mother, and sister, and he was able to explore, experience, and rethink them with me, his analyst.

George's wish to leave the analysis precipitously was driven by his fears about his attachment to me and his guilt about his wish to be rid of me. He agreed to stay longer when my personal plea for him to stay convinced him that he could now trust our relationship to contain and tolerate stronger emotions than he had hitherto been willing to entrust to it. When he left a year later, he was still aware of some undone work but felt it was more important at that time to pursue his professional life. When he returned two years later, although he had had a recurrence of his original symptoms from years before, he was able to work them through quickly thanks to our mutual understanding of his conflicts and our familiarity with each other. At the time of his second departure, he could love and work in equal measure and experience ambition and intimacy without the previously overwhelming conflicts that had constrained him. This view of George's analytic progress—a view from the outside as it were—focuses on the way patients may learn to understand their conflicts through skillful and timely interpretation by the analyst of feelings and thoughts of which the patient may not be aware.

The second way of looking at this analysis is to focus on what was particular to George and me in our work together. I was a psychoanalyst in training, intimidated at first by George's intelligence and challenges. George knew from the outset that I was in training and therefore an inexperienced analyst. His surprise that I was so young indirectly expressed his doubts about me. I needed my supervisor, the experienced analyst to whom a trainee reports on his work and who can provide perspective and sometimes guidance, to reassure me that George's feelings had been evoked *by the analysis* and that, although to him they felt powerful and real in relationship to me and might to some degree be a part of our real relationship, they could be understood to relate to other aspects of his life as well. Of course, my supervisor's suggestions about how I could improve my conduct of the analysis also contributed to my feelings of incompetence—a paradox inherent in many training situations. The most dramatic emotional moment of the analysis occurred when I asked George to stay in the analysis for another year. This was an important personal encounter for both of us. Unlike many of the other things I had said to him, this one expressed my feelings about him directly. I believe that my openness gave him the confidence that he could continue with me and safely allow himself to expose more intense feelings than he had in the past, secure in my regard and in the experience that I could help him resolve them. My own willingness to be so personal probably reflected an increase in my own confidence in my analytic capacity—as is usually true in a good analysis, both of us were growing. His return after a two-year interruption to finish the analysis was a testimony to the strength of the analytic process and to the connection that can exist between an analyst and a patient. We had been able to establish a mutual trust strong enough to weather a long hiatus and then permit us to work expeditiously on his conflicts when they reappeared. Conflicts are seldom completely resolved, even in analysis, and throughout life may reappear in new guises and circumstances. A successfully analyzed person may well, at a later time, seek further analytic work on new conflicts or on old ones that arise in new circumstances (such as the death of a parent or a professional crisis). But analysis will have given that person the tools to do the work well and effectively. George's return to analysis when his symptoms recurred led to a quick resolution and ultimately an excellent outcome the lasting nature of which I have been able to observe over many years.

Both patient and analyst have to realize that analytic technique must encompass both an awareness of conflicts and a realization that these conflicts must be resolved in the analytic work between two specific people. For this to happen, for two people to work together over several years in an intimate relationship, they must develop the capacity to trust one another. Fortunately for both George and me, after the analysis was over we had several opportunities to follow the unfolding of his life and see how it progressed. For me and, it is hoped, for George, his analysis was a most gratifying experience. In what other setting does one have the opportunity to listen or be listened to so attentively?

CHAPTER 3

Laila: Treatment of a Patient with a Serious Chronic Disease

Laila, a 24-year-old single woman ballet dancer from the West Coast, came for psychoanalytic therapy while undergoing tests for some frightening physical symptoms. In January she had almost passed out from dehydration due to vomiting. The same thing had happened in the spring in a steam bath and then in the summer on a river trip. Now it was September, and she was about to go on tour with her dance company, and she was nervous about the possibility of fainting on stage. She was very worried. Her internist thought at first that the problem was a mitral valve prolapse. But the tests revealed instead a collagen disease characterized by exacerbations and remissions; it was determined that the condition had actually been present since the age of nine and was now quite advanced. Laila wanted to figure out how to cope with her fears. She was also feeling blocked in the work she was trying to do—her ultimate goal was to make her mark as a choreographer—and she wanted to feel better about herself. She hoped that psychotherapy would make her stronger.

Laila had a sister three and a half years older than she. Her mother had stayed home with the children full time. Both parents were healthy, outdoorsy, adventurous people. They had taken the children on many trips and outings, some connected with the father's work. Laila reported an idyllic childhood, although her family seemed to me to have been overly casual about her fairly severe physical symptoms. She had had headaches as a child, for example. These were bad enough to cause her to hide herself away from family boating activities. Her parents responded by encouraging her to be a good sport and try to have fun. She continued to suffer from nausea and headache on boats, but her parents continued to plan sailing vacations and did not pursue the cause of the symptoms.

As she described her family life in these first weeks of consultation, Laila said critically of herself that she "did not have her feet on the ground." She reported

33

that her parents did not approve of her boyfriend, who, they complained, was constantly either stoned or drunk or both. He was trying to be an artist but would not show his work or support himself by getting a job. He was reclusive and would not take part in her family's social activities. Laila thought that her parents hoped that psychotherapy would cause her to leave him. Thus, while they had different agendas for her treatment, both she and her parents believed that she needed help. They were willing to pay for it, and she was willing to do the work, so we began.

Laila had great difficulty putting her feelings and thoughts into words at first, and the first thing we uncovered was another divergence between Laila's own wishes and those of her parents. They thought she should talk about her illness, she said, but she herself did not think there was anything to talk about regarding that. (This was a stepping back from her initial wish to deal with her fears about her physical condition, but talking about her illness brought up feelings about her parents' treatment of her. Rather than confront these, she denied them and chose to "move on with her life.") Now she said that she only wanted treatment for her block in choreography. She was afraid that the only way she could create was by being alone with her thoughts, but to be alone frightened her. In some sessions she spoke only a few sentences, so fragmented that they were only phrases. Still, we slowly pieced together some facets of her attachment to her boyfriend. Together we figured out that the great thing about John was that he was always there. He never went out. No matter where she went, he would always be at home waiting when she got back. Loneliness was what she feared most, and with John she would never have to worry about being alone.

As she filled in her history, it began to become clear that Laila had been a very lonely child. Her parents had gone away frequently on long trips during which the children were left at home with housekeepers. Laila recalled bitterly the loss of one housekeeper of whom she had become very fond. She had no one else to play imagination games with her, and this woman played dollhouse with her. But as soon as her parents came back from their trip, they had sent her away. Laila had never compared this evidence of parental failure to accommodate to her feelings with her picture of an idyllic childhood, and she considered that my doing so was a vilification of her parents. She resented this. Although she told me at first that she believed her mother had sent the housekeeper away because Laila had become too attached to her, she became frightened when I reflected this back to her—as she had when we tried to address her feelings about her childhood symptoms—and she quickly revised her narrative. The housekeeper had left of her own accord because she had a little girl of her own to bring up. This reversal of the story comforted her, and for the time being I decided to let it stand.

Even so, Laila believes that she "clammed up" after that. Her mother took her to a therapist for a year, but she had hated going and agreed to it only because she had her mother to herself on the long car trips back and forth to the therapist's office. She had not really wanted to come to see me either. But her parents had encouraged her to come in hopes that she would give up the objectionable boyfriend, and she herself wanted to be free of her own fears of illness and the pain of not having her own feelings available for her art or for her love life. So she came. But her feelings really were not available to her at this time. She had no real idea of what she felt about her parents, nor could she imagine what they felt about her. This lack of access to her inner world left her very lonely, and she coped with the loneliness by maintaining a fantasy that all was well and that their family life was just as it ought to be.

Another source of loneliness was her feeling that she was different from other children who got their own snack food and ate in front of the television. Laila's family had formal rules for meals. They also had a cook and a man to serve at table. None of the other children at school lived that way. Laila didn't know why her parents did things the way they did, but she believed that the other children saw her as weird because of it. Another great thing about John was that he never criticized her parents or their ways of doing things; he just kept away from them. Together he and she were a couple of young artists, not so different from other young artists. She could have friends visit their tiny apartment without feeling peculiar. Both with him and compared to him, she felt normal.

After a few months of therapeutic work, Laila went on tour. Her physical symptoms worsened. She began a course of medical treatment that included getting more rest, but she also managed to keep her heavy schedule of dance classes, rehearsals, and performances. We began talking about her feeling that her body attacked itself when she was under stress, and as we continued to work together in a four-times-per-week—later increased to five-times-per-week—psychoanalytic treatment using the couch for the next ten years, there were no further relapses. Over that time Laila became a successful choreographer, left the troupe she was dancing with, and formed a troupe of her own. In the seventh year she managed to part from her boyfriend and immediately found another one who was much better functioning and married him. In the ninth year of treatment she became pregnant. She gave birth to a healthy baby despite the additional risks posed by her illness and struggled with child-rearing issues and with the stresses of being both a mother and a working artist occupied with continuing her career.

However, those achievements were a long time in coming. As I have said, in the beginning of Laila's treatment, she had great difficulty in talking. Long silences characterized all her sessions. Also notable was her denial of any negative feelings toward me, her parents, her sibling, her lover, or anyone else. Anger, envy, jealousy, resentment—none of these found their way into her communications. The need to avoid expressing these feelings led her to keep herself from becoming aware of them—and many others that got too close. Two years into her treatment she dreamed:

> Two people were playing guitars in a village square. I liked it, so I joined in and played my guitar. Then crowds of people came, and I moved out to the edge. Then I couldn't hear them any more.

After she told me the dream, Laila was silent for more than ten minutes. I asked her how she felt. She said she didn't know. The context of the dream led me to understand it as an illustration of her feeling that her parents were the only ones worth looking at and the only ones worth listening to, while she was barely worthy of being in the audience. I did not say anything about that to her at the time, and her associations went in another direction. Her own confusion about the dream reminded her that talking to her mother was confusing. "They're trying to get me to sign something so I'll get a lot of money in my own name. It is good for them. It helps them with the taxes. My mother said if I would sign, I could use part of the money to go visit my sister in England. It's embarrassing."

We tracked down the roots of her embarrassment; her parents had just made such a huge fuss about paying my fee that I had lowered it. And now it was clear that they could very well have afforded to pay me at my usual rate. She said, "Yes. It is two messages. They pull me closer, and now they push me farther away. I don't know if I can take all that from them."

We elaborated her confusion. Laila was aware that her parents were putting her in an embarrassing position. She had to tell me the truth about their financial situation and hers, but at the same time she had to be loyal to them because they were paying for her treatment. She believed that they were treating me unfairly, yet she could not be angry at them over this any more than she could over anything else. To be angry at them or independent left her feeling pushed away, so she adopted their point of view so as to be pulled close once again. The next day she commented, "I spoke to my father. I told him I would sign, but I know I won't."

I asked her if she was afraid of the independence of having her own money, of not having to ask her parents for everything. She said, "Well then. I always thought all I had to do to be independent was to refuse them. It's their money, not mine. I didn't earn it."

Of course, independence means much more than refusing money, but money was an acute focus for her struggle with her parents over autonomy, so we talked about money for many sessions. Laila had been anxious about the difference between the way her parents lived and the way the families of her peers did because she was aware that her family was much richer than theirs. Here was another instance in which feelings of confusion and weirdness related back to her feelings about her parents' money. Her feelings of "being different" had to do with her fear of the envy her peers and her larger extended family experienced at the display of her parents' wealth, yet she could not talk to them or to her parents about her fear. It was less awful for her to think that her friends thought she was weird than to think that they envied her. At last after several weeks of talking about the money that her parents were offering, I said that to take this money would be like winning a lottery; I wondered if she thought that there was a danger that I would envy her and her parents. She decided to sign for the money when she reflected that it *was* like winning the lottery. If she won that, she wouldn't have to give the money back just because she hadn't earned it. She said, "I still have the same feeling inside, only now I recognize it as a wish to stay close to them, in the nest." The feeling she was referring to was her wish to refuse the money that they had offered her. She had not directly addressed my question about my envying her, but she did say that she was afraid to take it and be even more envied, yet she was also afraid not to take it and continue to be totally dependent. Now she recognized the guitarists of her dream as her parents, always singing and having good times. Yet she felt that her wish to join in with them was being thwarted by me. She experienced my interpretations of her feelings of anger and envy toward them as pushing her away from them. Because those feelings were hers, not theirs, they differentiated her from them, which Laila at that time could understand only as a kind of distance.

This interchange had a real therapeutic effect. It allowed her to move on to the next level in her career by starting her own company. It had been fueled by my own anger at having been cheated of my fee. A psychotherapist works with her own feelings as much as her patient's; my anger led me to the thought that my effectiveness in the fee negotiation had been hampered by a fantasy of my own—that charging high fees was unnurturant and thus unmaternal and unfeminine. I recognized that I too had been envious of Laila's parents—specifically, of their ability to provide such freedom for their child and of their apparent comfort in hanging on to their money while taking advantage of my interest in continuing the treatment to get me to accept a lower fee. And I was envious of Laila—that she did not have to earn money in her work and could thus be able to be what she experienced as comfortingly feminine, living as her mother did on the income provided by her father. Once I had worked that out, I was more able to help Laila accept the very large sum that would give her independence. I did not tell Laila any of this directly, but I was able to convey my comfort with the envy I felt by my tone of voice and by persisting in discussion of the money issue without avoiding it or changing the subject as I might have if I were not comfortable with it or acting "weird" about money the way her parents had, to Laila's great social (and private) discomfort. I could deal pragmatically with the idea of this money, likening it to a lottery win, a piece of good fortune that could happen to anyone. Her fear of being envied was mitigated by my mastery of my own envy, which showed Laila that her money did not have to alienate her from me or from her peers or her boyfriend. It made accepting the money less dangerous, at least in the external sense. But explicit talk of envy, anger, and alienation from within was still impossible for us.

After a year of exchanges like this, Laila was more accustomed to being heard and having her feelings, especially her negative feelings, valued. As a result, she was worrying less about saying what she needed to say, and she was becoming much more articulate—sometimes to her own consternation. One rainy day she arrived late. She said, "It was hard to get here this morning. My shoes are wet. I think I'll take them off." She turned around and looked to me for approval. "I had a surprise last night. I thought I was only going to sleep for a little while, but I slept right through. Now. . . ." After two minutes of silence I said, "You find it hard to talk again even though you surprised yourself here yesterday, too—by talking throughout the session." After another five minutes of silence, I said, "You don't want to talk to me?" She said, "It feels like I want to maintain my privacy." Two more minutes passed. I said, "By not talking to me, *you* are in control." Two more minutes passed. She said, "It feels like sleeping through." Another minute passed. I said, "Sleeping through?" Another minute went by. She said, "Last night. . . ." Another two minutes. I said, "How did you feel about that this morning? Another minute. She said, "Strange." I said, "Strange?" Several minutes went by. I said, "Are you treating me as you felt treated? Did you feel shut out when your parents went away on trips? Are you doing to me what you felt they did to you?"

It was clear to both Laila and me that her aggressive talk in the previous session had left her feeling uncomfortable. It was not the content of what she had been saying that caused her to pull back but rather the volume and extent of her expressiveness, which had made her feel close to me and therefore too separate from her parents. Her silence was thoughtful now, without the hostile tinge it had had earlier in the session.

When Laila was having trouble talking, postural cues were very important in expressing her feelings. Sometimes she was silent because words had been interdicted either by her parents or by her own internal prohibitions. But the expression of emotion through gesture and action was second nature to her—she was a dancer and a choreographer after all—and she was excellent at it. On that day I had a sense that we were connected but worried that the connection had happened at the price of shutting out her parents. Laila had been talking of them the day before as if they were not perfect, thus breaking their rules and thus exposing her to the loss of their love—hence her anxiety and her renewed silence.

Like all families, Laila's had ways of shutting some people out and keeping others in, and in her family these were very pronounced and often had to do with money and dependency. It was by now clear to both of us that her parents' way of organizing their family life in a way that their relatives and friends could not afford alienated them and shut them out. How could I avoid repeating that old pattern?

Laila's next session was four days later, and she started it with a dream:

> It was strange. Someone was showing me paintings—they were John's. Drawings really. I hadn't seen them before. They weren't really John's drawings. They had maps and lines drawn around like some states. Eastern states. It was the seaboard. That's all I remember.

She fell silent. I said, "Maps? Traveling? Are your parents traveling?" "Oh," she said, "strange that you should mention that." Her parents were now off on their boat. Laila still had to find a way to convey her feelings about their leaving without directly telling me that they were going. I understood from long experience with her that she used silence to protect her parents from what she still understood to be my (rather than her own) criticism. If she told me that they were away again, I might (in her view) fault them by commenting that their absences hurt her. Yet even her refusal to speak conveyed her thoughts. Since my main criticism of them was that they had sometimes neglected and deserted their daughter, it seemed clear that another departure was the secret cloaked by Laila's silence. Her own critical feelings about being left were still very hard for her, and even for me to speak my own was to tempt her into alliance with me against her parents and thereby shut them out. In her silence, therefore, she shut *me* out in an attempt to preventing me from voicing the fearsome but powerful anger that she was holding so fiercely at bay.

But now there were the beginnings of a change. Laila had spoken to her mother last night. The map in the dream had a line from New York to Puerto Rico, where her mother had called from. Laila said, "I had nothing to say to my mother. She said she missed me because she had nothing to do down there. No work or anything." There was a silence. I said, "You were angry that she only misses you because she had nothing to do. You had nothing to say because you can't say that you are angry." She laughed and said, "Well, you could say that. I never saw it that way. I never think of myself as *angry*. But it did bother me. It does bother me. She said she doesn't like the yacht club they are at. She chose it mostly for my father. There is another one farther down that she likes better. I think there can't be that much difference. She has so many nice things down there. It's hard to imagine it could be nicer down the street. It's like nothing is ever enough for her. Nothing is ever enough."

Laila had progressed far enough in her treatment to be able to understand and accept her own anger, at least some of the time. We began to talk about how anger and envy were difficult for her to see in others—because then she might have to see them in herself. The gaps in her talking were gaps left by the missing anger that she had feared to express to me or even admit to herself, lest it cost her her parents' undependable love.

As the years went by, Laila managed to establish herself more firmly in her professional circle, getting grants and awards, creating new work and showing it. The new ease with her feelings that had come from her work in therapy enabled her to deal with the working world in a new and more productive way. It is very difficult to earn enough money to live on in the field that she has chosen, but she was now able to support, by her own earnings, a modest lifestyle. Her interactions became more comfortable as she began to understand why she intimidated people. Just as her parents had intimidated people with their opulent lifestyle, she intimidated by her fragility. When she began her analysis, no one in her family dared to call her on the phone for fear of upsetting her. She kept them at bay with her illness. She induced a similar fear in me. I found myself scheduling my vacations to coincide with her tour schedule and planning to work on days I might otherwise have taken as holidays. Her frailty was as intimidating to me as it was to others. She was physically fragile; her illness had damaged her internal organs. In addition, her need to protect her family at her own expense had made her emotionally fragile as well. She seemed as vulnerable and in need of protection as an infant. But Laila never complained of her pains or swelling; she could have been ill to the point of death, and no one would have known it for all the vocal complaint she made. I had to be as attuned to her moods and as careful of her frailty as if she were always on the brink of death. She kept silent because she was afraid of being abandoned, and in time I was able to explore this terror with her. She related a family story about how she had been left in the care of an inexperienced young maid when she was less than a year old. Her aunt came to visit, saw the infant lying listlessly in her crib and not crying, and immediately took her and her sister to their parents at the resort where they were on vacation. The aunt believed that she had rescued the baby; the parents believed that she had interfered unnecessarily. This story gave me a context for my feeling that I had been taking care of a woman who was as fragile as an infant.

Laila told this story at a time when her parents were coming to believe that Laila was "well enough" and that the analysis was no longer necessary. They had clearly begun to notice that she was no longer as silent about her feelings as she had been earlier, and this upset them. In turn, their disapproval upset Laila, who still did not always recognize the degree to which she felt compelled to comply with their wishes. By bringing it repeatedly to her attention I helped her become aware of how powerfully not only her parents but she herself believed: that analysis was unnecessary. If I were an intruder, I could be shut out and kept from upsetting the family balance, as so many intruders had been shut out before. If, however, I were the voice of Laila's own unspoken thoughts, fears, and wishes, who knew what the results might be?

In order to work with Laila on this dilemma I had to think about my own feelings about abandonment. It was painful to empathize with the experience of the baby girl, left behind and feeling hopeless; but it was painful too to empathize with the parents, who had not actively intended ill toward her but who had been accused of neglect and may indeed have been guilty of it. How could I understand what had happened without threatening to alienate her from them? I had to emphasize the ways in which they were mindful of her welfare—paying for her treatment, sending her to excellent schools, going to her school-related functions, and including her in what they meant to be wonderful vacations together. By talking about her parents as less than perfect, I was breaking the family taboo on seeing them as insufficiently responsible for her welfare. I was encouraging her to side with the "bad" relative who had taken her to her parents when she was an infant and seducing her to take that side as well. Yet to see them in such a one-sided way was to devalue Laila's love for them and to deny the conflicting demands that real life makes on all of us. I had to find a way out of judgment to a position that honored both the suffering that Laila had endured and the realities of imperfect parents. How could I keep off the moralistic high road of condemning their selfish hedonism? How could I keep from feeling like the disapproving aunt? I had to face my own choices as a parent. Had I not sent the kids away to camp for my own convenience? Had I not chosen to pursue my own career at their expense? Or *was* it at their expense? I had needed money to raise them in New York, to keep them in good schools. How much of this was what they needed? How much was what I needed? How much was what I wanted? And how much of this could ever be untangled? Laila's parents had needed to take care of themselves as well. At the same time that I knew there could be no entirely selfless parents, I knew that I somehow fantasized being one. How many times I had said to my patients, "Passengers should fasten their own oxygen masks first and then help others." How could I know what her parents had needed or intended? What feelings did their long absences contain, allowing them to be present, at least some of the time, for their children? How much envy had these parents suffered that they now imposed it on others? Was it resentment toward the child, who had in some ways been treated better than they had themselves, that causes them to withdraw from her at times? I had to think through all these gray areas before I could communicate them to Laila in a way that was not black and white, and she had to trust me enough to hear them as attempts to help her dare to take a point of view of her own even when it clashed with theirs. To do this, to be able to differ with them yet remain connected, she needed a stance that took into account not only her anger but also her love and not only their selfishness but also their intentions.

My awareness of my countertransference feelings (responses to Laila and her parents that relate to some of my own personal concerns) allowed us to do the work that eventually gave Laila an understanding of how her family's tendency to push away others as intruders related to her own sense of isolation and alienation—the feelings that had caused her to cling to the otherwise unsatisfactory John. The requirement that others outside the family circle be pushed away so as to protect their nuclear family from the envy of the larger extended family had kept Laila from feeling close to her schoolmates or to the members of her extended family. It had hindered her connections with others in her social and professional worlds, keeping her too dependent on her parents for emotional support and therefore unable to tolerate their absences. In her current life it kept her tied to a man with whom she was living an extended adolescence, as she was afraid to be on her own long enough to find a man who could be a real partner to her. To stay with him was to keep the circle closed, and her attachment was fueled by her great sense of desperation in keeping the connection to her parents in the face of their absences and in the face of their attitudes toward the aunt, the nursemaid who had played dollhouse games with her, her boyfriend, and her analyst. Her fear of losing their love by betraying them to an outsider's envy had contributed to her choosing a boyfriend who could not possibly compete with them and who, being on perpetual vacation himself, could not criticize them for their vacations.

Over the next five years, Laila was progressively more able to talk, and with this she gradually became more able to perceive and express her own feelings. Each time I managed to articulate possible negative feelings toward me and not punish her for having them, she became a little better able to tolerate those feelings herself and therefore to express them to me in words. Seven years into the treatment she became aware of some erotic feelings about me that frightened her. (A sexual attraction of this kind in analysis may be intensified by concerns not solely sexual and when it happens is a useful clue to what those other concerns might be. This kind of "transference" experience is one of the ways that a patient's feelings—feelings that she may not even be aware of—are brought to the analyst's attention so that they can be explored and understood. The attraction itself is seen as natural and to be expected, but it is not acted on by either analyst or patient. It is analyzed instead.) The following is an example.

Laila reported some dreams she had had over the weekend:

> Friday night I dreamt I met a man I loved a whole lot. I told myself I wasn't good. You shouldn't love someone that much. That's all I re-

member of that one. On Saturday I was doing a job researching the history of a dance. I had access to a file I wasn't supposed to look at. I looked at it anyway. I felt kind of sneaky. I was with my friend Billie. Some man was making friends with us. He wanted to make friends with us. He wanted to make love with me. I didn't want to. I was being chased by people. I ran into the bathroom, realized I had my period, and started looking for a tampon. I was worried they'd break in before I put the tampon in. I felt kind of vulnerable, and that was that!

"I thought the dreams related to each other," she went on. "The place I rehearse in is a yoga studio. An Indian man runs it. He was presenting himself as a teacher, some kind of guide. I felt it wasn't good. I have had that feeling here."

I said, "It feels like a threat to your womanhood to have that feeling here." (Here I was referring to the danger of being invaded or raped in the dream and especially to the need for a tampon to protect her genital.)

She said, "The first dream was a threat to my will or something—that I'd be lost." There was a silence. "I just started thinking about the tampon dream. There was lots of turmoil going on, but I just had to take care of my body. I had to separate that from what was going on in the outside world. I heard Billie's brother had a baby this weekend. Billie's gay, but she would want a baby herself. It's the same with me. I would be jealous if my sister had a baby and I didn't."

I said, "Would you be in the same position as Billie? Having a baby without a man?" She said, "No. But I need money for a baby. I wouldn't have enough money."

"Is money the real issue?" I asked. "Wouldn't your parents make you the same offer they made your sister?" (The parents were eager for a grandchild and had offered the patient's sister money to pay for the services of a nanny indefinitely so that she would not have to give up her work an artist.)

She said, "She is going in that direction. She will be able to earn more. She is silk-screening her designs onto things. She and her husband do earn enough to make the mortgage payments on their house. She gets some commissions too."

I said, "So by being with John you can't even consider the idea of having a baby." (It went without saying that her parents would not support her having a baby with John. They believed that he would not be a responsible enough father. The irony of that assessment was not lost on either of us.)

She said, "I did consider it, but I rejected it for financial reasons. But if I said I'd like to do this and was focusing on it, I might really concentrate on doing something I could bring some money in with. But I'm taking all this medicine, and I'd want to clear my system before having a baby."

I said, "So since you can't have a child because of your illness, it doesn't pay to become independent and grown up. So you might as well not promote your career and stay with John, who supports your not supporting your career by not promoting his own." This was quite a harsh assessment of what was holding her back from achieving the real success that she desired in her career and her love life and settling for the barest minimum. It led to a long period of anger at me.

In fact I don't think that this was a particularly good intervention. (It appeared to support her parents' view that she was not choosing wisely for herself. I wanted Laila to become free to make her own decisions, not to have her comply with either her parents or with me, and this intervention was too close to being an expression of my own disapproval of John as a potential parent.) But it did open the floodgates of her anger and allow her to move ahead in being able to acknowledge and express "negative" emotions. During this period we learned that the erotic was Laila's metaphor for danger and her defenses against it a protection from that danger. She was expressing her deepest fear—that a baby would kill her—which had especial power in light of the complications of pregnancy posed by autoimmune disease.

It was through the exploration of her wish to have a child that we eventually worked through the struggle between Laila's desire for the freedom and self-determination that I represented and her last-ditch hopes that she could somehow still realize the perfect intimacy that she craved with her parents. They wanted a grandchild, and Laila wanted to give them one. She wanted to be in bed with them, to conceive a child with them as a token of her love. My concern about the medical implications of pregnancy was experienced by her—as many of my past interventions had been—as an intrusion, an undermining of the familial intimacy that she still clung to. Yet she wanted to be in bed with me too—conflictedly. It was in *my* bed that she could grow up and become the mistress of her own feelings and her own fate. Yet she feared that to have her baby with me would be a kind of incest and that I too could become a feared parent who would dominate her and make her decisions for her. We had to understand her negative view of me before she could give up her negative view of her parents. Should the baby be mine or theirs? This question was the metaphor for the entire analysis, and our working through it was the effort that eventually freed Laila to make her own relationships—with me, with her family, with others—on her own terms.

Laila was talking ever more easily, and as she became better able to put her feelings into her words, she became better able to put them into her work as well. At two points in the analysis I believed that she had achieved enough self-understanding for us to consider the issue of termination. One occurred in the seventh year just after she had begun an affair with a new man who she thought might become her boyfriend. Her career and her need for time to pursue it seemed to be the most important issues in her life. She began to miss sessions, and I no longer felt it necessary to change my schedule to meet hers because now that she could express her anger and sadness in words, she no longer seemed or was as vulnerable as before. When she said that the analysis was getting in the way of her life, I heard her. It did seem as though many of her goals had been met, yet she still required support in paying attention to her own needs and feelings. Was she ready? I told her that if she wanted to end the analysis, she should set a date, and we could work toward that. But Laila rejected that possibility in a dream. She asked a cab driver to take her to 14th Street and he let her out at 26th Street. When she refused to get out, he drove her to Queens and let her out. We understood that I was the cab driver who was not taking her far enough. Later she associated Queens with the cemeteries where some of her ancestors were buried. She articulated her dream of being able to be an ancestor herself; she wanted a child. With the understanding of this wish and how hidden it had been from her as well as from me, the idea of ending treatment now seemed premature.

In the eighth year of our work, Laila managed a very painful separation from the extremely inadequate boyfriend to whom she had been loyal since high school. Hitherto she had felt that only with John, who was too passive to leave her, could she find the unconditional acceptance that she thought she needed to feel that she was a worthwhile person. But her growing experience that she could be angry and not lose me allowed her to be less dependent on him and to believe that she could attract a man who had enough self-respect to feel that he had a choice. My respect for her feelings, even when they were critical and rejecting of me, generated respect for her own, and this self-respect made it possible for her to aspire to a better relationship. John had a violent outburst when she told him that she wanted to separate. He smashed some furniture and frightened her, but she was able to recognize that she used *his* temper as a substitute for expressing her own anger. She not only projected her feelings (that is, she attributed them to John) but also induced the behavior that expressed them as well by making him angry. For example, Laila had never told John that she was angry that he had not shared the rent on the dingy apartment that they had shared but had relied on her to earn all their money. Once she left, he could not afford the place but would have to go back to his parents' home, where there really was no room for him. She, on the other hand, moved into a family house that contrasted elegantly to their depressing old place, and it was there that she asked him to come to give her back the apartment keys. When she refused to continue paying his rent, he became enraged and broke a chair.

Laila's career was now progressing both creatively and financially, and she found a new boyfriend. She understood now that she had tolerated John's addiction and paralysis because she had believed that she was just as imperfect as he was and that she could not criticize him because she was no better than he. I had pointed out how well his behavior had met her needs and that she must have encouraged him in it whether the two of them were aware of it or not. She now recognized this, recalling how much better she always felt knowing that she would find him at home after her absences and the many times when she had found herself feeling better after his tantrums.

In the following years Laila changed her life radically. She arranged her career so that she had time and energy to devote to her love life. She began dating men in her own field and found one who was very devoted and loving and who enjoyed talking with her parents. He became part of their family when she married him. She no longer saw him as an outsider who would come between her and her parents. The long-standing distrust of strangers or outsiders now came into focus as an internal prohibition against the choice of a love object other than the parents. She felt secure enough to try to have a child. I now understood that her wish for a baby had been tied to continuing the analysis because she needed the psychological support to get pregnant and maintain the pregnancy. Her immunologist had insisted that she remain in analysis to minimize psychic stress in order to maximize her chances of tolerating the stress of pregnancy. She cut back on her work schedule and managed to become pregnant. Like all autoimmune diseases, hers increased the risk of miscarriage and of premature labor, and she was closely monitored throughout her pregnancy, but her doctors were amazed. She was the first person they had seen with her illness to maintain a pregnancy long enough to give birth to a healthy baby. After the birth she shifted her work life again so that she could spend more time with her child. Her husband took on more of the responsibility for the family. Again it was looking like she might be ready to finish treatment.

Her physician encouraged her to continue doing whatever she had been doing, which included her psychotherapy, but this recommendation posed a difficulty. Laila's analytic goals—as we had reformulated them over the years—of understanding her own motivations and becoming aware of her conflicts and fantasies had been adequately realized. She had become able to articulate her life goals of marriage, motherhood, and career, and those goals too seemed to have been met. According to these criteria, it made sense to terminate the analysis. The only question left was how she would deal with her physical illness. Although she had not had an exacerbation of her symptoms since the second year of analysis, she was still taking medication and could become actively ill again at any time. We could continue the analysis as a prophylactic procedure, and I thought this might make sense. But Laila did not want to continue to spend the time or money that analysis takes. I agreed that we could terminate; we set a date and proceeded—as often happens—to go through a condensed repetition of all that had happened in the analysis. Her angry feelings about abandonment, disloyalty, fear of death, and longing to create were reawakened, and her old tendencies to set up arguments between her parents and me that served to distract her from her own internal conflicts came back to haunt us. She became stubborn and pushed away my attempts to help her as though I were once again an intruder, bent on separating her from all she loved. She also invited me to see her dance and admire her. This invitation, asking me to be her audience, made it clear that she was going to be able to fulfill her erotic wishes and her wishes to be admired by channeling them into her work rather than acting on them in ways that could have been damaging to her marriage. Finally she made the choice to end the analysis herself, knowing that she would miss me and miss her treatment.

After termination of the five-times-per-week analysis, Laila asked for and I agreed to a twice-a-week schedule of a more supportive treatment geared to helping her maintain her self-esteem in her difficult struggle not to repeat with her own child what her parents had done with her. Although I wanted to believe that she had enough treatment to stand on her own, the reduced-schedule psychotherapy was less frightening to her than being entirely on her own. I had to struggle internally to accept that her analysis had not done everything she needed—like everything else human, analysis is not entirely perfectible. And analysts, like everyone else, sometimes find this hard to accept. For her part, Laila understood that termination and even reduction of the analysis would create a dangerous disequilibrium and that monitoring her symptoms during this time would take much vigilance on her part. While the analysis had enabled her to understand her own motivation and to act in her own best interest, both she and I knew that she was still not confident of how her body would stand up to the stress of losing a relationship that had been so supportive to her. She would need to keep working on accessing her negative feelings and expressing them in appropriate ways. She would need to keep watch on her tendency to deny herself what she wished for. She would need to remember to put loyalty to herself, her husband, and their child ahead of loyalty to her parents.

Dynamically, the major thrust of the analysis had been on dealing with her angry feelings about being neglected and refused permission to complain about it. At the new twice-a-week frequency, this aspect of the work alternated with support for her in her wish to be a good mother to her daughter. The psychotherapy was much more oriented to parent counseling than I felt was appropriate at the time. I still wanted Laila to feel independent enough to make decisions for herself in the parental role. When she wanted to reduce the schedule further to once a week, I chose not to go along with that because I thought it would reduce the internal work even further and turn it into mere advice giving, and we parted amicably, even if not to Laila's or my complete satisfaction.

Discussion

The questions I would like to consider with regard to Laila's treatment are the following:

1. To what extent did her psychoanalysis relieve her medical illness?
2. To what extent was her analysis affected by her physical symptoms?
3. What did her need for supportive treatment later mean in the context of her analysis?

The most striking aspect of the work with Laila was her silence in the treatment hours. This could be understood as either the inability to recognize what she was feeling or the inability to express her recognition in words. Marie Cardinal (1983), in a memoir of her own analysis tellingly titled *The Words to Say It*, details her experience of both of these problems. For her, in fact, analysis was a process first of finding words and then of exploring her feelings by means of the words she had found.[1]

It is also possible to understand both the inhibition of Laila's creativity as a choreographer and the inhibition of her speech in the analysis as different aspects of a single problem—an unconscious fantasy so threatening that it had to be "silenced" (Arlow 1969). For Laila, the unconscious fantasy, reflected in her early dream about the guitars, was that she was not worth looking at. She was not worth listening to. She had nothing to show, she had nothing to say. With this fantasy came the belief that her parents' love and protection could be won only by a self-sacrificing submission—a submission that was the only way she knew to suppress the terrifying rage she felt at her parents for the various forms of pain she had suffered as a child. That was a rage she had dared not express, and the need to inhibit its expression severely contaminated her capacity to express herself as a dancer and even in speech.

Now, however, Laila was aware of the rage she felt at her parents for their repeated abandonments, their indifference to her feelings and her well-being, and their undermining of the creative ways she found to make good their own lacks, such as in their dismissal of the supportive housekeeper. She was also able to see how they had tried their best and to know that their insistence on everything being happy and full of singing and dancing had not been intended to stifle her but was a reflection of their need to feel like good parents, especially in the context of the criticisms of their extended family. Laila's own wish for applause from an audience was a reflection of their need for applause from her. Now that she knew that, she could give them what she needed without having to give up ways of getting the kind of applause she wanted herself.

Does it make a difference to see this patient's treatment in one theoretical frame as opposed to another? Or does theory merely add a layer of words without changing the essential work that patient and analyst have to do? This is one question we can ask our patients, and some of those who have written about their analyses address it unasked. Daniel Gunn (2002) wrote a memoir of the termination of his treatment with a Lacanian analyst. He believed that he had achieved his goal of success in his academic career. But he had not settled into a relationship with a woman he could love. Although he forced the ending of his analysis by choosing to go on a sabbatical, his poignant awareness that he had not finished the work and that its riddles were as yet unsolved seems to have haunted him so that he could finish by writing only about the last month of his analysis. ("The Sergeant" was Gunn's name for his analyst, who, Gunn believed, would have continued with the work past the time when Gunn had arranged to leave.):

> The less time I had, the stronger my desire to hold solutions in my hand as I approached the gates of sleep each night. . . . Yes, I did want to turn my dream life into narrative to have a satisfying ending, kine into corn into years, worms into cows into goats. And if the narrative had a moral twist, or an allegorical turn, then so much the better. Oh, I wanted it all right and I sometimes almost got it. But in the end there was no end; the more powerful my own interpretations—and as for the Sergeant's, forget it!—the more the dreams just generated further new stories. (37)

Lucy Daniels (2002) also turned to writing to deal with the perhaps premature ending of her own analysis. She had achieved her most important goal: she had found her own voice as a female writer. The idea that she could write as a woman was very important to her, as she had previously been able to write only in a male persona. Her analysis ended a lifelong physical illness, so that she was at last able to act and feel like an adult who did not need permission to feel her own feelings. Her freedom to write and to be a female at the same time was hard won, and she treasured it.

But I don't know how Laila would have evaluated her treatment. Perhaps every analysis ends with more work that could be done in the future; perhaps she will be able to work out the unsatisfying termination of a very satisfying treatment in her art. I did not feel comfortable asking her to read and respond to this report. At the time I was writing, I attributed this discomfort to some personal connections between her circle and mine. Yet I had initially been inspired to write about her when I learned from the person who had referred her to me that her parents credited the analysis with saving her life. I also had an encounter with her doctor, who said essentially the same thing. He believed that her close adherence to rigorous but necessary dietary restrictions and medical regimens and her willingness to change to the less physically taxing career of choreographer rather than dancer were due to her analysis.

I thought that her ability to come to terms with the demands of her illness was the result of her de-idealization of her parents. Before the analysis, her illness had not been correctly diagnosed; compliance was not yet an issue. In the early days after the diagnosis, compliance was difficult in the context of her dancing and touring. As her self-esteem increased over the analysis, she came to see that she was taking care (or not taking care) of her valuable body and her valuable self. At that point compliance became both possible and desirable. When she was no longer so afraid of her anger at her parents that she had to see them as per-fect to keep rage at bay, she was able to be how *she* wanted to be. Thus, she had less need to achieve in her career the physical perfection she had imagined that her parents wanted of her; she began to understand that she was valuable even if she was not getting the kind of applause from an audience that they needed so badly. My constant presence and attention meant to her that I valued her and eventually that she could trust me; her willingness to talk about her negative feel-ings and to take in what I had to say came from that trust. These interpretations themselves had value for her because with their help she could construct a view of her own life that she experienced as authentic. Her gratitude to me and to her parents (for supporting her treatment with me even though it made her feisty with them) replaced the former envy of her mother that she expressed in the dream about the map. If her own envy was tolerable and did not kill, the envy of others could be tolerated and would not kill her.

Would I do anything differently now? The major regret I have about Laila's treatment is that I insisted on ending it totally. At the time that she and I worked together, I still thought, as psychoanalytic theory once held, that a successful analysis ended with a patient in no need of further treatment. Laila wanted to continue in a once-a-week psychotherapy, and I was still too much in the thrall of my idealization of psychoanalytic treatment and training to see that what she wanted was what she needed. Given the chance to do it over, I would agree to that. In the end, perhaps the reason that I have not asked her to write about her treatment is because I believe that I made a wrong decision at the very end. Per-haps I would have done better to continue at any pace she wanted. But this is something that neither of us can ever really know unless I get up the courage to contact her.

Note

1. Cardinal recalled a childhood marked by longing for the love of a mother who spent all her time tending the sick and weak. She recalled how her divorced mother had

cared for the grave of an older daughter who died before Cardinal was a year old and how her mother had used her as a screen against men. Her somatic symptom had to do with the fear and fantasy of death as a consequence of giving birth—a fear and fantasy that Laila shared and had conveyed to me and her doctors in her somatic symptom rather than in words. And she recalled her feelings of disgust and fear at her own bodily processes, especially her menstrual blood. Thus, the analysis led to a hypothesis that her initiating symptom, an excessive and unpredictable menstrual flow, was relieved by replacing the flow of blood with a flow of words—words that allowed her to access her affects, memories, fears, and moral strictures.

CHAPTER 4

Watt: A Case of Sexual (Dis-)Orientation

This chapter describes the six-year psychoanalysis of Watt, who was in doubt as to whether he was gay or straight and hoped that analysis would provide the answer. Watt thought at first that I would see through to the truth of his inner nature much as a radiologist might see right through his body to the bone. Of course, I had no idea whether Watt was gay or straight—how could I?—and I wondered why he thought I should and why he didn't know himself.

Watt said that he hoped he was straight because he wanted to have a conventional married life and wanted especially to be a father, but he felt he'd have no problem being gay if it turned out that he was, as he indeed thought more likely. The problem was being stuck in the middle and living in an equal-opportunity closet. He had had one brief homosexual fling as a teenager and one fairly long heterosexual relationship as an adult in his mid-twenties and had enjoyed both forms of sexual expression. But both relationships had ended unhappily. The faithless boy had left him, and he'd broken up with the cloyingly needy young woman. He rarely approached other women, certain he was too fat and too awkward to have any chance of success with them. His sexual fantasies and dreams were generally homoerotic, which was why he imagined he was gay, but for all that he wasn't sure.

Before coming to me, Watt consulted briefly with a gay therapist who believed that Watt was gay, genetically and irrevocably, and that his problem was in learning to accept the hand that nature had dealt him. He had also seen a straight therapist who felt the answer to Watt's question could be determined mathematically by assigning numerical values to his sexual fantasies and activities and coming up with a "scientific" score that would settle the issue once and for all. Both of these approaches only spiked Watt's anxiety, and he hoped a third opinion might prove the charm. But I told him that I had no answer. I could see that sexuality was a source of anxiety for him, but it was clear after we talked for a few hours that he was anxious about many things. He had panic attacks when he found himself in unfamiliar places, couldn't sleep at night unless the television was on, found it nearly impossible to regulate either money or food, and smoked three packs of cigarettes a day. And although he was nearing thirty, he had no serious idea about what he wanted to be when he grew up. That he didn't know how to think of himself sexually seemed merely one aspect of an overarching sense of confusion.

I told Watt that I didn't know whether he was gay or straight but that if we were to examine his thoughts and feelings in an unhurried and open-ended way, his understanding of himself would deepen considerably and this might bring him closer to answering his question. He thought this sounded promising, and so we began.

History

Watt's family history sounded like something out of *Bonnie and Clyde*. He had never met his father (a sheriff "somewhere out West," Watt thought), who had left his twenty-year-old pregnant wife—and Watt's two-year-older half-brother Nick—shortly before she was arrested for driving the getaway car for a boyfriend who robbed banks. Watt spent most of the first five years of his life living with his mother's stepparents, who were concerned that her wildness—not to mention the months she was in prison—made it impossible for her to provide a proper home for her sons.

Watt's grandfather was an angry and stingy man who worked in a factory. He was obsessed with money and hoarded what little he had. He preferred Nick to Watt because Nick was athletic and conventionally masculine, whereas Watt had no interest in aggressive play or sports. Watt remembered his grandmother fondly as "a good mix of sweet and sour." Ordinarily submissive to her old-country husband, she nevertheless stood up to him repeatedly in Watt's defense. The day the old man called Watt a "sissy boy," she told him she'd leave him if he ever said it again. Watt felt loved by her and protected, and she was able to soothe him when he was troubled.

When Watt was four, his mother married for the third time, and this union produced a third son, Jesse, when Watt was eight. Like Nick's father, this husband was an alcoholic. "My mother was an asshole magnet," Watt said, accounting for the procession of drunken losers she was always either planning to marry, married to, or breaking up with. His mother boasted that she never hit her sons, but unlike his grandmother, Watt remembered, she never protected him or his brothers either. He was thus often cruelly disciplined by frightening men that he scarcely knew. He thought his mother weak willed, depressed, and oppressively needy.

In school he did well until the fifth grade, when his mother moved them unexpectedly to an especially unwelcoming neighborhood. Watt had difficulty making friends at the new school, found the lessons boring, and began to cut classes. He didn't like being teased about being fat. By eighth grade he was cutting all the time. While his mother was at work, he'd practice the guitar and watch cooking shows on TV. They lived in a studio apartment, and his mother brought men home to sleep with, dividing her bed from her sons' with sheets she hung across the room from a clothesline. When Watt woke up needing to pee, he would have to pass her and her boyfriend to get to the bathroom. Then he ate the candy and cookies he hid under his bed to distract him from the things that were always going bump in the night. He never slept well.

At sixteen, Watt dropped out of school, and at eighteen he found a job with a company that ran tour boats along the city's shoreline. The owners, a married couple, took Watt under their wing and soon recognized his potential. He worked for a while as a deck hand and maintenance man, and then they trained him to become a captain. He took and passed the GED exam because a high school diploma was a prerequisite for the captain's exam, which he also took and passed. Watt was extremely successful in his new role, although the daunting task of piloting a large vessel filled with passengers through a maze of sail- and power-boats led to his first panic attacks. He also got second job as houseman for a professional couple with two young children. These people virtually adopted Watt and provided him with his first experience of secure family life as well as access to a world of art and culture he'd never dreamed existed. Watt was still living with them when we met. During the summer he worked for them part time and drove the boats. For fun he played guitar and sang for a little garage band. He also wrote songs in which he tried to express the feelings that always seemed so bottled up inside him.

I.

During his first hour on the couch, Watt reported a dream. He looked in the mirror and discovered to his astonishment and joy that all his hair had grown back. (Though still in his twenties, Watt was completely bald.) He wondered what it meant. I said that I thought the dream contained his hope for the analysis, namely, that something lost from his head—from his mind—would be restored, that he would begin to grow again emotionally. "Cool!" he said, clearly pleased. The dream made me feel hopeful as well because I saw it as tantamount to an oracle, an announcement not from the gods but from Watt's unconscious that he believed the analytic path on which we were embarking would take him where he wanted to go. Such hope is of enormous significance in analysis, as it is in growing up. Like a child, a patient must feel that however overwhelming life may seem at times, he will grow and ultimately prevail.[1] Watt also reported that on the previous evening he had rented the Andy Warhol film *Flesh*. He said he wanted to see it because he was turned on by the beautiful hero, Joey Dallesandro, which proved he must be gay. I asked him which part of the movie he'd liked best. "The scene where Dallesandro is naked on the floor holding his infant son," Watt said. "He's very tender and plays with him as he feeds him. That's my favorite." I said it was interesting that the scene he liked best was about a father lovingly nurturing his little boy, precisely the sort of experience he'd so painfully missed growing up. Watt was surprised; it had never occurred to him to think of it that way.

His fixing on the image of the beautiful father playing with his child strengthened my assumption that the analysis would reanimate Watt's longing for a tender and nurturing father—a father who would want to touch him emotionally, who wouldn't be afraid to let his own feelings show (Dallesandro's nakedness), and who would lovingly teach him to be a man. The physical perfection of the movie star brought to my mind the possibility that Watt longed for a father whose perfect masculinity would provide an antidote to the confining emotional attachment Watt felt to his weak, depressed, and depreciated mother (Kohut 1991). I thought Watt's confusion about whether he was gay or straight probably spoke to his question as to whether he was doomed to experience himself as depressed—which to him meant like a woman, that is, like his mother—or whether he could come to feel energetic and competent, which for him meant like a man.

On the surface Watt was open, friendly, and at ease, but beneath this veneer there was something guarded and opaque. He *seemed* to trust, but he trusted no one. It became clear before long that he assumed I would soon want to be rid of him. He was, after all, a low-fee patient, and although I might need to use him for a while in the service of my training, I'd kick him out the first moment I could or the first moment he pissed me off. He'd been a "charity case" all his life, relying, like Blanche Dubois in *A Streetcar Named Desire*, on "the kindness of strangers" (Williams 1947, 178). But such kindness had strings attached. Strangers always expected something in return.

The question for Watt was, What did I want? He was sure that if he didn't come up with whatever it was pretty quickly, he'd find himself on the street. He had dreams of fellating powerful men, never with his own pleasure as the motive but rather in an effort to placate and control them. He believed that these dreams proved he was homosexual, but to me they seemed to have little to do with sex. What they suggested rather was the sexualization, that is, the sexual expression, of a nonsexual need to take the strength of a father into himself and his view that masochistic submissiveness was the only way he might do so. Fantasies like these came up most often during breaks in our schedule or after small derailments in our rapport—times when the connection between us on which he had come to depend felt weaker. This indicated to me that his longings to connect with a strong father figure served crucially to ward off anxiety and depression.

From the outset Watt found the basic analytic rule of free association terrifying. He didn't want to say, without censoring, what came to his mind; he wanted to tell me what I wanted to hear. He assumed that I wanted to hear that he was straight because he assumed that I was straight, and it quickly became more important to him to please me than to seek to discover his heart's desire. So he was soon talking about his attraction to various female television and movie stars, and he began once again seeing and sleeping with his former girlfriend Carla. After a while he reported a disturbing dream in which he and Carla were having sex until Carla began to morph into his mother. Watt woke up in horror at this "Freudian" dream. "I guess you'll say the dream is about my sick oedipus complex," he said. But I said nothing, so he went on. "After we have sex, Carla always wants to talk about her problems, and I mean for hours. And she expects me to give her advice. Like I have any! I just want to go to sleep." I said, "It sounds like your dream came true." He didn't follow. "Carla turned into a depressed woman who wanted you to solve her problems, just like your mother. No wonder you worry about getting involved with women."

Watt was surprised. He never thought of himself as rejecting women, even though it was he who had broken up with Carla the first time they were involved and he who was now thinking of ending the current relationship. He was convinced that any woman he might pursue would reject him because he was fat and bald and had a too-small penis. These ideas kept his darker fears of women far from consciousness—the fears about violence, sexual engulfment, and the collapse of self boundaries that had grown out of his long and traumatic exposure to his mother and her lovers in bed. But maybe this was true, maybe he did worry that women were finally all like his mother. He remembered reading *Portnoy's Complaint*. Portnoy told his shrink that he could never escape his mother, that as a child he'd leave her in the morning only to discover that she had somehow managed to transform herself into his teacher so that she could give him grief all day before flying home on her broomstick to bust his balls all night. Now that he thought of it, Carla was always needy and depressed and *did* seem a lot like his mother. Even the woman in whose home he worked, a woman who was cultivated, energetic, and rich—in short, everything his mother wasn't— became completely unhinged whenever a drain backed up or a fuse shorted out. Maybe it wasn't so surprising that he longed for the company of strong, competent men.

After eighteen months he did break up with Carla again, and he didn't attempt to date other women for a very long time. Nor did he get any closer to me. He appeared to enjoy his sessions and to look forward to them and to find whatever interpretations I made "interesting," but he kept his distance. He wasn't yet ready to risk admitting that I was important to him.

II.

Two years into the analysis Watt got very upset in the office for the first time. It was the Saturday morning (we were meeting on Saturdays then) before Father's Day, and he alone among his friends had no plans. "I have a giant black hole where all the Dad stuff is supposed to be," he said. He didn't want to be with his friends on Father's Day, and he didn't want to be alone. It would be a nice day to be dead, he said bitterly, especially inasmuch as he imagined I would be having a great time with my children. The following Monday he didn't show up, explaining on Tuesday that his alarm clock had failed to go off, his usual explanation for missed morning sessions. I said that I thought his clock was working but that an internal alarm had directed him to sleep through the session so that he wouldn't have to feel bad again about not having a father. He was surprised; he'd completely forgotten that we'd been talking about Father's Day during our last session and that it had been extremely painful for him. Watt didn't like thinking that things like the alarm clock not working happened to him because of feelings. It was better to think such things were beyond his control. I made it sound like he was entirely clueless, he said, the last to know what was actually going on inside him. He thought analysis was supposed to make him feel better, but it was making him feel worse. What was the point of dredging up awful feelings from the past when there wasn't a damn thing he could do about them? His hostility frightened him, and he quickly retreated to his default position of bland friendliness. Nonetheless, an angry cat had been let out of the bag.

The following Christmas I planned to be away for two weeks. Watt insisted that a break from the analysis would be a relief; it would allow him to sleep in and relieve him of the burden of having to come up with things to say. A week later he called the resort where I was vacationing to tell me that he'd tripped while going down a flight of stairs and broken both his arms. We came to think of this fall as his "Freudian slip," the one that gave the lie to his claim of self-sufficiency and dramatized his feeling of falling apart when our schedule was interrupted. His inability to acknowledge how "dis-armed" he had felt when I left had manifested itself entirely literally, as if to prove (the French psychoanalyst) Jacques Lacan's maxim that what is suppressed in the "Symbolic Order" of language returns in the "Real" of traumatic action (Lacan 1977). After two and a half years of carefully skirting its margins, he had fallen down the rabbit hole and into the wonderland of the transference—that is, the relation with the analyst that evokes the thwarted feelings and longings of earliest childhood, feelings and longings that are the source of the analysand's current problems. Analysis cures by bringing these lost emotions into the lived relation with the analyst, allowing the issues bound up with them to be worked through and ultimately resolved. Feelings then that Watt had tried so hard to keep "at arm's length" had forced their way first into his actions and then into his consciousness.

Watt couldn't work for a time, but the family he was living with cared for him and nursed him. After the casts were taken off, he required extensive physical therapy to regain the use of his hands and arms. He loved physical therapy because he adored his physical therapist, Marie. Being with her made Watt think of a baby's interactions with a perfectly responsive mother. The feeling of being touched, manipulated, and for a while even fed reminded him of Joey Dallesandro's baby in *Flesh*. Suddenly he was himself the envied baby, experiencing a sort of "polymorphously perverse" pleasure (Freud's term for an infant's erotized response to all forms of its own functioning and to all forms of parental manipulation) in response to Marie's hands, voice, and smile. She was patient, gentle, and encouraging; he struggled to please her whenever they were together and exercised faithfully according to her instructions between sessions. Her competence, her devotion, and her delight in his progress lifted his spirits, and like a schoolboy with a crush on his teacher he found excuses to extend their time together—a minute here, two minutes there. He couldn't believe how lively, intelligent, and funny she was and that she liked his favorite movies and bands. As the weeks passed he found himself also noticing how attractive she was and wondering if she might not have more than a purely professional interest in him too, especially after she showed up one night at the bar where his band was playing to hear him sing.

Marie reminded Watt of Mike, his best friend and roommate for four years while Mike was in graduate school. Mike had worked summers with Watt on the boats, and they had gotten a place together. During that time Watt commuted to his houseman job, except when his employers were out of town and needed live-in child care, and he moved back into his old room. Mike was Watt's inspiration. He encouraged Watt to lose weight, work out, stop smoking, and think seriously about his education and future. Watt did all of these with increasing enthusiasm until one day Mike announced out of the blue that he was moving out of their apartment so that he could live with his new girlfriend. Watt was devastated. He admired Mike; indeed, he imagined that he was in love with him. And then Mike just split. Watt gained back all the weight he'd lost, went back to smoking three packs of cigarettes a day, and quit the health club where he and Mike had exercised together. These memories frightened him because he worried

Marie might tell him that she, too, had someone else—as indeed she did as Watt learned when he found the courage to ask her out. He was heartbroken, and again he crashed, losing interest in the exercises he was doing to strengthen his arms and shoulders and the diet he had undertaken to make himself more attractive to her. Bad as he felt, however, it encouraged him to know that his attraction to Marie was real and unlike any sexual longings he had ever felt for a woman before. Indeed, Watt had clearly loved Marie (unlike Carla, whose most recent appearance in his life seemed to have been largely staged for my benefit); his intense sexual feelings for her had arisen out of admiration, as had his love for Mike.

Watt almost never reported sexual thoughts or fantasies directly involving me. After breaks in our schedule, however, he often dreamed the familiar dreams of fellating older men, which I thought pointed to his disillusionment with me for abandoning him and his regressive wish for enlivening contact with father figures to ward off his anger, loneliness, and depression. He always worried that such dreams meant that he was homosexual, but again, I was convinced only that they spoke to his need to manage his disappointment. The fact that they weren't accompanied by feelings of arousal lent support, I felt, to my hunch that their manifest sexual content wasn't where their chief significance lay. Interestingly, Watt's homosexual fantasies and dreams were exclusively directed toward heterosexual men. Homosexual men in his eyes were tainted with effeminacy: he saw them essentially as women who needed from men exactly what he needed and were thus incapable of providing him with what he lacked. As a result he found it impossible to desire them.

This phase of the work, on the idealized figures who lifted Watt up before failing him and causing him to crash, began to make sense of his fear of flying. Merely thinking that he might have to travel somewhere in a plane could bring on a panic attack, and he practically had to put himself in an alcoholic stupor before actually boarding a flight. Flying meant putting himself in the hands of a stranger he didn't know but had to trust with his life, which of course he found impossible. Ordinarily Watt's lack of trust wasn't a problem because he was good at looking trusting when the situation called for it—another of his ways of placating people. But flying wasn't about convincing the pilot that he trusted him; it was about convincing himself.

In this context Watt realized that in his best efforts to idealize people, he often *didn't* convince himself that they could be trusted; he always held something back against the likelihood that they would disappoint him. But he was finding it increasingly difficult to resist his growing longing to trust me unreservedly, as he had Mike.

Watt began watching sports. He'd never been interested in them, but because he knew I was, he began taking note of the scores and finding ways to tell me he was keeping up. Then he began watching games on television and would ask me questions about rules, strategies, and players as he headed for the couch or the door. I enjoyed answering his questions and sometimes imagined taking him to a ball game or teaching him to throw and catch properly, as my dad had taught me and as I'd enjoyed teaching my children. Of course, I'd very much liked Watt from the first, but it was curious to find myself thinking of him with the particular affection of a father for perhaps a nine-year-old son. What was going on? The psychoanalyst D. W. Winnicott talks about how important it is for parents to allow the child to place them where the child needs them to be (Winnicott 1971), and I think what put me in this place-of-the-father was Watt's touching expression of his forever-thwarted yearning to share with and perhaps in some sense to be "just like" the father he never had. He conveyed in these exchanges a quality subtly but compellingly different from his ordinary friendliness, a quality of vulnerability and hope beneath the casual surface.

I seldom commented on these moments because I didn't want to make him feel self-conscious and because I knew he was using the margins of the sessions in part to escape such scrutiny. I was also confident that we'd have plenty of time to frame things down the road. At some point, however, I did say I thought that in these liminal moments "before" and "after" our sessions, as it were, we were enacting something together and that something was an expression of longing— his longing to connect with me as he had never been able to connect with his father and my reciprocal longing to be a father to him.

Watt felt so happy and excited about the way we were relating that he worried there was something "wrong" with it. To bring himself down from this unfamiliar and somewhat dizzying "high" (and with it the fear that what was happening between us was merely a cruel setup, a too-good-to-be-true from which he'd come tumbling down as he had when Mike had unexpectedly rejected him), he decided that he was simply trying to manipulate and control me by talking about things I'd be sure to find more diverting than his pathetic life. Maybe we were just using one another this way? Maybe it was all a kind of blow job? It was clear, however, as we discussed his anxieties, that what was going on wasn't a blow job. Indeed, during this period Watt rarely had fantasies of fellating powerful men, and I began to think his questions about sports represented a transformation and desexualization of his wish for carnal knowledge of an idealizable male figure and a rekindling of his earliest wish for knowledge of his father's essential masculinity.

Watt began to feel more and more secure. His nightly cookie binges slowed down—no longer an automatic and necessary device for making it through until morning, now they were a comfort he resorted to only in the aftermath of specific disappointments. He began to sleep better and to find effective ways to manage his time and money. Perhaps most important, he became increasingly able to experience and talk about what he thought were unacceptable feelings. He no longer slept through his alarm clock when he was upset about something that was happening between us; he would dream of oversleeping but come in and tell me the dream. This made it possible for him to talk about the feelings that had given rise to the dream rather than splitting them off.

A major breakthrough occurred after Watt saw a movie in which a prison guard helps a prisoner write his life story by breaking the rules and providing him with forbidden paper and pens. The prisoner, a brutal murderer, is transformed by writing about his life and the knowledge that the guard will read what he writes. Watt was struck by the analogy of the movie to the analysis. The prisoner who makes a story of his life comes to see his experience—including his crimes—as effects of the violence that was done to him rather than as evidence that he is the inhuman monster he has always believed himself to be. Everything turns for the prisoner on the fact that the guard takes an interest in his life—his past and his future as well as the seemingly interminable present. Watt thought that telling me about his life not only gave it a shape it had never had but somehow and for the first time made it seem his own. The fact that I wanted to know and that I remembered what he told me helped him find words for what he'd lived through; and he could see that the words were producing a story—a history—that was his but also ours and that made him feel more connected to me. What he had suffered could never be undone, but the fact that his suffering for the first time had meaning and an enduring form in and through time changed everything. He felt he'd found a new voice. His sense that I was watching over him and remembering him made him feel both held and held together, and his sense that I was able to accept him—indeed to like him even when he wasn't playing a role—made him feel he might begin to like himself.

This new sense of coherence in time past and present carried with it a new sense of hope for the future. He decided to go to college and get his degree so that he could become a therapist and work with children. Until then his only plan had been that his little bar band might be discovered and signed by a major recording label. Writing songs had been especially important to him because he felt he could only express real feelings in his music. As he was able increasingly to face and share his feelings in the analysis, the rock star fantasy began to fade. He continued to write songs, but his daydreams of being adored by countless women who would dig him because he was famous started to strike him as adolescent. He thought that if he could play music with and for his friends, he'd probably be happy. Grandiose fantasies, however, tend not to go gently into any good night, so occasionally he'd imagine opening for Bruce Springsteen in Madison Square Garden, destined for stardom after all. Then he'd laugh and say, "Naahhh!" which made me think of Kohut's description of humor as a "transformation of narcissism" (Kohut 1978): that is, as a way to forgo archaic wishes by playing with and finally mocking them.

The thought of becoming a child therapist became more real and exciting to Watt every day. His chief responsibility in the household where he worked was child care, which he loved. He was friend and confidant not only to his own two charges but to many of their friends and even friends of their friends who came to talk to him because they'd heard he was someone who could help kids in trouble. He was encouraged to think his suffering might not have been entirely in vain. It seemed clearly the link connecting him to suffering children.

The major work of this long middle phase—years three through five—of the analysis continued to center around Watt's ambivalence about experiencing rather than splitting off his feelings—importantly his rage but also feelings of longing and love. His habitual approach to powerful feelings had always been to suppress them as much as he could by eating, smoking, and buying himself presents he couldn't afford. Then he'd berate himself for being weak and disgusting, someone no one would want to be around. Everything, he said, was his own damn fault. I said that blaming himself for things he could help, like eating, smoking, and recklessly spending money, distracted him from the ones he couldn't—namely, the traumatic disappointments of his childhood. Rather than experiencing the full impact of his rage and depression over his father's forsaking him and his mother's inadequacy, he protected himself by imagining that they hadn't failed him but that he'd failed them and that if he'd only change, the support he'd been denied would somehow still be forthcoming.

His approach with me was the same. He wouldn't let himself see that he felt hurt or angry when I disappointed him; he'd simply announce that he was furious with himself for some sin of indulgence or sloth for which he deserved whipping. Invariably it was possible to link these sins to some recent failure of mine that he barely remembered or considered irrelevant to his distress—maybe I was late for a session or failed to remember the name of one of his friends. Nonetheless, for a long time he refused to believe he was mad at me. He was mad at himself and not because of anything I'd done but because he was weak. He would say he was feeling better because he was sticking to his diet and smoking less or feeling worse because he was not sticking to his diet and smoking more; and I would say that I thought his varying ability to stay with his diet or not to smoke had everything to do with his feeling that he could rely on me and that we were connected or that he couldn't and we were not. Back and forth we'd go, Watt editing me out of his script, me writing my part back in. Eventually he came to see that his various excesses represented his efforts to self-medicate when he was in pain. Still, it terrified him to think he could be so dependent and needy, and he worried that when I realized the truth, I'd leave him.

Watt didn't mind telling me that he was angry with his mother or his bosses; they depended on him too much to forsake him. His mother in particular could tolerate his hostility because she was so cowlike and out of it that she scarcely noticed he was upset even when he was trying to tell her off, and even when she did "get it" and tried to retaliate, she could never stay angry long. But Watt was terrified to be angry with me. The way he understood his father's incomprehensible absence was to imagine that his father had known from the first that Watt's emotions were unendurably oppressive. Certain that I would see the wisdom of his father's point of view and abandon him myself, Watt sought to be as agreeable with me as he possibly could. He was thus relentlessly "pleasant." He'd repeat Jay Leno's opening monologue from the previous evening's *Tonight Show* hoping I'd laugh or lay out the intricate plot of a movie he'd seen on video because he knew I liked movies and hoped I'd be interested. But in contrast to my always-engaged reaction to his questions about sports, which came from a growing and newly vulnerable part of him, I often found myself bored with the material he presented out of his old defensive fears. I listened with a sense of dutiful politeness, angry at my inability to do anything other than mirror his false and self-protective blandness with my own version of the same thing. For a while I would get as caught up as he in scenarios of being entirely too "nice" to each other, but eventually I'd find myself ready to scream, and this would force me to shake things up by making an interpretation. I'd say that in being so "pleasant" with one another we were colluding to keep strong feelings out of the room, thereby confirming his conviction that neither of us could tolerate them. Such interpretations gradually allayed his anxiety—and mine—and we'd begin again to move ahead.

III.

As we increasingly understood how Watt tried to split off painful affects with various forms of "misbehavior," he began dreaming of horrible beasts on rampages, destroying everything in their path. I said that the beasts were his feelings. He insisted they were just meaningless dream junk, but after a while he could see that the dreams followed sessions that upset him as those preceding his misbehavior did and that they were offering us a vision of angry emotions he'd not known how to acknowledge. He bought himself a copy of Maurice Sendak's *Where the Wild Things Are*—a story he'd often read to the children he cared for— to celebrate his evolving acceptance of the fact that the wild things were in his heart.

On a day when I announced I needed to be away unexpectedly the following week, Watt couldn't conceal his rage from either of us. "Don't I matter at all?"

he fumed. "Couldn't you have given me more notice? This is really going to fuck me up!" I said that I was glad he was able to let me see how betrayed and angry he felt. The next day, however, he missed his session because he had such a frightening panic attack that he drove himself to a hospital emergency room, convinced he was having a coronary and was about to die. I said that the "heart attack" was an apt metaphor for his feeling that because he had attacked me, I would banish him from the analysis and he would die of a broken heart. He then remembered the Christmas vacation when he had insisted he felt nothing but had later fallen and broken his arms. His expression of rage—and, more important, our coming to terms with the panic it inspired in him—seemed a crucial breakthrough to us both. From totally denying that he had negative feelings, he had come first to recognize feelings of rage and depression concealed in various of his actions and dreams and finally to be able to experience rage and depression directly.

Watt also found he was able to express loving feelings. He began talking about how much he wanted to be special to me, indeed, how much he wanted to belong to me. Both of the couples he was employed by (the people he lived with and did housework for and the ones who owned the boats) insisted he consider himself "one of the family," but he knew he wasn't. He remembered the Uncle Remus tale in which Br'er Rabbit gets caught in Br'er Fox's "tar baby" and begs Br'er Fox not to throw him in the briar patch, pretending it's the place he most fears. Br'er Fox falls for the trick and sets Br'er Rabbit loose in the briar patch, where, of course, he immediately escapes because the briar patch is his home. Watt said that my office felt like the briar patch to him, and he wished it really was his home, his room, because if it was, I could never send him away. Kids in "regular" families have rooms they get sent to when they are bad, but they are never sent "away." He'd never had a room of his own and had always been sent away, but if the office were his room, it wouldn't matter how bad he was or how mad I got because we'd just talk about it next time in the briar-patch office that was his room.

IV.

As the fourth year ended, Watt began to feel that he finally had what he needed to grow up. He remembered his grandmother and recalled being safe as a small boy huddled under the bridge of her legs when she rested them on the ottoman in front of her chair. His sexual fantasies about fellating physically strong men had all but disappeared, replaced by a longing to incorporate what he saw as my moral strength into himself. He began to stand up to his bosses over matters of conscience, although he feared that doing so would get him fired. At the boats he witnessed a near disaster when a crew member came to work drunk and carelessly left open a hatch on the deck through which a small boy fell. Luck saved the child from serious injury or even death, but the boss let the man off with a warning, more worried about being short of help during the brief high season than in the safety of his passengers. Watt told the boss he'd quit on the spot if the deckhand was allowed to work even one more day. The boss fired the man and thanked Watt for bringing him to his senses. After this Watt told his other employers that they were copping out on their children by too often expecting him to discipline them. Again his stance met with gratitude rather than hostility. Later, Watt's troubled nineteen-year-old nephew asked if he could stay with him over the summer and work on the boats. Watt took him in and got him a job because the boy promised to get himself together, but he was soon busted for smoking pot at work, and Watt caught him stealing money from his wallet and prescription drugs from his medicine cabinet. It was clear that giving his nephew second chances only enabled his misbehavior, so Watt told him to leave, and despite the boy's pleading, he stood his ground. It was painful to say no, but Watt was proud of himself for sticking to his guns. He felt that in the past he had always compromised his integrity to maintain relationships, but now he thought relationships were worth keeping only if they allowed him to keep faith with himself.

He remembered the story of "Pinocchio," one of his favorites as a child. It was funny to think of the little wooden marionette's metamorphosis into a real flesh-and-blood boy. Watt had always been a flesh-and-blood boy—far too fleshy as he reflected ruefully—but like Pinocchio, he'd never been fully "real." Indeed it occurred to him that he'd always been a sort of marionette, manipulated by invisible strings that others controlled. Now, however, he seemed to have shed his strings. But where Pinocchio had been too wooden and stiff to be real, Watt had been too soft. What he'd needed was a solid backbone, and somehow it seemed he now had one. The masculinity he'd dreamed he could take into himself only homosexually (and temporarily) from a strong man was something he now felt had become a permanent part of himself.

After a long period of failed efforts at dating, each against a terrible gradient of anxiety that he would be rejected, he began to date a woman he really liked, a new hire at the boats. She seemed energetic and kind and made it clear she was attracted to him. He could see that the relationship would soon become sexual and worried about having to expose his naked body to her and perform in the role of a lover. What if she found him repellent or anxiety wilted his erection? What if she thought he wasn't any good in bed? He decided to get himself a prescription for Viagra—which it was soon clear he didn't need—while we discussed his anxieties. The idea that he was "performing" for his girlfriend led to talk about whether lovemaking was something he was doing for her or something he was doing with her but because it was what he wanted himself. As the relation to her grew in importance, Watt realized that what had kept him from connecting with women wasn't that they found him unattractive as he'd always imagined but that he was afraid of being subjected to the neediness and depression he believed they all shared with his mother. Like Marie, however, Quinn seemed completely different from his mother—lively and funny and hopeful rather than depressed. But then one day Quinn's sister attempted suicide, and she began to unravel. Suddenly Watt found himself in the role of her shrink as he had with Carla, and again it made him uncomfortable. Now, though, he told Quinn that he wanted to be there for her but that he could be there only as her boyfriend. She agreed that she needed a therapist; she found one, and they grew closer.

Around this time Watt had a dream he thought important. He was driving his car in an unfamiliar mountain region. The weather was stormy, and he was worried about what might happen if he got stuck. No one else seemed to be around. On a hairpin turn, one of his front tires ran slightly off the road and sent the car into a skid. He didn't feel panicky, as he was sure he would have in the past, but expertly slowed the car and then discovered that all the equipment he needed to fix the damage was in the tool kit. He thought the dream pretty much announced his self-state: he didn't have to worry about derailments in life because he had what he needed to set things right. This made him think about terminating, an idea he'd always found impossible to contemplate but one that now seemed the next logical step. He thought he'd be able to manage it because he no longer thought it would mean the end of our relations, just their taking a new form.

V.

Watt was happy to think of what we'd accomplished. He realized he did feel that the office was his room even if it was mine, and he joked that he was planning to build a doll-size replica of it in his apartment so that he could go there in his imagination whenever he needed me or just when he wanted to feel peaceful. But in fact, he said, the peace was already inside him. This was why he was no longer afraid of flying. He trusted the calm in himself because we had worked through his assumption that anyone he might rely on would fail him. I'd stayed with him despite his certainty that I wouldn't, and now he thought I was in some way permanently his. "It changes you," he said, "having someone come through with you. I'm more than I was." And this was true. He was full of hope for the future and had started college. He had a girlfriend he really liked and had promised himself he would stay with her for as long as they were good together, not out of a wish to please her or, for that matter, me. He could see that his dream of being the father he never had was going to come true. He felt he wasn't entirely free of homosexual longings, but these occurred rarely, usually when he was upset with Quinn or with me, and he didn't think they were likely to disrupt his life. He'd learned not to be afraid of his feelings, so if he was a little more inclined than the next guy to appreciate the image of a male model's washboard stomach in an ad on the side of a bus, so what? He loved Quinn's body and didn't have homosexual fantasies when they made love. He rarely had homosexual dreams, and when he did, they were no more a problem to his relationship with Quinn than the fleeting heterosexual attraction he felt to women he encountered on the street every day. Indeed it occurred to him that anyone in a relationship—whether homosexual or heterosexual—was going to be attracted to other people at times, and those who were happy in their relations lived with those attractions without being undone by them. Feeling attracted to a person outside the relationship but not acting on it didn't mean you were living a lie, it meant you were committed. He no longer worried about whether he was gay or even bisexual, although he thought Freud had been right to recognize such potential within us all.

We talked at some length about what our relations would be following termination. I asked what he would like them to be. He said he certainly thought of me as a friend but that it was perhaps more important for him to think of me as his analyst. He expected we'd run into one another socially from time to time as we had on occasion through the years, and he said he looked forward to that. He also wondered if he might come to see me or if that would violate some rule. I said I would be delighted to see him any time he might wish to be seen and that the only rules were rules we made together. He wondered if he ought to come back periodically as it were for tune-ups. I said that he ought to come in if he felt like coming in and that he ought not to if he didn't. What if he just felt like calling to tell me what was going on in his life, he wondered. I said that would be great but that I would think of him warmly regardless. He was pleased and said he'd certainly always be thinking of me.

He didn't often become terribly sad during this time; his focus was more upbeat than mournful, perhaps because for Watt a deep consideration of loss carried too great a threat of unendurable pain.

As we moved into the final days of the analysis, Watt had three dreams. In the first, he saw himself with dreadlocks. This reminded him of his first dream on beginning analysis, the one in which his hair had grown back. He guessed the dreadlocks suggested both the idea of dread—he was confident about being without me but a little anxious nonetheless—and the idea of strength—dreadlocks suggested the hair of a warrior. He wasn't afraid; he was one to be feared. Well, maybe he was both. In the second dream he found himself in an old hotel. His computer was set up in his room. With the computer he could somehow look into other rooms that housed strange and lonely souls he felt he knew and didn't know. He thought they were his family and all the people he'd lived with and been abandoned by growing up, even forgotten aspects of himself. He said he thought the computer was his memory and that with it he could access his history and the people he'd known. He didn't need to be with them, and he didn't have to wall them off to keep the feelings they inspired in him from overwhelming him with despair and rage. The third dream was again about his car. He was driving and noticed the ashtray filling up with oil. There seemed to be a leak somewhere. He thought the leaky ashtray meant sorrow. The car was wet, as it were with tears. He said he felt sad to be leaving me but happy because the sadness was sadness, it wasn't depression. And it meant he was growing up, so he felt sad and happy all at once.

As did I.

Thoughts and Conclusions

What conclusions can be drawn regarding the question with which this analysis began, that of Watt's sexual orientation? I think it's clear that Watt's sexual orientation was not something he had simply been "born with" and somehow lost, something that we rediscovered intact as treasure hunters might find buried pirate gold. Rather it seems that his sexual orientation came into being as the analysis progressed and Watt's sense of self became increasingly coherent. Even if I could have "answered" his question as to whether he was straight or gay at the outset, whatever I said would have been meaningless, because his problem wasn't fundamentally a lack of knowledge but rather his inability to feel comfortable in a sexual context until his sense of self was sufficiently coherent to allow him to manage the intense feelings attendant on sexual relating. "Not knowing" was his way of trying to explain his anxiety, his near panic, over the idea of having to participate in a world of adult relationships that—given his traumatic exposure to his mother's sexual behavior as a child—he thematized as sexual relations. In other words, his doubt about his orientation was akin to his fear of flying, a way of avoiding experiences that might cause him to crash and burn.

Because sexual attraction for Watt represented the erotization of admiring feelings and because he tended to idealize men who stood for him in the place of his absent father, his desire was predominantly homosexual, but it was exclusively for heterosexual men. His idealization of me during the analysis, however, was accompanied not by increased homosexual feelings but rather by an increasing sense of masculinity and attraction to women. I might have understood this as his way of escaping from his homosexual feelings for me into heterosexual fantasies out of the worry that if he expressed sexual feelings for me directly, I'd rebuff or criticize him. But his heterosexual feelings seemed such a joyful expression of his increasingly coherent sense of self and burgeoning delight in feminine sexuality that I trusted their authenticity. What all this suggested was that Watt had turned away from his heterosexual feelings not because he was essentially gay but because such feelings had posed too great a threat to his sense of self.

As Watt gradually came to accept the fact that I could disappoint him at times and still be worthy of his admiring regard and as he came to feel integral, competent, and strong, his dream of being the sort of family man and father he had always longed for seemed within his grasp, and the question of his sexual orientation ceased to be in doubt. He began to express a new capacity for intimate relatedness, seeing women no longer as depressed and degraded but rather as lively, capable, and self-sufficient, in a word as desirable.

It appears therefore that Watt's sexual orientation was the product of neither nature nor nurture, a pure expression neither of his genes nor of his education—although it is reasonable to think that these factors influenced his orientation, as they do everyone's. Rather it seems that his sexual orientation was the construction of his experience of both nature *and* nurture, that is, of what he made of living in the particular physical and relational worlds he alone finally occupied. In other words, it was about meaning—"sexuality as textuality," in Bonnie Litowitz's fine phrase (Litowitz 2001).

Sexuality had been a problem for him because the homoerotic desire he felt clashed with his deep and abiding wish to function heterosexually. Watt was caught between two impossibilities. To be heterosexual required that he identify with a father who'd abandoned him, with a rejecting grandfather, or with his mother's bad men. To be homosexual for Watt (although not necessarily for anyone else) meant giving up his wish to be a father himself and accepting a vision of himself and the other as damaged and degraded (Freud would say castrated) as his mother had been. Homoerotic desire functioned for Watt as the sexualized expression of his need for an internalized sense of masculinity. He might have made similar use of heteroerotic desire—that is, he might have used the idea of physically perfect and sexually available women to counter his depression over the lack of inner perfection and strength he perceived in himself; but he didn't because for him women were compromised by his experience of his depressed mother. Heterosexual desire was thus a source of frightening fantasies of paternal violence, maternal engulfment, and the collapse of self-boundaries. In short, it was a source of terrifying anxiety. There is nothing inherent in either homosexuality or heterosexuality that dictates such uses; rather, it was Watt's particular experience that dictated the use he made of them—all of which is to suggest that our sexual samenesses may be merely the stalking horse of our infinitely complicated sexual differences.

Sexuality serves and expresses the overarching needs of the self. As these change, the uses and forms of sexuality may change too. What the analysis cured wasn't Watt's homoerotic feelings per se but rather the fundamental fragility that required him to use sexualization as a defense against anxiety and depression. Eventually it was heterosexuality that offered him the best solution to the complicated problem of defining his existence in his own uniquely significant world.

We don't know exactly when and by what alchemy a self constructs its goals, ideals, and aspirations, but early in his life Watt came to have a vision of himself as a husband and especially a father, a vision that remained constant for him before, through, and after the analysis. Despair accompanied his fear that this profound inner goal might never be realized, even as a profound sense of joy followed his awakening confidence that such a future could indeed be his. The same despair and joy, as we know, follow the thwarting and the realization of other such deeply held aspirations, as, for instance, when one becomes strong enough to leave a job one hates and venture bravely forth to pursue work based on an inner dream. Those able finally to do what they feel they were "born" to do or to live as they believe they were "born" to live feel a special sense of "at-homeness" in the world, of being where they are "supposed" to be, of being lucky or even blessed. Sexual orientation, like other aspects of identity, character, and personality, is one representation of our efforts to solve the problems with which our lives and experiences confront us. As we develop we rule "in" various possibilities for vitalizing experience, while ruling others "out"—the self's cost, as it were, of doing business with the world.

Afterword

Four years have passed since the analysis ended. Watt hasn't come in to see me, but he calls perhaps once or twice a year to let me know how he is, and it seems things are going well. He's about to graduate from college and go on to graduate school; his plan of becoming a child therapist is intact. He's still with Quinn, and they are planning to marry soon. He asked if I'd come to the wedding, and I said I'd be greatly honored to. I called to tell him I had written this chapter and to ask if he would read it and let me know if he would be comfortable with my publishing it. He said he would be happy to read it and after doing so told me he liked it and would be happy to see it in print. I asked if he would be willing to write his own report on the analysis, and he said he thought he would like to do so very much. His account follows.

DISCOVERY: WATT'S PERSONAL PERSPECTIVE ON ANALYSIS

I never thought that writing about my experience of analysis would be as difficult as it proved to be. I thought that after spending so much time organizing my thoughts and emotions I would be able to turn out three or four pages of thoughts in no time. This was not the case. It was much more difficult than I thought it would be.

I have had many conversations with friends and family about my years in therapy. I have always been able to describe the experience rather easily. When I think about those conversations now, I find those descriptions to be a bit superficial. I would describe the process in terms of organizing my "internal filing cabinet" or "deleting viruses from my hard drive." In many ways these seem to be accurate metaphors for the desired result of therapy, but they don't really cover my personal experience of the process.

I remember having many mixed emotions when the idea of analysis was presented to me. I was intrigued and anxious. I wanted to explore my emotions and the way those emotions affected my interactions and relationships, but I was very worried about the intensity and the time commitment that I perceived to be inherent in an analysis. As I look back at the anxiety I experienced, I think that it was based on the fear that I would have to connect with someone on terms that were not entirely my own or expose feelings and thoughts that were better left unexposed and not the idea of seeing someone four times a week. After all, repressing those feelings was the only way I had made it through to adulthood.

I remember many images flowing through my mind when I considered starting analysis. I, as I assume most people do, acquired most of my ideas about analysis from television and films. I thought about the television ad in which the therapist sneaks out of the office for a cup of coffee and a quick check of the sports page while the patient is on the couch rambling on about his problems. The therapist then returns just in time to say "time's up." This might seem like a silly image to bring up, but it was of some importance to me. Deep down inside, I didn't think anyone would really be interested in anything I had to say about myself.

The other image that really stood out was the relationship between Judd Hirsch and Timothy Hutton in *Ordinary People*. I think that this relationship brought to mind the full range of hopes and fears that I had with regard to therapy. I was very afraid of unearthing some long-buried pain that might completely disrupt my life. This was not an attractive idea, even if I was less than happy with my current life. On the other hand, I think that there was such an internal longing for the emotional connection to a father figure, like the one that was developed in the film, that I was a little overwhelmed with the possibilities of analysis.

When I began my sessions I found the environmental design of analysis to be a bit strange. I was disoriented at first by the couch, the lack of eye contact, and the disembodied voice of my therapist. I wasn't used to being so disconnected from people when I was speaking to them. I also felt that I was "under the microscope," as it were. It took quite a while to feel even remotely comfortable in the setting. I think that I was the type of person who needed to see the face of the person I was talking to in order to judge my responses to questions. I needed to be able to see if I was giving the "right" answers. Throughout my life I had never told anyone what I really felt about myself. I always believed that if people knew what was really going on inside my head (or, more to the point, how screwed up I was), they would head for the nearest exit as soon as possible. My whole life was about not rocking the boat. So here I was in a situation where not only was I supposed to start rocking the boat but I was supposed to trust the guy in the boat with me not to let me drown if I fell in, which I was certain that I was going to do. Needless to say, the boat rocking didn't start for a very long time.

When I finally got to the point where I felt I could talk about some of the things that had happened to me in my childhood and some of the issues that brought me to the point of therapy in the first place, I used an interesting method of communication. I simply discussed all of these horrible things as though they had happened to someone else. I remember talking about the fact that that was what I was doing and trying to understand why. The simple fact was that if I had to be connected to these feelings, they weren't going to see the light of day. I think that before I could connect myself to my bad feelings, I first had to connect my self to my therapist.

Developing that connection seemed to happen in an odd way. The primary reason I started seeing a therapist was the need to know if I was gay or not. I had had one brief homosexual encounter with another boy as a teenager but had never had what I'd call a homosexual relationship. But I couldn't help feeling that I was "different" from other guys. I also felt very attracted to members of the same sex. So the question "Am I gay?" seemed like an appropriate one to ask in therapy. Upon reflection I think it was the wrong question.

When I say that my feeling connected to my therapist came about in a strange way, I mean that what started out as a way of avoiding making that connection became the impetus for the connection itself. I think I became tired of talking about feelings and emotions. Especially when I didn't feel terribly connected to what I was talking about. I started to talk about anything but my problems. I knew that my therapist was very into basketball. I figured maybe if we talked about something that he was interested in, we could forget about me for a while. I'm pretty sure he saw through this thinly veiled ruse, but we talked about basketball nonetheless. The remarkable thing about these conversations was that I began to learn about sports. I began to learn about sports from a man. I began to learn about sports from a man who didn't make me feel stupid or inferior for not knowing the things that I assumed every man should know. I began to not only feel that there was a place in the "man's world" for me but that there were men in that world who would welcome me there. I think it was at this point that I really began to feel connected to my therapist and that our place together was a safe place where I could really begin to find out who I was.

Suddenly, the issue of being gay or straight was replaced by questions like "Why didn't the men in my life care about me?" or "Why did they always make me feel like baggage?" It was through this relationship with my therapist that I began to understand that what I wanted from men was love, acceptance, and a sense of inclusion in their world. Who knew that you could learn so much about yourself by avoiding talking about yourself?

As I write these thoughts down, I am a bit astounded by the changes in my life. I am pursuing a degree in psychology. Going to college was not something I ever thought would be a possibility for me. I found the strength to quit an abusive work environment that I had been in for nearly twenty years. And finally, my fiancée and I are in the process of planning our wedding. I have a very hard time imagining that any of these changes would be happening if not for my experience in therapy. I can't say that I feel like a different person because of analysis, but I think it's fair to say that I feel differently about the person I am.

Note

1. Usually it's the therapist's job to keep hope alive during the times when the patient can't. Yet the very fact that the patient shows up and pays his bill gives the lie to even his most despairing pronouncements because, of course, if he believed things were completely hopeless, he wouldn't keep trying. Paradoxically, though, and interestingly, at times when I feel I have gotten caught up in a despairing patient's despair and have begun to feel that the work might indeed be pointless, it is invariably the patient who pulls me out of the depths and lets me know that what we are doing is a source of light—however faint—in a life of otherwise near-total darkness. This rekindles my ability to hope, and we soldier on.

CHAPTER 5

Caroline: "The Same but Forever Changed"

Caroline came to therapy because she felt depressed and anxious much of the time. "Everything's really wrong and nothing's really wrong," she said. "My life just isn't going the way I want it to." At twenty-six, she had graduated from college and was making progress in her chosen career in the arts but at the high price of always feeling behind, like she wasn't doing a good enough job, like "the bottom is about to fall out of things." She constantly felt that she was about to make the critical mistake that would show her boss, a much admired older woman, that she had made an error in hiring her and trusting her with increasing responsibility.

Her love life, meanwhile, had gotten really complicated and confusing just when it should finally have been sorting itself out. After two serious boyfriends in high school and college, she'd become involved with Nick, four years her senior. When she came to treatment, they were engaged to be married, but she had the niggling sense that something just wasn't quite right between them. She noted that she sometimes found him moody and selfish, that he tended to criticize her in public in embarrassing ways, and that her friends and family sometimes found him distant, a quality that they interpreted as arrogant. Nevertheless, he could be wonderful, fun, and loving, and they had many interests in common. He was a successful entertainment attorney, and she envisioned them as a powerful personal and professional team. Still, she found herself fantasizing about other men she would meet through work, curious about what a life with them might be like and whether they would be less demanding and selfish than Nick was. Although Caroline did not see this as a problem at the beginning of our work together, I also noted that she seemed not to have much capacity just to play, to let loose and enjoy herself, to pursue her leisure activities with gusto. Partly this was a result of long work hours, but it was also partly due to her tendency to feel she was spinning her wheels on the weekend, sleeping too much, or simply not doing much with her free time unless it was completely and in-flexibly scheduled. Leaving room for spontaneity in her schedule seemed almost inevitably to give rise to depression and anxiety.

Following an initial consultation, I recommended psychoanalysis to Caroline because of her long history of mild to moderate depression and anxiety (for which she did not want to take medication) and because her issues extended into multiple areas of functioning, including work, love, and play. She'd had a twice-weekly psychodynamically oriented psychotherapy in college that ended when she graduated and moved to another city, but she understood that the work she had begun there was unfinished. She opted to begin twice-weekly treatment with me with a goal of progressing toward analysis "if the work went well."

Caroline was the older of two sisters born to a mother who was bitter about her role as a housewife and frequently depressed and a father who was a highly successful businessman and "lived for his work." Her four-years-younger sister Cheryl had never wanted to have a career. She had married young and started a family; Caroline felt simultaneously both disdainful and jealous of this. Though she was tempted to marry Nick and "live happily ever after as Betty Crocker," she was afraid of giving up her career and work identity because "I don't know if I could ever trust him—or anyone—that much."

Just when we were about to begin analysis, about a year and a half into treatment, Caroline came into a session and opened with a dream. The day before, she had announced that she would be away on a big business trip on the official "first day," thereby delaying our start, and she prefaced the dream with the off-hand comment that the trip, beginning analysis, and the dream were probably related.

"I dreamed I was at your office. I was sad that it was the end of our session, the last one before I was going away for a week. As I left, I accidentally jarred a glass table by the door. I saw the sheet of glass fall off the table as if it was falling in slow motion. I wanted to catch the edge but I couldn't move. The glass hit the ground and shattered into thousands of shards. I was afraid to look at you; I thought you would be very angry. When I finally looked up I saw that a gash on your right palm was bleeding. I felt scared and sad."

When Caroline tells me her dream, I find myself glancing anxiously at my right palm. And then I begin to wonder, why the *right* one? I feel for a moment like the analyst in the *New Yorker* cartoon who, when his patient says "Good morning," thinks "I wonder what he meant by that?" But as I reflect on it, I realize that it is my custom to shake hands with Caroline at the end of the session when there is to be a break in treatment and to wish her well. The handshake is a rare moment of contact—of literal, physical connection—in a treatment that stresses putting thoughts and feelings into words rather than actions. I wonder if the gash on my hand in Caroline's dream means to her that I would not or could not make the gesture of the handshake before her big business trip, a gesture that probably helps solidify her sense of connectedness to me as we part. Is Caroline afraid she will wind up leaving me mad and hurt instead? And does the dream hint at what Caroline was afraid of within the analysis: that getting closer and knowing her better could be dangerous for me, resulting in hurt and anger?

These thoughts run through my mind, but I say nothing and wait to hear what Caroline will say about the dream images. She notes, laughingly breathing a sigh of relief, that I do not actually have a glass table in my office. She speaks of our impending separation, ruminating about her business trip and whether she will be able to make a successful presentation at the upcoming important meeting. She jokes that she wishes I were coming with her in her suitcase, saying that she would feel more certain of her abilities if I were with her.

But having expressed this wish to carry me with her, Caroline seems surprised as she begins to realize that her joke has led us right back to a topic we have been focusing on recently, her relationship with her mother during her teenage years. She recalls, more solemnly, that she did in fact hurt her mother as she grew up and became more independent, literally and figuratively leaving her mother behind. "She needed me to need her," she reiterates somewhat angrily. "She would get her most depressed, angry, and withdrawn when it came time for me to leave her, like to go to camp or to college. She would always say she didn't want to get in my way, that she wanted to let go of me when the time came, but I think it was hard for her. And she made it hard on me."

"Do you think our impending separation relates somehow to the image of the shattering glass in the dream?" I ask. Caroline pauses for a moment, then says, "My mother used to say that I was like a bull in a china shop, barreling around the house. I was too much for her, energetic and lively as a child. I guess that same energy ultimately propelled me away from her, into a career that involved my moving far from home." She looks quizzical for a moment. "And there's a story I remember that really involved broken glass." Although I am always eager to hear such stories, I find myself momentarily distracted, caught back at the idea of Caroline as a bull in a china shop.

A bull in a china shop. What are the origins of this expression? I contemplate the masculinity of the bull and wonder: did Caroline's mother see her athletic daughter's vim and vigor as somehow masculine and threatening? But this question will have to wait as Caroline careens off in another direction. "I don't think I've told you this, but as a toddler I broke the last of three milk glass dishes that my mother had on the coffee table. I think they were some of the few household trinkets my mother and father could afford at that point in their marriage. My mother was particularly attached to them. I broke them in order, first the largest, then the middle-sized one, and finally only the smallest one was left.

Mom later told me that when I broke the last one, she practically threw me across the room and into my crib. I think she must have felt really guilty about it afterwards. The story seems vaguely familiar to me, though I don't know now if I actually remember it or if it seems familiar from baby pictures."

"How does it show up in baby pictures?" I ask, puzzled. "Well," she says, "there's one of me at about eighteen months, fingering the last of the three glass bowls. It was heart shaped with tiny pearls around the edges."

I find myself wondering why Caroline was allowed to play with the dish, even captured doing so in the photo as if it were cute, if her mother didn't want Caroline to break it. After all, if you lead a bull into a china shop, the results are predictable.

This first glass story reminds Caroline of another one. In this second tale, a three-year-old Caroline slips away from her parents' cocktail party, climbs up on her bed, and snags a jar of petroleum jelly sitting on her dresser. The jar slips to the floor and shatters, and Caroline is found sitting on the floor, surrounded by broken glass, gamely chomping on a large piece. A party guest holds Caroline upside down and shakes her, attempting to dislodge any pieces of glass caught in her mouth or throat. In the family lore, it is an episode that captures Caroline's adventurous spirit and natural curiosity yet hints that these qualities are potentially dangerous, even potentially lethal.

I decide that it's time to try to tie together these themes of fragile relationships, natural curiosity and independence, and shattering glass. "We've discussed how your adventurousness and curiosity and maybe even your competence threatened to disrupt your relationship with your mother by making you not need her. She needed you to need her. If you didn't, she would feel angry and hurt. It's as if the relationship itself, the bond between you and your mother, was fragile and easy to shatter. And now," I remind Caroline, "you're going off on your own, without me, on a big business trip that is the direct result of your effective efforts at work. I think you're concerned about whether I can tolerate your capabilities and your independence. I think you're concerned that one or both of us—or maybe our relationship—will get hurt the way I am hurt in the dream. And maybe you feel like the more intense things get in analysis, the bigger the risk to our relationship will be."

I feel certain that my interpretation has touched a nerve when Caroline begins to cry. "In a way I feel like I've spent my whole life trying to make up for hurting my mother by leaving her. Maybe part of holding myself back at work has been that I want to be sure I'm not too competent and don't leave her too far behind. I guess it's possible that I'm also worried that I'll hurt you, too, even though I get the sense that you're stronger, you don't need me to need you as much. But when I start analysis, all bets are off about how much each of us might need the other or demand from the other."

I say, "I think you're very worried that you can't be competent and independent and also remain close and connected to your mother and to me as well. Perhaps you're worried that that conflict will intensify as our work together becomes more intense in the analysis."

"It's funny because when I was coming here today, I was tempted to buy flowers for you," Caroline says, "maybe as a kind of going-away present, a way to be sure you're not really angry or hurt while I'm gone. I guess they'd be a sign that I do still need you, even though I'm going off on my own for a while. And a reminder that I still want you to want me back when I'm ready to come back and start four times a week."

"We do need to stop here for today," I say, rising from my chair to open the door for Caroline. "I hope you have a good trip."

"Thanks," she says a bit shyly, looking down at my hand as I reach to open the door for her. Then we shake.

This session with Caroline demonstrates some of the hallmarks of psychodynamic treatment, whether psychotherapy or analysis. She reports a dream that we explore together in the session using the technique of free association. That is, Caroline tells me whatever comes to mind, and I associate silently along with her, noticing what the images in the dream stir up in me and trying to figure out how to relate these to what I already understand about Caroline and her relationship with me and others. We attempt to relate the story of the dream and its themes to the transference—that is, to the view of me and our relationship that Caroline holds at the moment. In addition, we speculate about how the dream relates to Caroline's childhood relationship with her mother. We pay special attention to areas where Caroline has strong feelings, suspecting that these feeling states are important to our understanding of what Caroline is saying. In short, what Caroline and I are doing is what the many therapists and patients engaged in psychodynamic psychotherapy and psychoanalysis around the world do. But just what are we trying to accomplish, and how will we know when we've accomplished it?

I believe that each of our brains contains models, maps, of how relationships work; they tell us what our own role is in our relationships as well as how relationships are likely to make us feel and what to expect from others. These maps probably reside in the cerebral cortex, the thin gray uppermost layer of the brain that is the most evolutionarily advanced. I've seen how these maps guide my patients' behaviors within relationships as surely as the motor strip of the frontal lobe of the brain guides the movement of their hands. Our models, or brain maps, of the rules that govern relationships are formed through early experiences with important caregivers. Encoded in early life, then modified and elaborated with later developmental experience, these rules are repeatedly reenacted in our adult relationships, including the relationship with an analyst. There is nothing special about the so-called transference to the analyst as compared to other relationships, except that in psychodynamic psychotherapy and psychoanalysis it is explored in depth.

Our cortical models of how relationships work have connections to the limbic, or emotional, center of the brain. These connections too are forged in early childhood as we interact with caretakers whose job it is to help us learn the tricky task of emotional self-regulation. When an infant smiles and his mother smiles back, this moment of engagement and emotion shapes the child's view of himself, of his mother, and of their relationship. When the infant has had enough stimulation from this interaction, he will avert his eyes from his mother, allowing his physiological reaction to the intensity of the experience to settle down. Gaze aversion is a nascent attempt to begin to learn to modulate his own internal emotional state—to learn to tolerate feelings without being disorganized by their intensity. Most mothers respect this aversion of gaze on the part of the infant and allow him to disengage, but in some mothers it seems to trigger feelings of abandonment that cause her to pursue the infant, trying to hold his gaze. A pattern ensues that Beebe and Lachmann (1988) have termed "chase and dodge"—the mother "chases" the baby and attempts to reconnect, while the infant "dodges" her attempts to meet his gaze in an effort to avoid being overstimulated. His early attempts to regulate his own inner states are thwarted. If experiences like this are repeated over the course of early development, they may leave the child with unpleasant or threatening views of himself, his mother, and their relationship as well as trouble regulating emotion in later life. I believe that most people come to psychodynamic treatment suffering from both disturbances in their models of how relationships work—which Schachter has termed "habitual relationship patterns"—as well as problems in how they regulate affective states, especially painful ones such as anxiety and sadness.

The network of neurons in Caroline's association cortex that encodes her map of how relationships operate is a problem for her precisely because it is a prototype—a rigid model—that straitjackets her approach to relationships. She does not learn from new experiences with people because her relationship prototype can structure new interactions only according to its own guidelines, based on relationships long ago past. She is primed to look for clues in how new people relate to her that fit her model of how relationships are supposed to operate. If we were to define the rules for relationships that Caroline's cortex contained at the beginning of her psychoanalysis, they might go something like this: "Other people need me to need them. For me to be separate and independent is dangerous to people around me and threatens to disrupt my connection with them. I must be extremely careful when I go off on my own, or they will end up shattered. I cannot be successful, powerful, and independent and also warmly connected to others. Therefore, my choices are to be depressed, needy, and incapable (like my mother) but connected or to be competent and self-sufficient yet all alone. My abilities are a constant threat to my fragile relationships with important others." Caroline's relationship map is like an organ grinder whose monkey can play only one tune no matter what the audience requests. To me, this is the definition of neurosis.

Caroline came to psychoanalysis, as most people do, because she felt depressed and anxious much of the time. She was unaware that she even had a prototype of how relationships work, let alone that it kept grinding out the same tale every time she met someone new. Nor did she know that the tale itself—the bind of being unable to be both comfortably independent yet warmly connected— was itself contributing to her feelings of anxiety and depression. Part of the task of psychoanalysis is to flesh out, in an increasingly complex way, the patterns of relating to others that are unconsciously and repetitively reenacted in relationship after relationship. With Caroline, I didn't have long to wait to show her another example of her cortical map in action.

When she returns from her business trip two weeks later, Caroline lies down on the couch for the first time. She starts out by telling me with excitement about buying a ceramic figurine for her mother while she was away: "I got it right at the beginning of the trip and carried it all around with me. In fact, I was running a little late to my presentation because I was waiting for it to be properly boxed. I made it on time, but it was close."

"What's the figurine like?" I ask.

"It's a peasant woman with a duckling at her feet. She's feeding it, and the duck's head is angled upwards. After I bought it I realized that I should have gotten it at the end of the trip so I wouldn't have to worry about it getting broken. The duck's beak is really fragile. I carried it around very carefully and got it back in one piece, but I worried about it the whole trip. My mother loved it, but I still felt really guilty that she hasn't ever been to Europe and I have. No statue could make up for that." Caroline looks guilty and begins to cry.

I try to bring her back to our last session, remarking, "Getting the figurine at the beginning of the trip sounds like a way of carrying your fragile relationship with your mother, and perhaps your easily shattered mother herself, around with you while you were gone. It sounds like buying the figurine caused you to attend all the while to the dangerousness of the trip and the fragility of the figurine. And it almost made you late for that important presentation."

"I got you something fragile, too," Caroline laughs, presenting me with a box that contained a tiny Limoges cigar box with a removable cigar. "It's to remind you during my analysis that sometimes a cigar is just a cigar, that you shouldn't make too much of everything I say. But it is funny that it's equally breakable as my mother's figurine and that it's also perhaps a way of appeasing you about being more independent, like the gift of flowers I contemplated getting you before you left. And now *you're* the one who'll have to worry about whether it gets broken or not, not me."

"It seems this analysis feels like a dangerous business to you already," I say, "full of fragile figures, tenuous connections, breaking glass, and the possibility of lacerating guilt over people or relationships that get shattered beyond repair." Caroline and I were, I felt, off to the races in this analysis already, focusing on a core theme of her relationships and relating it to our own connection to one another.

Through the slow and meticulous process of exploring her fantasies, her dreams, and the complexities of our relationship to one another, Caroline began to change in subtle but important ways. Fast-forward two years into analysis, and her dreams and associations to them had begun to sound quite different. One session, she reported the following dream from the night before:

"I go to a large club which to my surprise has a swimming pool. The sides of the pool are transparent; they allow you to see the legs of a person swimming underwater, to recognize who they are. I am surprised someone has spent the money to build a pool like this. I have heard it cost two million dollars to build. I notice a woman at one end, beckoning me into the water. I am a little frightened to jump in and wonder if the pool will crack, but when I test the water with my toe, it is warm. I get in, swim toward the woman, then float comfortably on my back."

I am surprised as I listen to this latest dream to find myself thinking about the very beginning of my work with Caroline. When she first began psychotherapy, she felt concerned about whether she could actually be in therapy twice a week. Would she run out of things to say, her verbalizations waning to a slow trickle? Would she be overwhelmed by feelings she had been warding off for years? She compared beginning psychotherapy to diving into water that was cold and uninviting, that took her breath away when she entered it. She didn't know whether she would sink or swim. Only when I reminded her that I would be with her in the water, swimming alongside, did she begin to be relieved. Now I wonder if this dream contains a possible reference to that earlier interaction. Only this time, the water into which she dives is warm and welcoming. There is a hint of the image of glass in the transparent pool; Caroline feels concerned that it might crack if she dives in, perhaps a reference to her old tendency to see her assertiveness as potentially damaging. But this time it does not shatter, a testimony, I believe, to the greater strength and resilience of Caroline's connections to me and to important other people in her life.

Caroline's own associations run along these lines as well, a sign that we are on the same wavelength. She comments that this time we are linked by our enjoyment of the warm water rather than by the cold, hard, fragile glass that used to represent our bond.

But psychoanalysis, despite its focus on the relationship between analyst and analysand, does not operate in a vacuum. When it goes well, the work has far-reaching implications for a patient's inner life and relationships outside the office as well. And in fact Caroline's relationships had indeed shifted significantly by this point in analysis. Her relationship with her boss had become more personal and intimate, and she had progressed at work, getting several rapid promotions and gaining increasing responsibility for artistic choices within the office. Caroline was beginning to find that things between her and her boss no longer felt so tenuous; connections had begun to feel to Caroline like rubber bands, not cold, hard glass that would shatter unless handled with extreme care. They could, potentially, be stretched to the snapping point, but generally there was more flexibility and give, more margin for error as well as more warning before things got out of hand. "I used to relate to the line in *Evita* in a song called 'High Flying, Adored,' in which Evita has climbed so far in her life and the lyric says 'Don't look down, it's a long, long way to fall.' But now I feel there's a floor under me at work, a history there that can't be erased by one error, even a big one. Maybe," Caroline now says, half joking, "it's that I don't feel a need to be quite so high flying or so adored at work myself. I don't need adulation in the same way, and so there's less riding on the relationship itself and less that can go wrong than there was before when my self-esteem was depending on it."

Through the associative process that Caroline and I have been pursuing in our analytic work, her prototype relationship map is becoming visible to us. Caroline was surprised, in the first session I reported, when her "joke" about taking me with her on her business trip led so acutely to her struggles with her mother over independence. But it is exactly connections like that that make clear to patient and analyst where the roads on that map connect, sometimes unexpectedly, with others. As Caroline becomes more aware of her mother's intolerance of independence—and her own anger at it and guilty wish to escape it—dampened her own autonomy and self-confidence, she can challenge these old inhibitions and begin to reclaim the heady right to stand up for herself.

Undoubtedly my affection and respect for Caroline also played a role in her increased self-esteem. Analysis works, I believe, in large part because the exploration of old, engrained patterns of behavior occurs in the context of a new, intense, and highly emotional relationship with the analyst. The patient can experience his or her being in *all* its dimensions, perhaps for the first time ever, in the presence of another who regards those dimensions with unconditional positive regard. This makes for deeper and broader self-knowledge and a firmer and more respectful awareness of the "self" with which one encounters the world.

I think that Caroline is telling us with this imagery that being separate, independent, and competent at work now feels more natural than it did earlier and doesn't seem to threaten to disrupt or undermine her connections with others.

As she says, there is more margin for error. Further, as Caroline's sense of herself has solidified, she no longer depends on others to fuel her positive view of herself with constant praise and admiration.

Much of the middle portion of Caroline's analysis involved a trip back to the china shop—a sifting and sorting through of what constituted aggressive and assertive traits and how they related to being "masculine" or "feminine." Caroline spent much time in treatment trying to construct a new self that would feel adequately feminine without feeling weak or too soft. She wanted to be able to be self-assertive and tough with others when the situation required it without feeling that she was turning into "a ball-buster, a bitch that no man would want to deal with." During this period, we addressed repeatedly feelings about her father's insistence that men hated women who were "too much" and her own belief that she needed to be soft and agreeable, not a handful, neither too needy nor too tough. Her mother's embittered, depressed perspective on what it meant to be female—that she had to put up with a husband who gave very little emotionally and had to put aside everything of interest to her in the service of being a mother—had colored Caroline's perception of what she could expect in her own relationship with Nick.

Caroline began to see how this coupling contained familiar remnants of her parents' relationship, with Nick "putting her in her place" when she became too cocky or independent. As Caroline grew more comfortable and less constantly careful of and attentive to Nick's every whim, he grew more jealous, more tyrannical in his attempts to control her and keep her close to him. The more confident she felt, the more likely he was to try to tear her down, to make her feel badly about herself in ways that would inhibit her personal growth and growing independence. Caroline came to see that she had chosen a partner who fit her fears and fantasies about her relationship with her mother—someone who wouldn't, and couldn't, tolerate her independence yet remain close and warmly connected to her. In addition, she came to see that her father's distance from her mother and the seeming lack of affection and partnership in their marriage had limited her own expectations about what a relationship could be. Nick, in her final analysis, was someone whose self-esteem depended on always being "hard"— in control of himself and his emotions and unaffected by others, much like Caroline's father. After postponing their wedding several times, Caroline ended the engagement to Nick during her fourth year of analysis.

Newly single, she began a self-improvement program that seemed to be an attempt to reconstruct herself both inside and out. She continued her analysis. She went to a personal trainer several days a week, tested out looks that were newly feminine and sexy, and began to pay more attention to her hair, makeup, and clothes. These changes were made possible by a new inner feeling that she was doing what she was doing not for anyone else but for herself because of how it made her feel—in other words, that it was the result of an enhancement in her own sense of self and self-esteem.

Within the treatment during this period, Caroline's earlier reverence for me and her sense that I "had it all and was all put together" came into question for the first time. One day she admitted that as she followed me down the hall from the waiting room to my office, she had the thought that I looked fat in the pants I was wearing that day. This first admission of some competitive feelings left Caroline embarrassed and alarmed about what my reaction would be. After all, her own thighs and buttocks were increasingly toned from working out. She was quick to counter the implied criticism with reassurance that she loved and admired many of my other attributes, such as my sense of humor and the way I smiled at her as she left the office every day. We began to explore why the criticism had made her so anxious and found ourselves elucidating another piece of her relationship map, a new road leading back to Caroline's experience of her mother's dependency.

While some patients experience long periods of intense anger with their analysts during analysis, it became clear that Caroline experienced being different from me in and of itself as an expression of hostility toward me. Making her own choices about what kind of woman to be was not only dangerously independent but also a secret way of criticizing aspects of what I had chosen for myself in my own life, who I was as a person, as a woman, and as a romantic partner. For instance, Caroline couldn't praise her own choice of suit without feeling an obligation to say something nice about mine to neutralize her sense of covert criticism of me, competition, and ultimately, superiority. What went for the suit went doubly for the important others in our lives as she began to wonder more openly about my own romantic and sexual life, trying to imagine what kind of partner I might have chosen and what my life outside the office would be like. Yet at the same time, Caroline was careful to avoid learning more about me lest she have further fodder for her growing critical feelings, and she once put down a magazine in my waiting room when she realized it had an address on it different from my office address—in case I might live in a "disappointing" neighborhood.

We began to see that Caroline's mother experienced Caroline's desire to be different during adolescence as an attack rather than a natural phase of teenage separation and differentiation. When her mother felt attacked, she would become depressed and angry, and Caroline would be left holding the bag—either trying to make up with her mother (attempts to which her mother responded icily) or feeling enraged at her mother's unwillingness to let her be her own person. In time as I tolerated her attacks, Caroline realized that not everyone was as rejecting of her wish to be an individual as her mother had been.

During our fifth year of analysis, my pregnancy challenged her fantasy that I would never want children and so be distracted by them from pursuing a powerful career. As I became more round and soft during the pregnancy and also revealed that I planned to return to work half time after maternity leave (which necessitated some shifts in our appointment schedule), Caroline began to think that perhaps she could successfully combine aspects of being soft and hard, stereotypically feminine and masculine, into a mosaic that would work for her. But further work revealed that Caroline was also secretly angry about and resentful of these changes in me and especially of the idea of being displaced by my baby, to whom she imagined I would ultimately be more attached and devoted than I was to her.

As this work continued, Caroline began dating a man who was himself "softer" than Nick—more emotional, more overtly loving and tender, more appreciative—but who managed to be assertive and successful as a businessman in an artistic field related to Caroline's own. Their relationship quickly became serious, and Caroline found herself thinking for the first time that perhaps she might like to have children after all. She hadn't wanted to before, out of concern about whether she could have a different kind of relationship with a child, and especially with a daughter, than she and her mother had had.

Perhaps most important, as Caroline's work and love life became less constricted by conflicts, and she experienced them as more fulfilling, Caroline began to expand her capacity to play. This began when her new boyfriend Dave dared her to try to learn to play tennis with him on one of the first vacations they enjoyed together. Caroline took him up on his offer, but at first she was working at playing, studying what she was supposed to be doing on the court and practicing attentively. Over time as they played together, she became more able to simply let go, get engaged in their volleys, and have fun. The moments of depression and anxiety she had experienced in "downtime" in the past also seemed to evaporate as she became more comfortable simply hanging out in the park reading the paper or riding her bike around New York City with Dave. As it became clear that "spinning her wheels" all weekend was rapidly being replaced by lazy Sundays of dim sum and bike rides, we agreed that Caroline was ready to stop analysis.

It was in the context of our discussions of termination (that final-sounding term for the end of analysis), approximately three months before we actually stopped, that I approached Caroline about the possibility of participating in this book project with me. She was at the same time delighted, apprehensive about whether she could do a good job, eager to have an excuse to work with me in a different setting, and able to explore the question of whether my offer was appropriate, somehow exploitative of her and our work together, or unnecessarily revealing of the details of her treatment to the world. While she initially jumped at the chance and agreed, I urged Caroline to let the idea percolate and let us explore it together.

We focused especially on what such a project would mean about contact with each other after termination. Caroline had often sent me postcards during her travels and had generously brought me small gifts, the meanings of which we always investigated. She had said that she planned to keep me apprised of her life after analysis, perhaps by returning at times to fill me in on what was happening and perhaps by dropping me a note—or a wedding invitation! While like many patients Caroline appeared to long for posttermination contact ("Couldn't we just have coffee or a drink and you could talk about you for a change?"), by the end of the analysis she had also come to appreciate that our relationship was unique, and she desired to keep some of the reasons for its uniqueness—including my relative neutrality and lack of involvement in her day-to-day life outside my office—intact. "I might want to come back to work on something, and if we'd totally shifted to a different mode, I might have lost an analyst even though I'd gained a friend."

After much discussion of how contributing to this book might fit into our analytic and posttermination relationship, Caroline continued to wish to participate. She liked the fact that it would keep her in the front of my mind after we had ended, and she liked the fact that ultimately I thought that our work was important enough that I wanted others to understand how it unfolded and what made it valuable. Doing the project together was a way of both documenting our work together and thinking about its importance to each of us. While she understood that my asking her if she would like to participate was an atypical thing for an analyst to do, Caroline was pleased that I took my work seriously enough to want to convey its essence to others. We agreed that I would not send my own write-up to Caroline for several months after the analysis ended, during which time she was certainly free to change her mind about participating. If she did not, we would meet once she had read what I had written and I had read her contribution to discuss the impact of the writing and of this shift in our relationship.

The night before analysis ended, Caroline dreamed that she and I were alone on a terrace of an apartment building watching a sunset together. She proposed a toast to the sunset, and we clinked our tiny liqueur glasses together before sipping a bright orange substance that had the intense flavor of tangerines. The liquid stunned her tongue and mouth, for it was fragrant, tangy, tart, and sweet all at the same time, almost too intense to bear. She could feel the substance running down her throat and into her stomach and had the sensation of warmth emanating from her very center. The taste woke her up and she found herself in tears at the prospect of our relationship ending. In telling me of the dream, Caroline remarks on this final transformation of glass imagery into something positive that united us. She feels that the dream had the tone of a Caribbean postcard, with the tropical drink and the intensity of the sunset, and that it was like joining me on a minivacation before we parted ways.

I wonder if the minivacation might also be the plan of working on this chapter together, and I worry whether the romantic imagery of the dream means that I have been seductive in suggesting that Caroline work on the book project with me. But when I raise these possibilities with Caroline, she jokes about the movie *What about Bob?* in which a patient follows his therapist on vacation and shows up unexpected on his doorstep. The book project, it seems, pales in comparison to what she really wishes she could have with me: a vacation evening together, watching the sunset and toasting each other in exotic liquids. In fact, the feeling of the intensity of the tangerine juice and the warmth in her gut that it produced was sort of orgasm-like. It was as if the liqueur could curl your toes the way a good orgasm might. Perhaps the dream was her way of having an intense sexual relationship with me before she left? Even though we had explored Caroline's sexual feelings for me at other points in the analysis where they seemed relevant, I find that she is speaking now with a new openness on the subject. To Caroline, the dream was a marker, a toast to our work together. Yet it carried also the wistful feeling of all that has been left not fully explored—even after the six-year analysis that has taken her so far—and of all the possibilities that can never be captured on paper, either. It was a culmination and a good-bye, but one that left lots of feelings open, lots of issues to be profitably explored.

"I may just want to seduce *you*," she remarks, "not the other way around. So that you won't let me leave. I'll be too fascinating to let go of, and we'll have to continue. I think that's why I'm bringing you this juicy dream—literally juicy—as a kind of gift in our last session." She recalls the end of the movie *The Prince of Tides*, when Nick Nolte drives back over the bridge to his home in South Carolina at sunset, leaving psychiatrist Barbra Streisand, with whom he has had an intense—and intensely therapeutic—relationship behind, to rejoin his regular life with his wife and children. In the movie, Nolte and Streisand spend their last evening dancing at the Rainbow Room, and Streisand cries because when Nolte leaves, she will be all alone once again without love in her life, without a partner. "I think you have love in your life, a partner and children that you love," Caroline says now. "And I think that you love me, but you're not *in love* with me. You'll miss me, but your life will go on. Meanwhile, I'll be doing all the old things, but in new ways. I'll be the same but forever changed."

"So the drink together in the dream was like the night Tom and Dr. Lowenstein shared at the Rainbow Room, knowing they had to part and yet not wanting it to come to an end?" I ask Caroline, picking up on her associations to the movie. While it's true that analysts and their patients don't spend their last moments together doing something as overtly sexual—and boundary violating—as dancing at the Rainbow Room, Caroline's dream indeed contains erotic elements, and I find myself seduced, analytically speaking, by her dream and my own associations to it. Questions and theories spring to mind as I enter the spirit of the analytic dance that happens when analysts and patients are working well together. But then I glance at the clock and find myself feeling deflated and sad as I have to recognize that we'll be stopping our work together in a few minutes. Perhaps the erotized imagery of the dream is a defense against loss for Caroline, just as engaging in one last analytic dance had served to prevent me from realizing quite how much of our last session together has already passed.

But Caroline and I have each incorporated representations of one another into our neural networks, connections etched in our brains and minds that will endure for both of us once we stop meeting. We will literally be carrying parts of one another with us for the rest of our lives, just as we carry those important early life relationships that help us form our views of what it means to be a person, what it means to have a relationship with another living being. I realize that I want Caroline to think of me, to feel connected to me when this is all over, that I feel attached to her and will think of her fondly as well. I think about the power and fun and sometimes the scariness of being an analyst, of allowing someone else's mind to reverberate with and ultimately take up permanent residence in mine. Before we both know it, the session has come to an end. "We do need to stop here," I say to Caroline, rising from my chair to open the door after conveying to her how much our work together has meant to me and reminding her that my door is always open to her. We both chuckle, recognizing that I have used my usual tired old "shrink" line to end our session once again. As we'd anticipated our parting, Caroline had mused about whether I would say the line this way even on our last day together, and now I have, without even thinking about it. "It's reassuring that some things never change around here," she says. We walk to the door, both with smiles yet with tears in our eyes, and I recall for a second the dream of the broken table and our tentative handshake so long ago. But there is no hesitation this time as we hug good-bye, both of us now soft enough to be affected by each other and sturdy enough to stand apart.

Caroline's View

It's a funny experience to see yourself written about by your analyst. Unexpected and unusual but not unwelcome. It's interesting to see both what seems similar in how we think about what happened between us those six years and also fun to note what's different. For example, for my analyst, the story seemed to start, at least in the retelling, with my dream about breaking the glass table in her office. To my mind, it starts earlier than that, with the dream I had the night before I went to see her for the very first time. In that dream, I'm at the piano, being forced to play some dramatic Chopin number that was never my favorite growing up but that I did use to play when I was taking lessons and doing recitals. On the horizon there are the rocket's red glare and the bombs bursting in air—a huge war is going on, perhaps the Revolutionary War, and I'm not that far from the front lines. There's a stern, demanding man standing over me whose job it is to police my piano playing. If it's good enough, it will stop the war from happening or else help my side win. If it isn't, I'm in danger, at personal risk. I think the dream says a lot about how much pressure to perform and how much threat I felt about everything when I started analysis—the pressures and threat of my daily life that led me to feel that "nothing was wrong and everything was wrong." There's more than a hint of narcissism in the dream, of course, since it's about being able to save so many others or change the course of history if I play well, but the main feeling in the dream is one of dread and pressure, that so much is riding on my shoulders. The song I had to play in the dream wasn't of my own choosing, and yet I had to play it well or suffer dire consequences. At the beginning of analysis, I wouldn't have been able to play my own tune, organ grinder's monkey that I was. I do know that analysis changed all that, but I honestly don't know how.

Perhaps what I can most usefully convey to complement what my analyst wrote is that from my perspective as a patient it didn't feel as clear-cut and coherent as it seems to have felt to her, those themes and how the work unfolded. It was murkier and messier than that for me and yet somehow, like a rock that has the waves wash over it for a century until its shape is different even though there's no perceptible change from each wave, I did change.

The most important way in which I'm different is that I walk around feeling happy and centered for most of the time most of my days. Rather than feeling a dark cloud of anger or sadness or anxiety, which I used to live in, I'm more comfortable in my own skin and more confident of who I am and what I want. I'm also more comfortable letting people know when I don't like what they do or how they act toward me, and I'm generally less leery of confrontation than I was before I had analysis. I think I'm this way because I am more certain of who I am and what I think of myself independent of the evaluations of others than I used to be. Since I'm not depending on looking at how they see me to decide how to see myself, what they think simply doesn't matter as much. Like a rock gradually shaped by a wave, this way of being different came as a result of a gradual shift during treatment rather than because of some thunderbolt of insight. I'd say my analyst values pattern recognition and insight or at least highlights it more in our work as she writes about it than I do. To me what stands out most over the course of time are moments of mutual intense feeling, moments where we both had a good laugh about something that happened or something that one of us said. And there were moments of intense connection where I realized she was moved by my story. Once when we ended with something difficult that had happened as a child with my mother, I saw that she seemed teary-eyed when I left and that stayed with me, the notion that I could actually move her and have an impact on her. I think it was in part that absence of deep feeling, of communication of both laughter and tears, in my family that brought me to analysis in the first place.

I found it funny that the two things my analyst left out of her own account of the analysis had to do with sex and money, especially since I think that she was generally attuned to and interested in both topics during our work together. As I thought about it after reading what she had written, I felt that the main reason she probably didn't include either had to do more with protecting my privacy than avoiding the issues, especially since they were not avoided in our work. In other words, I think it was out of respect for my privacy that she glossed over both topics, but I feel fine about filling in some of the details myself, and I think that being sexually freer and making more money, being less conflicted about wanting to make money, were important aspects of the analysis that haven't been discussed.

When I started analysis, I rarely had an orgasm when I masturbated, and I never did during sexual intercourse. I always felt that the closer I came, the more I scrutinized my own reaction, and, in short, by pushing myself to let go, I actually inhibited myself. Because of my difficulties trusting others, I also felt that I didn't want Nick to see me in an out-of-control way and that in a sense I worried about letting him see me with my guard completely down. Perhaps I was worried that I'd be a mass of naked desire and intimidating or unlikable for that reason or else that he'd find my being out of control threatening and off-putting. Practical things happened as we talked about my difficulties achieving orgasm, like I felt less conflicted about buying and reading erotic stories that fueled my fantasy life and I bought a vibrator, which for the first time in my life actually made it easy for me to reach orgasm and allowed me to have multiple orgasms. The practical and experimental changes I'd make would then get woven back into the analytic work, like my feeling that wanting more and more pleasure was greedy and somehow problematic. My analyst never made direct suggestions like why didn't I use a vibrator, but I found that when the internal conflicts were highlighted and worked on, then I was able to see or find more readily the practical answers that had been there all along. Having better sex with another person was partly the result of increased sexual self-knowledge about what I liked and didn't like that I'd gained through fantasy and masturbation and partly a result of all the work we did on issues of trust, independence, and interdependence in relationships more generally. As my analyst notes, feeling that I could do my own thing and be independent from another person yet still close to them was instrumental in developing my relationship with my husband. It was also instrumental in how my sexual relationship with him has been.

Being able to play with being attracted to my analyst physically and also wanting to be able to seduce her were things I felt more comfortable exploring toward the end of analysis. The many meanings of sexuality in relationships grew clearer then, for I could see that I might want to engage her interest so that we wouldn't have to stop or for her to fall in love with me so that I'd be her favorite—it wasn't just that I actually wanted to be sexually involved. The sunset drink of the glowing tangerine substance that warmed my insides is a kind of melding of a romantic image, a sense of inner heat that goes with sexual arousal, with the warmth that comes from close relationships. Before analysis I could never comfortably put these two together, and though it took until the end of analysis to express the wish and desire to put them together with my analyst, I was finally able to do it. As she notes, by the time I was able to do it, I had also come to realize that our relationship was already special and the only one of its kind in my life, so that however much I'd longed for actual friendship or even romantic involvement over the course of it, it was actually a more special relationship than those because I knew she would never act on my wishes and fantasies, and therefore I felt more free to have and to explore them.

Like sex, money is something that got better and better over time in my analysis. I once calculated that based on the promotions and raises I'd received, analysis had more than paid for itself; I would never have anticipated doing so well financially without analysis. As I felt less ashamed of and conflicted about my own financial ambitions and my desire to be a real player in my field, I found it easier to stand up for myself in asking for the money I needed or deserved for the jobs I was doing. I also came to be much less judgmental of other people for being interested in or motivated by money, whereas before analysis I would feel that someone who was manifestly interested in money was crass or boorish, and I would think ill of them. My narcissistic ambitions came to seem more healthy to me and like they didn't have to be hidden under the cloak of being forced on me by torture as they were in the first dream. I could *want* to make music that would stop wars and influence people without having a stern and demanding taskmaster that I had to please standing over me; I could own up to my ambition and recognize that I was my own taskmaster. Of course, as I succeeded more, I also paid my analyst more, so she was also financially rewarded by our work together, and I enjoyed being able to pay her full fee by the time our work together ended. I think people might have a different perspective on paying for treatment if they were able to view it as an investment in themselves that might literally pay off—but then I guess that if they were comfortable seeing it that way originally, they would already be partway through their work and financial conflicts!

Let me close by saying that analysis was definitely the most important single thing I ever did for myself. I see myself continuing the work we did on my own now, a few months after ending, and while giving up the relationship itself was difficult and sad, I do see my analyst's continuing presence in and influence on my life. Analysis literally changed everything, from how I feel inside and how I think about myself and my relationships to how I behave in relationships, how much money I make, and how my sexual life is with my husband. Nothing I have done has had such a marked impact on so many areas of my being, and for that I am profoundly grateful. It remains hard for me to explain to myself exactly how analysis does what it does, but I see in a daily way in so many thoughts and feelings and actions that it does work even if I still can't quite explain how. I found it very hard to dive in at the beginning, but I hope that this book will encourage others to have the trust in the endeavor needed to take the plunge. I can pretty much guarantee that it'll be the swim of your life!

CHAPTER 6

Sarah: "This Aplysia . . . Makes Me Sick to My Stomach"

> This aplysia . . . is so shapeless and sluggish, so squashy and
> slippery, that it makes me sick to my stomach.

My first meeting with Sarah is preceded by a telephone call. A person who introduces himself as an old friend of hers urges me to take her on as a patient. The friend warns me against letting her slip away "because Sarah," he says, "is a person who offloads problems onto other people, but I'm afraid she might withdraw if she is offered real help. Moreover, she gives the impression that she can deal with any difficult moment she is going through because she is a very active and resourceful person, really full of energy. I guess she would tell you she is going through a difficult moment, but actually I can tell you that her life is just a sequence of difficult moments! Every time she appears to get herself together, but it is only seemingly so because shortly afterwards she gets into another mess. She starts something with a lot of enthusiasm, and then at the first sign of difficulty she makes a scene and gives up. This is the way she is. I'm afraid she could do the same with the analysis; she could even say she wants to do it but then drop out because she has gone off on another tangent."

Sarah comes for her appointment. She is a woman in her forties, not really beautiful but with elegant features, soberly and tastefully dressed. She strides into the office and immediately, without any preamble, starts talking about the difficult moment she is going through. She has an intense gaze; it reflects the liveliness of her inner life and the effort to express what is going on inside her more than it does an interest in the person she is talking to.

She talks heatedly, without stopping, and usually without finishing her sentences. A new subject takes the place of the previous one, which has been barely outlined, so that after I have been listening to her for a while, I feel submerged by disparate fragments of subjects started and dropped. I don't have the elements

I need to understand what she is talking about, and from time to time I try to remedy this with some short question or comment, but this doesn't improve the situation much; Sarah almost ignores me, giving short, vague answers and then immediately plunging back into her thoughts. She doesn't seem interested in locating her intense affective (that is, feeling) states in factual reality—she gives no information about where, when, with whom, or why. Nor does it occur to her that I may not be understanding what she is talking about.

During the intake interviews I learn that she has always worked—as a regular salaried employee or as an unpaid volunteer—in international humanitarian agencies that bring assistance to people in trouble: victims of disasters, wars, poverty, abuse. She has sometimes moved from one agency to another because of conflicts with her superiors and her criticisms of their political and organizational choices.

When Sarah was twenty years old, she was married for a year to a fellow student. They decided together to interrupt their studies and to set up a literacy and health education project in a developing country, but fierce disagreements about how to realize the project led to its termination as well as to the end of their relationship. From that time on, Sarah has been uncoupled, living on her own or sometimes with a roommate.

Sarah was the only child of very young parents. She remembers her mother, who came from an Eastern country and got married mainly to escape from poverty, as glamorous and charming. About her father her memories are more vague; she remembers him too as a charming person, but a general opinion that he was a rather immature and childish man was probably right. Soon after their marriage, Sarah's parents lost interest in each other, and neither seemed to be interested in looking after their child. The mother was probably affected by a psychic disturbance that led her to drink too much, so that she spent long periods in nursing homes.

Sarah talks reluctantly about her childhood. Her most acute and vivid recollections are of how alone and neglected she felt. Though she frequently says that she is feeling very distressed, she doesn't say much to make her present suffering understandable. She does state that she doesn't like the word *treatment* at all: she has been being advised to "get treatment" since she was twenty, and she resents this suggestion a lot. She still maintains that she isn't ill, and anyway she is skeptical about official medicine. Nevertheless, she thinks she needs someone to help her because she feels on the point of doing "something desperate"—as she once did ten years before, when she struggled against the impulse to drive off a bridge in her car. She needs someone to help her realize herself, but this time she wants to do something different from the things she has tried in the past: "I have had enough of going round with people practicing forms of meditation and self-consciousness! This time I have to go deeper into my mind and understand what really troubles me. Maybe psychoanalysis is right for me because it is not really a treatment, is it? It is mainly a way of understanding oneself, isn't it?"

She says that now something is upsetting her life again, something she has already experienced and thought would not occur again. It is an intense emotion, like an urgent need to change and to run away from anguish, but it is also something physical, "something," she says pointing to her belly, "that sits there like a dead weight that won't dissolve." It seems to me that this weight, made up of emotions and of physical sensations—a true psychosomatic tangle—apparently develops when Sarah is involved in relationships with people she feels both attracted to and rejected by. It is not clear to what extent she is reticent on this subject and to what extent she is incapable of expressing her overwhelming distress in words.

Undoubtedly Sarah's distress is intense, and it is clearly visible through her expressive gestures—she is restless on the chair, she puts her head in her hands, she gets up and walks up and down. She behaves like a panicked animal shut in a cage, and one understands how a person in such a state might try, as she once did, to free herself from such urgent and explosive pressure through a suicide attempt.

From the first interviews, Sarah shows what turns out to be a typical feature of her way of communicating, a feature that was especially evident in the first year of analysis. While her communication has a strong affective quality that conveys a reasonably understandable meaning, the meaning of her *words* is much less clear and intelligible; her speech tends to be incoherent, chaotic, with overlapping subjects. For instance, usually Sarah doesn't introduce people she refers to, so that they appear and disappear from her narrative just on the basis of her need to express—or rather to free herself of—unpleasant feelings.

So when I can understand that she had a quarrel with someone, it is not because she has told me what happened, or how, or—even less—who was involved but only because I can guess from some detail of her narrative that she had an argument. Things become even more complicated when it turns out that there are two important people in her present life who have the same name. Their name comes up often, but Sarah gives me no indication of which one she is referring to.

Her way of speaking resembles the way children tell you what happened to them when they are deeply worked up. They are too excited to make the facts clear; the listener has to know already what happened and who was involved in what. With Sarah, the more intense the emotions involved, the more chaotic and incomprehensible her narration becomes. The emotional upheaval breaks the uncertain boundaries between herself and the external world, resulting in a lack of separation between herself and the person of whom—as well as *to* whom—she is speaking. This inability to contain and represent within herself feelings, wishes, and thoughts indicates an identity weakness of which she is herself sometimes sharply aware, as, for instance, when she suddenly exclaims with a mixture of regret and anger, "I don't exist! I don't exist!"

The Containing Function of the Setting

During the first interviews with Sarah, I thought a lot about how I should answer her request for a psychoanalysis. On the one hand, I was aware that there were aspects of her personality and pathology even besides her poor aptitude for reflection—such as impulsiveness and inconstancy in her relationships and life choices—that argued against a capacity to maintain the heavy commitment in time and money necessary for an analysis. On the other hand, it struck me that although emotional discharge was more typical behavior for her than organized discourse, Sarah wished deeply to understand herself and was committed to this idea. This made me suppose that perhaps, if she had access to an intensive psychoanalytic process, she would be able gradually to relinquish her discharge mode of communication. When I told her what psychoanalysis was like—certainly a rather long and intensive undertaking—she accepted immediately, even enthusiastically. Remembering what Sarah's friend had told me in the phone call, I wondered whether she would have second thoughts. But never throughout our work did she question her choice.

In fact, except for some turbulence at the beginning, the analysis had a stabilizing effect on Sarah, as she herself acknowledged by saying repeatedly that at last she had found "something to keep her firmly on course." The analytic setting very soon turned out to be what she needed to contain her disparate states of mind and begin to put them in order: "I don't think! I can't think on my own. You make me think. . . . No, actually, *this place* makes me think!" she said after the analysis had been going on for a while. "It's enough for me to come in here to start thinking! It's incredible! Why can't I do it on my own, outside of here?"

Sarah took considerable advantage of the environmental and relational aspects that are typical of psychoanalysis—the sense of security of the regular daily appointments, the absence of contact between patient and analyst outside the therapy, and the interested and benevolent attention of the analyst, who maintains toward the patient as neutral and respectful an attitude as possible and who abstains from sharing with the patient any aspect of his or her own personal life.

Not that Sarah entirely appreciated the analytic setting at the beginning of treatment. On the contrary, she repeatedly objected: to the fixed schedule of the sessions and to my failure to give advice, tell her about my private life, or express opinions about social, cultural, or political events.

At the beginning she couldn't put up with all these frustrations and met them with criticism and sarcastic commentaries on rules and authority, but after a while she began to take the rules of the analytic setting in better part. Her annoyance at having to adjust to a situation under someone's else control—she tended to rebel against anyone who was "in charge" of her—changed quite soon into acceptance and then even into a special kind of appreciation. The analytic situation (that is, the rules of the setting and my person as guarantee of them) eventually came to mean an assurance of stability, security, confidence, reliability—everything that her childhood had seemingly lacked.

In the initial phase of our work, Sarah made use of the analysis in "impersonal" or "nonspecific" ways rather than specifically analytic ones. By that I mean that our early work was not directly aimed at detecting or understanding unconscious mental contents and processes (making the unconscious conscious).

The arrangement of the analytic situation as a whole—I mean constancy of time and space together with the sympathetic and caring attitude of the analyst—provides the patient with the experience of a baby being held in a secure environment by a good-enough mother. Of course, this "holding function" isn't set in motion automatically just because one lies down on the couch for forty-five to fifty minutes and talks to a listener; for the patient as for the baby, a caring figure is necessary. But if properly carried out, the holding function of psychoanalysis is highly effective for mobilizing psychic resources and particularly self-reflective mental activity.

In Sarah's case, the capacity to think about herself and to scrutinize the implications of her own feelings—what is called the *self-reflective function*—was able to be reactivated, stabilized, strengthened, and eventually built up. This happened through a complex process of mutual regulation of our relationship during which, for instance, I came to understand how to choose my interventions; how to pace them; which words, expressive style, and tone of voice to use; when I should actively help her deal with her feeling and thoughts; and when I should listen quietly to her discourse without interfering.

This complex work of regulation of the relationship is like the gradual weaving of a web of interpersonal meanings, like the way a baby grows up in a good-enough family environment—that is, an environment in which a reliable parental figure is basically present in spite of occasional "disappearances"; who is capable of giving support, guidance, and comfort; and who has the achievement of the child's potential at heart. The analyst too—though without explicit expressions of affection toward the patient—nevertheless is able to convey interest and concern through his or her words.

As that sort of facilitating environment is a prerequisite for fostering the development of the human baby, so it is for making an analysis proceed. To facilitate the analytic inquiry into the unconscious mind, a vast array of relational devices is set up in every analysis, even though there may not be much explicit focus on how this occurs. Often the holding activities remain in the background of the analytic investigation, but in some treatments—namely, when primitive mental functioning is prominent—they perform an important primary role.

Sarah was one of these cases. The holding function of the setting—not only the material, concrete setting but the setting in the wider sense of the quality of the relational atmosphere—was in her case crucially important because she was often prey to a chaotic succession of different affective states and purposes that kept undermining her capacity to live as a subject responsible for her own actions and intentions and throwing her into a state of mental and behavioral disorganization. These states can be imagined as reactivations of a primitive level of mental functioning, something that Sarah presumably experienced over long periods of her childhood, when she only occasionally had an adult near her who was interested in her development, aware of dangers, and able to help her make her feelings understandable by putting them in a meaningful context.

Thanks to the feeling of safety and containment that the analytic setting provides, Sarah's anxiety decreased. Her narration became more consistent and orderly. It was as if she had attained a new point of view, a sort of "observing eye" on her internal world, that let her carry out a dialogue within herself as well as with the analyst. She began to recall some episodes from her childhood and to portray the climate of neglect in which she had grown up. She talked about her mother, whom she remembered as beautiful and charming when she was well and ugly and disgusting when ill. She remembered her mother as a self-absorbed young woman, basically uninterested in her little girl except in the rare moments when she related to her as a plaything—as, for instance, when she enjoyed combing Sarah's curly black hair or dressing her in black velvet for a festivity or a party.

Sarah didn't care too much, she said. "I did whatever I wanted to!" When she didn't go to school (this happened frequently because she was rather undisciplined, had problems studying, and would invent excuses for not going), her mother barely noticed it and didn't really scold her. Her father was a dandy who liked to lead a good life, going to parties, playing bridge, riding, and occasionally working in the family import–export business. He took even less notice of her than her mother did; Sarah did not remember a single occasion in which her father was involved in her life.

The only person she remembers really looking after her a bit was her grandmother (her father's mother). Sarah felt that she did this with an ambivalent attitude since she alternated affection toward her grandchild with detachment or even aloofness and that her grandmother often considered her "a bitch" for her rebellious character and "a bastard" by virtue of the grandmother's ill-concealed rejection of her beloved son's disliked wife.

In this family environment, by report quite neglectful if not overtly damaging, Sarah grew up in an atmosphere of great freedom—a "little wild girl," as her grandmother called her. For her strong-willed and assertive character many called her a tomboy. Not only did Sarah not care about this, she was proud of it. She much preferred boys as playmates to girls, who in her view were weak while boys were strong. For similar reasons—her rebellious character and lack of discipline— she was considered a bad student, even though some of her teachers were able to appreciate her curiosity and fits of generosity.

Given the apparent absence of a sympathetic and caring adult figure close to her, her intolerance of any restriction, and her innate inclination to search for the new and interesting, it is no wonder that Sarah attracted the attention of men who abused her. These encounters, which began when she was quite small and stopped when she was around twelve years old, made her feel uneasy. Several times she thought about talking to someone about them, but she always eventually decided not to because she was ashamed.

Two facts characterized her adolescence: the appearance of nervous crises for which she was put through a number of medical examinations and an intense bond with a teacher. This woman, the first person she ever trusted, became her confidante and counselor and got her to put her mind to her studies. The nervous attacks she suffered showed themselves in fits of crying and rage during which she hurled insults at everyone and smashed everything she could get hold of. In the midst of one of these crises she would sometimes disappear for a day or more and come back home on her own while the police and everyone else were still looking for her. She remembered that during these flights she walked a lot, mostly through woods, crying floods of tears and finding in this relief from her unhappiness. (In the analysis, Sarah didn't say much about what, or how, she *felt* but talked mostly about what she *did*; she recounted these things without much participation, with a kind of mild detachment.) On these occasions some attempts were made to get her to talk with a psychologist, but Sarah always refused; the only person she was willing to talk to was her teacher. When I suggested that she might be reliving with me a kind of relationship very similar to that one, she agreed enthusiastically. "You are my guide and my anchor," she said, "because you think and you make me think. I have the feeling that when I'm here I become able to think, and this makes me feel stronger than when I'm outside."

This impassioned declaration reflected Sarah's joy at seeing for herself, for the first time, how containment and support reduced her anxiety and the disorganizing effect it had on her thinking. She saw a new skill growing in herself, a capacity for slowing down her emotional reactivity and therefore reducing her impulsiveness. Her confidence in me strengthened, and we approached another step in our exploration.

It soon became clear that our "good relationship" was helping Sarah go deeper in her internal world. But it also served a defensive function. It gave her the feeling that she had a primitive, magical bond with me, a merger with (what she unconsciously thought to be) an omnipotent figure. This gave her a feeling of power and unassailability. In addition, Sarah considered our relationship *utterly* good. She rejected anything that she felt might damage this perfect goodness, as if all goodness had to belong to us, and any badness had to stay outside of us, in the "external" world. So, when I said something that hinted at a forbidden impulse inside of her—such as an aggressive feeling or a sexual interest—she would became uneasy, even physically restless, and would say in a peremptory tone that she couldn't bear me speaking that way, that she didn't want me telling her what made her feel separate from me.

These were crucial moments in the analytic relationship because they embodied all the ingredients that made her life so painful and turbulent. When she was confronted with an unpleasant issue, she became affectively and behaviorally disorganized, as if she were devoid of the mental tools to handle it. She complained of an unbearable tension and anxiety that urged her to react immediately, either by fighting against the source of her distress or by running away from it or both; in fact, these opposing reactions would occur in such rapid sequence (both in her mind and in her behavior) that a great deal of confusion ensued.

When I touched a subject that Sarah found unpleasant, she would react at first by warning me against going ahead; I should turn a blind eye to it, she implied rather intimidatingly, in order to preserve the absolute goodness of our relationship. She would keep her eyes firmly closed and put her hands over her ears as if to show me that she couldn't bear to listen to me. But these gestures were highly expressive, and they showed me at the same time that when her anxiety increased, she had to resort to body language. Sometimes she was so upset and angry that she left before the end of the session or skipped the next one.

The Crises

This primitive defense mechanism of *splitting*—living in the "goodness" of our relationship and rejecting anything perceived as bad—and Sarah's expectation that I shared it and was her ally in the wish not to explore her fears came up several times in the first period of her analysis. Later on she found—more accurately, there emerged—another protective device, one that did not interrupt the communication with me but kept her from feeling responsible for what she said. Her way of speaking would suddenly change; it was as if she were falling into a sort of hypnotic trance, while her consciousness became ever more narrowly focused on her inner reality at the expense of her contact with the outside world. She looked as if she were plunged in a rich sensory experience, the movements of her body intensified, and her talking seemed to come from a dream; she also often laughed or sobbed. When she was like this, in what we call a *dissociated state*, she lived simultaneously in two experiential worlds. She was on the couch with me, but she was also in the tangle of affects, thoughts, and bodily sensations that could be set off in her by reference, even in a single word, to a conflicted issue whose importance pressed for awareness but whose fearsomeness demanded that it be kept out of consciousness.

These crises were a turning point in Sarah's therapy. From one point of view they were regressions, reeditions of similar crises that she had suffered during her childhood and adolescence to the point where she was treated for a while as an epileptic. From another point of view, however, they were an occasion for going deeper into the ways her mind worked, without her knowledge, when she was afraid or overwhelmed. Her dramatic, even theatrical I might say, displays of distress weren't only a primitive mechanism by which Sarah defended herself from "the unbearable"; they were also a way to make me acquainted with it. In this sense they marked a progress in Sarah's therapy. Thanks to the crises—or, better still, thanks to Sarah's efforts to communicate with me during and after the crises—we were able to gain more knowledge about the two critical points affecting her psychic functioning: the childhood sexual abuse and her loving attachment to women.

The topic of "women" was the first and most powerful trigger of the crises. For years Sarah had been trying hard to conceal from herself (as well as from others) that there might be anything more than generic female friendship in her long-standing relationships with girls and women. When she entered analysis it was harder to maintain her denial: her apprehension, uneasiness, and embarrassment while talking about her female friends was palpable. But when I brought this subject up, however cautiously, she held out against confronting it. Instead, she asked me explicitly to help her control her disturbing wishes, saying, "You must be a guide for me! You shouldn't talk about this part of me, you'd do better to help me to repress my impulses!" On another level, however, she was expressing these same impulses in her self-induced hypnotic states. They emerged as Sarah talked with deep sighs and moans and in fragmented sentences as if to an imaginary presence. This enabled us, after the dreamlike state had ended, to go back to what she had said and to give it meaning by making connections between the two dissociated parts of herself.

As we worked through the crises and what Sarah said in them and strove to discover their triggers, it became clearer why Sarah was so ambivalent toward me, why she presented such a tough resistance at the same time that she wanted me to investigate her unconscious world. She felt that her sexual desires, which on the one hand she needed to have recognized and accepted, had on the other hand a nasty and offensive quality. She worried that I wouldn't carry out the "necessary" task, which she had assigned to me in fantasy, of keeping a watchful eye on her: "You don't understand how dangerous I am!" she cried out once as she was talking about how intense her craving was for physical contact with a friend of hers. She felt that her longings were so desperate and somehow frantic that she might seduce and hurt her friend. By assigning me the function of an authoritative and repressive guide, she could make sure that no harm would be done.

When she perceived her desire in such an exciting and alarming way, it was as if she was unconsciously reliving what had happened when she was a child with the men who had seduced her and had sexual contact with her. Yet she reenacted those experiences not as a child passively suffering a sexual approach but as an adult actively seducing a child. In other words, in her fantasy, when she got sexually aroused, she forsook the passive role for the active one; she identified with (that is, felt subjectively akin to) the men who got round her, enticed her, and seduced her. It was as if their excited and frantic behavior had left a sort of a template in her psyche that was reactivated whenever she felt sexually attracted by someone. This process was at first utterly unconscious, and it took quite a long time for her to work through it consciously.

Although it may appear obvious that sexual abuse suffered in childhood will have an impact later in life, this wasn't so obvious to Sarah. She was not interested in talking about it. For a long time she exhibited toward her childhood sexual experiences a detached attitude. She would mention them hastily and in an expressive style that was definitely laconic, especially when compared with her usually emotional way of speaking. (This is quite a typical reaction in traumatized people, in whom affective indifference toward the traumatic event is a form of psychological protection from otherwise overwhelming feelings. In cases of seduction and sexual abuse, shame and reluctance to go back over those experiences are also common.)

It took us a long time to work through Sarah's traumatic history, and there were many reasons for this. The first, as I just said, was Sarah's evasiveness and resistance. When I suggested some connection between past experience and what she was living at present, she often reacted defensively: "What's *that* got to do with it?" she would say. At other times, it was guilt that hindered further exploration since Sarah tended to take on herself the responsibility of having seduced the men who abused her.

A second important reason was that I had to be cautious myself. I had to take into account another side of Sarah's personality: her suggestibility, her complaisance. It seemed that this was a vulnerability that had played an important role in the past experiences, when she had trusted in an adult who had then seduced her and imposed on her his affective (sexual) language. Sarah tended to fall easily into seducer–seduced relationships (not only the sexual sense but more broadly as well), and this kind of relationship could be reactivated with me too. Every time that Sarah accepted an interpretation not because it explained something to her but so as to maintain a live and tight affective bond with me, we were involved in a seduction—again, seduction in the broad sense.

The last but not the least important reason for care in our search for historical reconstruction was my conviction that what is therapeutic (that is, what leads to integrative processes in the personality) is not so much the mere retrieval of repressed memories or even the general reconstruction of what really happened in the past. Rather, it is the construction of a narrative of one's vicissitudes—a narrative made plausible and coherent when meaningful place is given to present and past affective experience.

So I was careful and respectful when digging into Sarah's traumatic memories. But from time to time I wondered whether I wasn't behaving in *too* respectful and cautious a way. In other words, was I reenacting the well-known "impartial" and "neutral" role of the parent (usually the mother) of an abused child, who in practice colludes with the abuse by not looking at and not seeing what is taking place in front of her eyes? And if so, I wondered whether that attitude came from my own reluctance to explore this area or whether it was to some extent unconsciously induced by Sarah in the service of maintaining her pathological equilibrium.

I wish to point out here that the variety of Sarah's attitudes toward her past experiences and the variety of my own perspectives in understanding and interpreting them were not surprising. That kind of variation is inherent in the way knowledge is attained in psychoanalysis. Far from developing in a linear way, the analytic process moves along many fronts. It starts from disparate points of departure and progresses both backward and forward. Now new understandings are opened up, then defenses are tightened. The analyst's task is to understand not only which aspect of the patient's internal world is most important at any time but also when, to what extent, and how the patient is activating feelings, thoughts, wishes, fears that belong to the analyst's own personality: that is, which aspects of the analyst's own subjectivity are involved in the interaction. When a very little child has a need, he doesn't know what kind of need he has. He just behaves in such a way that something happens in the mother's mind so that she can understand the baby's need and take care of him. Something similar occurs within the analyst, who becomes the container of the unconscious, unrecognized parts of the patient's mind. The sicker the patient (that is, the more significant and extensive the parts of the mind that are unconsciously defended against and therefore unrecognized), the more these feelings may flood the analyst's mind. Of course, it is important to distinguish the feelings that belong to the analyst's own personality from those that belong to the patient. Therefore the analyst must scrutinize carefully what analysis stirs up within him- or herself.

The Autohypnotic State

In time, as we repeatedly worked through these episodes, Sarah overcame her ter- rified fantasies of destruction and abandonment. She developed a more reliable sense of safety, the crises became less dramatic and her dissociation took on a milder form, and a kind of autohypnosis replaced the gross dissociations. When she went into such a minicrisis, she deliberately closed her eyes and in a few words let me know that her way of speaking was going to change. Then she would begin to talk in a fairly comprehensible way, as if she were describing a scene she had dreamed. She often made use of a peculiar linguistic device: in- stead of speaking in the first person, she used the third person or an impersonal form. For instance, instead of saying "I wish" or "I worry," she would say "She wishes" or "She worries." Instead of saying "I am feeling something," she would say "There! A feeling [anger, passion, fear] is coming out." In other words, she talked of herself (certainly of a primitive part of herself) as if she were looking at something from the outside. At the beginning, for a while, this third person was rather indistinct; it was a "person" mainly at a grammatical level, an entity whose particularity was somewhat overwhelmed by a tangle of sensations and affects.

These minicrises were quite frequent, and it became clear that they served to help Sarah feel safe while talking about unpleasant matters. Addressing ques- tions and comments to these *(id)entities*, as I privately called them (because they seemed to fall somewhere between an "entity-out-there" and a subjectively felt state), was more successful than it had been in the earlier crises, and I came to act as a stable partner in a sort of multilevel dialogue. This made it possible to give a narrative structure to the dissociated experiences, so that a more compact, less fragmented identity could begin to take shape.

On one very important occasion this more structured and recognizable identity acquired a name. Something was stirring up deep disgust and agitation in Sarah. When I asked her where such feeling came from, she hinted at "some- thing shapeless, stupid, fragile, living down there in the darkness." It seemed to me that these adjectives could be describing a part of her (female) body as well as the most helpless and powerless aspects of herself. I told her that what she called "stupid and fragile" might be something like a little girl who felt stupid be- cause she didn't know what the adults know and who therefore felt insignificant and inferior to them. I told her that what she called "shapeless and living down there" might correspond to an important, though without a definite shape, part of her (sexual) body.

The absence of shape was the equivalent of the absence of a name. Sarah still wasn't able to name the entity because this part of her body—along with the shocking sensations and feelings associated with it—was apparently distant from the way she thought of herself. While trying to portray this entity, she talked of "something smooth, mushy, slippery, like a mollusc . . . like . . . how can I describe it? . . . Yes! I've got it! Once I saw a picture of it: the marine worm studied by a famous neuroscientist, a worm called *Aplysia*. This Aplysia—when I think about it—makes me feel sick! It is so shapeless and sluggish, so squashy and slippery that it makes me sick to my stomach! It makes me want to smash it!"

In every single analysis, a particular language develops between analyst and patient, and some words or expressions in this language are packed with meaning. *Aplysia* became one of these words for us. Referring to a very simple and primitive living being with an elementary nervous system and a very simple shape, the name seemed fit to represent some elementary sensations of Sarah's internal world. From this point on, "the Aplysia" became a crucial character in our dialogue. We used it for many things. We used it to refer to the female genital, which Sarah perceived as shapeless and "living down there." But it also helped us put into words Sarah's experience of feeling fragile, impotent, and inadequate, bereft of the power, the strength, and the visibility with which others—above all, men—were seemingly endowed. This misshapen and awkward marine worm provided us with a metaphor that organized into a meaningful narrative a number of experiences of humiliating inferiority—the inferiority of children with regard to adults as well as the inferiority of women insofar as they are seen as deprived of male attributes.

The Working Through

Once acknowledging that she harbored in her mind such a flawed representation of femaleness, Sarah could begin to consider her special friendships with women from a new perspective. She understood that other women had for her a twofold attraction. On the one hand, she was bewitched by powerful and prominent women who in fantasy represented redemption from powerlessness and inferiority to men. On the other—that is, when she felt such intense attraction that she was frightened of inflicting pain—it was as if she herself got possession of the power and the superiority she so longed for.

As Sarah's scattered bodily and affective experiences took the form of organized verbal expression, as we constructed a coherent narration of her life and its vicissitudes, another flawed aspect of her mental functioning improved: she became able to distinguish how "imagining" was different from "doing," how "thinking" was different from "feeling," and how these in its turn were different from "perceiving." Once she appreciated that what went on inside herself didn't necessarily coincide with factual reality, she freed herself from the anxiety and confusion of mistaking her feelings for the "real world." She began to understand the capacity of the human mind to produce and use symbols. Now she could allow herself conjectures, imaginings, and make-believe situations and keep them separate from her self; she no longer fell into confusional anxiety because she could now feel the distinction between her own identity and the external world.

As Sarah experienced such new feelings of safety within herself, her impulsiveness (that is, the urge to express herself through action) became less of a problem—she discovered that thinking about what she might do, what she was going to do, what she might have done, was a safe alternative to acting it all out. Thinking even acquired the flavor of a pleasurable activity. Sarah had lived in a world in which pleasure came from acting, from being engaged in actions or in sensations; "thinking" had barely existed beyond its meaning of "not acting." Before analysis, this "not-acting" was a sacrifice for Sarah because only by acting out could she feel the sense of omnipotence and realized self-assertiveness that she craved. Yet for her as for all of us, thinking is a way of delaying action as well as of relinquishing it; analysis let her discover the positive values of not acting (that is, of thinking) and the possibility that effective and productive self-assertiveness was possible without having to feel omnipotent or without having to lose touch with reality.

Now the analytic situation was no longer needed to contain her within its setting or to purge her of her overwhelming feelings; it became a place where thoughts could be experienced and worked through as trial actions. The less Sarah had to feel omnipotent and split the world into good (herself) and bad (everything else), the less she had to project the "bad" parts of herself into other people and blame them for her problems. She could take responsibility for her thoughts and actions. Relinquishing her most primitive defensive techniques implied that the most regressive forms of gratification would have to be abandoned too; Sarah couldn't demand anymore to be treated as a domineering little girl to whom everything is permitted and everything is forgiven. But for the first time she could do something else. She could work through her depressive feelings—remorse for the damage she might have done, sorrow for her faults and limitations, sadness for the inevitability of compromise. The principal arena in which these new aspects of Sarah's personality came to light and were put to the test was the burning issue of her fondness for women.

Though she came from a rather open-minded family, and though in her work environment being homosexual would easily have been accepted, Sarah had denied on principle having homosexual inclinations. Her attitude about this had been very firm for a long time, as if even to consider the possibility of affectionate feelings toward women were a sort of collapse of her identity. Besides, it must be said that in this area she still resorted to the same primitive defenses that she had once used to deal with other troubling issues—dissociation, denial, and projection ("I'm not this and this . . . , I don't feel this and this . . . , he or she wants me to be/do/feel this and this . . ."). We analyzed these defenses again, as we had when they had occurred in the less frightening areas of her life, and as she tried out again how it felt to do without them, we could gradually move closer to the issue of sexual choice. Arduously and bravely confronting those parts of herself that she had denied and disavowed for so long, Sarah came to accept that her sexual longings were longings for women.

She eventually met a woman a bit older than herself who fell in love with her. Sarah accepted the relationship, and she accepted her love for this woman. But she also became very anxious; what she found most difficult was not so much loving someone as being loved. To be receptive in a real relationship—both the possibility and the actual experience—was for Sarah loaded with very negative feelings: she feared that it meant fading away—losing strength, power, and control, being so overwhelmed by intense sensations as to feel almost paralyzed. She was accustomed to protecting herself from these fears by taking an active role. It was clear that Sarah's fear of receptiveness (which she disdainfully called *passivity*) also had to be referred to the Aplysia story: it was a reedition—undoubtedly at a much higher level of psychic organization—of her fear of accepting the receptive side of her femaleness, the side that, when she was a child, had been ill treated by men.

In the last year of her analysis, Sarah committed herself completely to working through this issue, and she did it with a thoughtfulness inconceivable in previous years. She wanted to give solid roots, she said, "to the first relationship in her life in which she felt dependent in the right way." Before analysis, Sarah had been so afraid of feeling impotent that she projected impotence into others and behaved as if she were all-powerful; in her omnipotence she denied any form of dependency. As more effective and realistic forms of self-assertiveness replaced her reliance on omnipotent fantasies, she could begin to understand "dependency" not as a way of being powerless but as a way of accepting good things from someone else. Her increasing capacity for receptivity too allowed her to understand "taking" as an act of integration as opposed to a helpless surrender to something imposed from the outside.

Sarah's analysis lasted four years. We could have gone on longer—and perhaps that would have been advisable—but "life couldn't wait," as Sarah said. She was working on a project with the woman she now lived with—a nursery school in a Third World country for children who had lost their parents—and she wanted to realize it. This wish precipitated the end of her analysis.

About a year later, Sarah came back from the foreign country where she was living and asked to see me for a few sessions. She told me how satisfied she was both in her work and in her relationships. Since she had become able to think about her feelings instead of acting them out, her propensity to dramatize and exaggerate conflicts had diminished. Her life was calmer and less troubled than before because she felt much more in control of external events as well as internal ones. She told me that what helped her most when facing any potentially anxiety-provoking event was to bring to mind what she had experienced in her analytic work; when she was tempted to plunge into desperation or to discharge anxiety into some impulsive action, she would get back to the atmosphere of our dialogue and think about what she had learned.

During these follow-up meetings I could see that Sarah had acquired a stable capacity to resort to a mental function—a sort of "third person," I would say—that helped her step beyond the immediate intensity of her experience and consider what was going on outside herself separate from her own wishes and fears. She could grasp the distinction between the immediate experience and the mental state that underpins it. And she could represent her own feelings, beliefs, and desires with sufficient clarity to experience a core sense of herself as a functioning mental entity, adjust the fulfillment of her needs to the requirements of reality, and modulate her emotions. In short, I had the feeling that the analysis had provided Sarah with the self-reflective function that she had previously lacked[1] and that she had sought the posttermination meetings to refresh this function.

"I liked our work and sometimes I miss it," she told me a bit jokingly and a bit seriously during one of these visits. "Now that I have learned to reflect within myself, don't you think I'm ready for a second, higher-level analysis?"

After four years of analysis, Sarah was no longer the fragile and stormy person who had battled so valiantly but so helplessly against the fear of being overwhelmed by dissociated and repressed parts of herself. Now it would indeed have been possible for her to undertake a new, different kind of exploration of her internal world. However, since the major therapeutic results we had already achieved were enabling Sarah to carry on her life quite satisfactorily, we considered her idea of a "second, higher-level analysis" more a wish to deepen her knowledge of herself than the expression of a need for "cure."

Note

1. According to Fonagy (2000), the analytic treatment enhances the development of reflective function by improving the patient's control over his or her system of represen-

tation of relationships. The gradual and constant adjustments of the representational models facilitate the development of an internal world where the behavior of others may be experienced as understandable, meaningful, and predictable. This reduces the need for splitting of frightening and incoherent mental representations of mental states, and new experiences of other minds can more readily be integrated into the framework of past relationship representations.

CHAPTER 7

Jacob: Climbing Out of the Dungeon

Sometimes it takes a long time to learn how to love another person, another separate person. Many people never learn how and don't recognize what is missing or know in any real sense what those words mean. How do people develop the capacity to love? Why do some people succeed in love while others don't know how to begin? Why do some people try over and over again and repeatedly suffer the same disappointments?

My patient Jacob had spent his entire life frustrated in his search for love. A man in his mid-forties, he began psychoanalysis because of strong feelings of isolation and depression and intense dissatisfaction with his twenty-five-year marriage. Jacob and his wife had stopped having sex after their first five years together and had had literally no sexual or physical contact (not even hand-holding or perfunctory hugs) in the twenty years since. Jacob was the one in the couple who longed to be touched; his wife felt violated or intruded on by physical contact.

Jacob came to analysis after years of couples therapy and once-a-week individual psychotherapy for himself. Nothing seemed to help him or his wife Elizabeth move beyond a distantly cooperative but empty partnership focused almost exclusively on the needs of their two (now adult) children. Jacob didn't know if he was a sexual, potent man; he didn't know for sure if he had needs, perceptions, or opinions of his own, let alone what they might be. He became aware in analysis of how dependent he was on Elizabeth and how much he needed *her* to set the boundaries for what could or couldn't happen and who he could or couldn't be.

Jacob's story illustrates how the approximations and permutations of love that linger as carryovers from childhood make indelible marks on future relationships, sometimes in stiflingly destructive ways. Speaking of his distaste for oatmeal one day, Jacob stopped suddenly with a shock of recognition. "But *who* hates it? I don't know whether it is me or my mother. I realize I cannot tell yet." Scars of this sort suggest a history of parents who subsume or take over the child's separate aliveness, drawing him or her like a satellite into a tighter and tighter orbit of imprisonment. As Jacob learned more about himself in analysis, he began to articulate his understanding of this psychic "dungeon," the prison of not knowing what you want, how you feel, who you are.

In the early phases of analysis, Jacob luxuriated in a loving adoration of me. He praised my wisdom, my beauty, my compassionate listening, my common sense, and, more than anything else, my aliveness. He was exquisitely sensitive to momentary flickers of feeling that registered on my face in the hallway or as he was leaving the office, and he spent large amounts of time speculating on what these facial expressions "really" meant. Slight shifts in my voice between a warm or engaged tone and a relatively more matter-of-fact, casual, or neutral one caused a great deal of anxiety in Jacob. Had he hurt my feelings? Was I bored with him, mad at him, thinking about someone else?

Gradually, Jacob came to understand the reasons behind this extravagant devotion. He became aware that he was so anxious about the feeling of being separate from the me—about his awareness that I had an autonomous existence that couldn't be predicted or controlled—that he felt that only a state of perpetual gratitude would keep me around. At first, this was an intellectual understanding. He knew that he had been traumatized by his parents' many abandonments of him, and it "made sense" to him that he would bring those fears to his relationship with his analyst.

Jacob was the eldest of his mother's four children, all of whom had been fathered by different men. Each time his mother found a new man, she left Jacob, for months or for years, to join the husband or boyfriend who was in a different city or traveling around the world. For much of his childhood Jacob was without parent—either mother or father—although both his parents stayed with him, unlike his half brothers and sisters, until he was nine. From the age of nine on, however, Jacob felt (or felt that he had to feel) desperately grateful to the loving members of his extended family who took care of him during his mother's absences. Among other things, the experience of being a guest in his own home meant that he was never really able to relax and be needy, demanding, critical, or even just grumpy in the ordinary daily sense. Even more painful, Jacob realized that he never felt free enough to let himself feel or think about what he wanted—or even to try to ask the question, *What* was he thinking or feeling or wanting?—because he really wasn't sure there was any chance of getting it. As he was coming to see it, his mother had been extremely needy and self-absorbed. Jacob's survival had depended on his ability to be a chameleon, to fit his needs to her needs and the needs of others around him. In fleeting moments of self-awareness, he described this feeling as not even knowing when he was leaning against a burning-hot stove. He knew he had been burnt only when he noticed the scars many hours or even days later—and that was only when it registered at all.

Why couldn't Jacob tell when he was being "burnt"? Why wasn't he sure if he liked the taste of oatmeal when he tasted it with his own mouth, his own tongue? Why didn't he feel his own body clearly enough to know if he did or didn't want sex? He was eventually able to take responsibility for the fact that a wife who was comfortable not having sex saved him from the complicated and terribly risky task of freeing his own desire. But the road to this understanding was long, and it was not simple.

Jacob had grown up without parents who could nurture his sense of his own identity or help him as he grew older to sort out his own tastes, ideas, and values from theirs. In fact, they probably didn't recognize themselves that he and they were different people. They used him to fulfill their own needs without regard to his, as if he were a part of themselves and so had no needs (separate from theirs) at all. He had never had the chance to feel loved as a whole person, to love another who could appreciate him for himself, or to love himself enough to develop a real joie de vivre. He never had an opportunity to develop the perceptions and skills that allow people to recognize what they want in the world and go after it with desire and gusto. Jacob had what analysts call a deeply impoverished self.

Until about twenty years ago, many analysts did not know if psychoanalysis could help people like Jacob. But today, problems like Jacob's are the bulk of an analyst's work. How does analysis facilitate the birth of a separate person when there has been a childhood history like Jacob's, a history of only the most tentative—or sometimes exploitative—kinds of relating? How does a history like that get remembered, rethought, reworked, rebuilt? I will tell you how I saw it, and then Jacob will tell you how it looked to him.

The Initial Phase of the Analysis: Identifying the Internal Space

Jacob slowly began to use his analytic hours to carve out and articulate his inner feelings, his interior landscape—who he was. This was the kind of experience that had been so sorely missing in his growing up years, and it was a long time coming in his analysis.

It was hard for Jacob to break through his isolation (and what I guessed was his despairing fear that he would never be able to communicate with me) and simply tell me directly what he was feeling. There were many long, superficial descriptions of events or circumstances; these made me and probably Jacob feel very lonely and empty. It felt like there wasn't very much going on between us on an emotional level. If I asked him what he was feeling at those times, he would tell me that he didn't know. I sometimes tried wondering aloud if perhaps he were feeling sad or despairing or lonely, but although he might agree in the moment, ultimately those kinds of interventions didn't seem to be very helpful; they never led to new or deeper feelings. Much of the time Jacob was so intently focused on what he thought *I* was feeling or thinking that he could not spare any attention for himself. He didn't know how to experience himself except by reference to me. He also became very anxious when he wasn't able to feel, as he put it, that we were "together" on something or "side by side." He was uncomfortable lying "all alone" on the couch; he didn't like it that he couldn't see me because when my face was out of his view, it was harder to tell if we were "in agreement." I told him that I thought his need to be "in agreement" with me was hiding an even deeper anxiety—about finding out the contents of his *own* mind.

After a while, Jacob did find a way to elaborate his feelings. As his analyst, can I say how or why he shifted to a place of greater self-expression? I'm not sure I know a definite answer to this question. Our analytic theories would probably say that Jacob felt I had accurately understood his inner conflicts about having a self and needing to be more separate or perhaps that he was learning to trust me and feel safer. I do know that Jacob was trying to find words of his own to describe what we both palpably felt as a gulf between us—a gulf that he felt with everyone—or the intolerable sense of being alone in each other's presence. He began to elaborate a fantasy of being alone in a dungeon.

In the fantasy, some of the people in his life were prison guards; they lived on the other side of the prison wall or above him in the world of the living. It became clearer and clearer to Jacob that the dungeon was the psychic prison that symbolized his lack of identity, his lack of connectedness in the world. His proclivity for losing himself in other people's perceptions—the only way he knew of trying to feel close—had a frightening and paradoxical flip side. It kept him from knowing himself and so kept him essentially alone in his dungeon. The deep gulf, the distance that he felt between himself and the rest of the human race, was the measure of his alienation from himself.

The elaboration of the dungeon metaphor filled up a great many of Jacob's analytic hours. Listening to him during these times was often very painful. I knew it was important for him to "get it said," as he put it. But as time went on, I tried to talk to him about how in his repetitive descriptions of the walls of his prison I also felt as though he were trying to imprison *me*—to deaden me, to fill me up with his despair, because my aliveness, as much as he valued it, was so threatening to him. It reminded him too acutely of his own menacing potential aliveness. It sometimes felt like he wanted to pull *me* down, too, to escape the risks of aliveness. I didn't want to stay in the dungeon with him, I said, but I didn't think that was the only way for us to be together. I wasn't sure that I could find a way to drag him out, which he also sometimes seemed to want. But at the same time, I was trying to convey to him (nonverbally as well as in words) that our capacity to survive and overcome these feelings together—to preserve our sense of our aliveness even in the dungeon—would, if we really faced them, make us stronger.

Why did I share these particular feelings with him? I was trying to put into words the feeling of deadness and entrapment and being pulled down into a dark place, just as Jacob was. And I wanted to show him that I could feel it, too—that he could convey a true feeling of his to another person. In addition, it happens sometimes in analysis that the analyst is asked to feel and bear a feeling that emerges because it seems, for a while, too overwhelming for the patient to bear it alone. It seemed to me that Jacob needed two things from his analysis just then: an experience of not being alone, so that these painful feelings could emerge, and an experience of his capacity to be a strong and separate person, someone who didn't need to be rescued and who could find the words for his own experience. As you will also hear from Jacob in his section here, these discussions about "rescue" were a pivotal part of the analysis.

One day Jacob began elaborating in more detail a new part of the dungeon fantasy—a wish or a daydream about changing or being transformed. In the daydream, a woman outside the dungeon throws down a rope for Jacob and invites him to climb out. He told me the next day that he thought I was the woman and that the fantasy about a woman throwing down a rope was partly a fantasy about being rescued by me. He also made clear that there had been many people at other times in his life (doctors, teachers, ex-girlfriends) who had thrown down "ropes" but that he hadn't been able to use them. He hadn't at the time seen them as trying to help, or else he hadn't felt capable of being open enough to receive help from them. He recalled a poignant example. A young woman friend whom he had known right after college had repeatedly invited him to go for a walk with her and her dog. Despite her persistent attempts to arrange meeting times and even what were probably some deliberate attempts to "accidentally" bump into him, Jacob never realized, until he talked about it in analysis, that she had probably had a crush on him. Recalling this memory and remembering his feeling of deadness at the time made Jacob very, very sad about what he had missed. The sadness felt huge and almost unbearable—like the walls of a dungeon in his mind, he said again—because he became aware for the first time that there must have been countless other opportunities for lively, passionate intimate relationships that he had also missed. At the same time and in the midst of his grief, Jacob realized that his strong feelings of connection for me had brought him a new feeling of aliveness. Now, maybe, he could "grab the rope" and climb out of the dungeon.

Now too a debate began that continued on and off throughout the rest of the analysis: had I in fact "rescued" him by reaching out and letting down a psychological rope? Or was he giving me too much power and too much gratitude, the coins in which he had had to pay for the limited attentions of his needy and insensitive parents? Perhaps Jacob needed to argue with me about this because arguing itself was so freeing.

Now that his energies were not going entirely into being a chameleon, Jacob was learning in lots of ways to recognize and identify his own feelings more effectively both with me and with other people. For example, he wasn't as preoccupied with conforming to his ideas about what would please his mother—she had been dead for many years—by going to church every Sunday or setting the table with the china he had inherited from her. His mother receded a bit into the past, and his conflicts about people in his present life and what he wanted from them now began to take center stage.

All these new feelings were expressed in terms of the dungeon fantasy. Jacob wondered if he could laugh and be happy like the people "on the other side," the people in his daily life from whom he had previously felt so distant. Could his "guards" become his friends? Would they be able to see him differently now despite his past? Was he the one who was changing, or were they changing, too? Did people change together in response to each other?

The Middle Phase of Analysis: Staying Out of the Dungeon

After Jacob's intense elaboration of his isolation, the imprisonment in the dungeon, there was a definite shift in the analysis. He felt consistently more confident and more alive. His analysis was his first experience of someone listening to his deep feelings, and the process of finding words to describe them—especially such painful feelings as being in a dungeon—had strengthened his sense of himself. For the first time Jacob had access to ordinary, everyday feelings that he could now recognize and tell me about. He felt stronger, too, because as he grappled with some of the desperate and painful feelings inside of him, they began to feel more contained and more bearable. Before, Jacob had been "lost" in the dungeon. Now, by contrast, he felt "found" again. That was what he called this next phase of the analysis, the time after his emergence from the dungeon—the time of being "found," of being remembered, of becoming real.

How did Jacob became a more separate person in analysis, a person with feelings and thoughts that he could really call his own? How did he and I become connected as two separate people instead of in the more confused way with which he had begun, when he didn't know when he was trying to please me or when he was doing something he wanted? The experience of being thoughtfully listened to lifted Jacob's spirits and helped him "lift himself up." (In this I include both being helped and helping himself, although about this, as you will see later, Jacob might disagree.)

Jacob was now describing some very different kinds of interactions and relationships with those around him: he felt new feelings of respect and interest in his friends and coworkers, for example, as well as a growing sense of interest and respect coming from them toward him. He began to look forward to bumping into coworkers by the Xerox machine, hanging out with friends at the gym, or running into neighbors. His intimate relationships became deeper despite the many times that he had almost given up on them, out of fear of their potential for pain. Now, when he fell back into a state of fearful withdrawal, he could sometimes talk to me about it and about the hard truth that although deeper relationships can mean joy and closeness, they also inevitably involve the risk of being hurt by other people or disappointed in oneself.

There were many long periods when we struggled with this painful reality. For example, we spoke a great deal about the "double-edged sword," the paradoxical and potentially self-deceptive way that Jacob used metaphoric language and imagery—the dungeon fantasy, for example. On the one hand, metaphor was a safe way to explore things, allowing him to share feelings that felt too threatening or confusing in their most concrete form. But Jacob was also very adept at stringing words together repetitively in a way that was initially seductive but later had a distancing or even deadening effect, pushing the other person away and alienating him from the immediacy of his own experience. Inside his own mind, Jacob could use evocative words and images as a way to retreat into a kind of a bubble or an illusion that was always to some degree comforting because it was completely under his control.

And he characteristically, we learned, dealt with the risks of relationships by a variety of defensive fantasies. For years, for example, Jacob had hidden from his wife the times when his business was doing poorly and exaggerated his success when the business was doing well. He had tended to exaggerate his importance in an effort to assuage his fear that he was really insignificant. Now, however, he wanted to be more honest with Elizabeth about how much money he was really making. He began to understand that he had felt so extremely vulnerable to being humiliated by her (or critical of himself) that he would get confused about the reality of his business status and replace the confusion with a fantasy.

As time went on, Jacob came to understand how such uses of fantasy undermined the connections he was struggling to make in the real world with real people. But thrashing this out involved the expression of a lot of anger. When I wondered sometimes if he thought he was using a fantasy as a form of protection or as a defense, strong feelings of hurt and anger came up. Jacob got very defensive, for example, when I suggested that perhaps he had canceled a session because he was ashamed of the feelings that had come up the day before. Most of the time he explained his cancellations in terms of how busy he was, or with elaborate explanations that had to do with important meetings at work that could not happen without him. Gradually he was coming to see that his distortions about being so important were actually meant to hide the fact that he felt himself to be very unimportant and insignificant to me, to other people, and to himself. Still, his first response was anger, more often than not, when I pointed out how he distorted things. On one occasion, for instance, he told me how much someone at work admired his knowledge of rare books. It happened that he had told me also that this same person had walked away from him just a few days before while he was in the middle of a sentence. After working through his initial anger at me for bringing this up, Jacob painfully acknowledged that he was probably exaggerating or perhaps even imagining this man's admiration in order to protect himself from the pain of the experience of rejection.

Discussions like this were stormy and uncomfortable for quite some time; we had many disagreements and much back and forth and pushing and pulling around the subject. They had to happen, however. Jacob experienced his distortions and fantasies as self-protective, but they were protective only in that they transiently buffered his self-esteem. They were destructive in their undermining of honest relationships both with others and with himself, and Jacob now really wanted those real relationships. At the height of these skirmishes Jacob would accuse me of not listening to him and of being mean. Later, however, he was able to see them in a more humorous vein and would jokingly compare himself to his teenage son. Later still he became able to talk more seriously, now comparing the interactions between the two of us to his experience as the parent of a teenager. His fantasies of being better than he really was, like an adolescent's heroic fantasies, had protected him from feeling less important than everyone else.

There were many more important developments in Jacob's analysis that I can only summarize here. He developed a more genuine pleasure in making money, and even as he became able to face with me, with himself, and with his wife the times when he *wasn't* making money, he was becoming much more successful. Earning more money and spending more time in what he had once disparagingly called the "rat race" of the business world now had a new meaning for him—a feeling that he finally belonged to the "team" and had a much stronger and more genuine sense of his own presence on it.

His sex life reemerged. He became interested in muscle building and working out, and his new image of himself as a masculine man with "definition"—the now literally firmer boundary between his masculine body and his wife's feminine one—helped him consolidate his sense of himself as a man who was entitled to have a natural and aggressive sexual drive. With many halfway and stalled attempts and many painful retreats and withdrawals, Jacob and his wife slowly began experimenting with their sexual relationship. His marriage began to change in complex ways that made it both more satisfying and real but also more painful.

The Termination and the Book

A year and a half after Jacob's analysis ended, I asked him if he was willing to write about it. We decided to meet in order to discuss the idea. Many feelings were stirred up in Jacob as we began talking together, and he said that one of the reasons he had wanted to come talk to me about writing about his analysis was that he wanted an "excuse" (he says more about this in his section here) to return to treatment for a while. Since his termination Jacob had sent me several postcards and a letter. I had responded to all of them. But had he needed the invitation from me to meet in person (to discuss the book project) before he could come in and tell me that he wanted to come back for more analysis?

We had discussed at length the timing of his termination, but it was not until afterward that Jacob had realized that he had wanted me to stop him from terminating. Or so he now said. Once we discontinued our sessions, he found himself feeling that he had "too much time" on his hands, "too much space." He vacillated between wishing that I had more forcefully told him not to terminate and the knowledge that at the time it was he himself who had been needing to stop. In other words, during the termination phase he had consistently demanded that I tell him that in my opinion he was ready for termination.

As analysts do, I had tried to explore openly a variety of questions about whether it was the right time to terminate. I wanted to raise with Jacob some of the issues that I thought were important, to help him to make his own decision. Analysts and patients often don't know, in situations such as this, how much of the analytic work the patient can do on his own until after the patient has stopped for a while. Sometimes patients are ready to terminate, and sometimes they just need to experiment with taking a break. However, when Jacob and I had discussed these issues, he had often gotten angry with me, as if I were doubting him. He had felt strongly that his life was on the upswing, and, understandably, he had wanted to see how it felt to live his life on his own, not in analysis. It was only later on, when things turned out not to be as easy as he had hoped, that Jacob had begun to feel angry at me for *not* having stopped him and for my "failure" to save him from some of his disappointment.

His reaction raised many questions for me. Had I chosen to ask Jacob to write because I was aware that our work together was unfinished? When the idea of asking a patient to write about his analysis was first proposed to me I had hesitated. There are complicated issues involved, and my first thought was that if I were to participate in this experiment, it might be better to pick someone like Jacob, who had terminated. But *had* Jacob terminated? On the other hand, I wondered whether it might be more helpful to raise the question of writing in an ongoing analysis where these issues could be analyzed. Neither choice had seemed ideal. Now I wondered if by inviting him to be part of the book project I had preconsciously been inviting him back to treatment. Was this yet another version of the debate about my "rescue" of Jacob?

Jacob's ambivalence about who should make the decision about when to leave analysis (like our debate about the throwing down of the rope) went back to one of his central conflicts—can he really know internally what he wants in the presence of the other? And can he do it for himself, or must someone else do it for him? On the most conscious level, Jacob prefers to think of himself as someone who needs to be rescued. He doesn't always attend to the other side of his feelings—his fear of having his independence "undermined," his rage when he feels his capacity to "do it alone" is doubted. He had had a hard struggle to know his feelings at all; he resisted for a long time the additional complication that most feelings have two sides. Only after he came back and talked to me about it was Jacob able to realize fully that he wished I had done the very thing that he had told me at the time that he *didn't* want. For the first time, in this context, Jacob was able to see that maybe "sometimes" he didn't want to be rescued. Thus, he opened up the door to the next, very important piece of the analytic work.

The Patient's Perspective

To begin with, I want to tell the reader what I've learned from this writing process. The first time I wrote about my analysis and met with my analyst to talk about this book, I realized that wanting to be a part of the writing project was partly an excuse for me to come back and see my analyst, or a way for me to realize that I wanted to come back and be in analysis again.

When my analyst asked me if I thought it was fair or right to ask a patient to write about their analysis or if I might feel used or taken advantage of, I said no because I felt flattered and I wanted to do it. It also seemed like it might help other patients. But then I realized it was more complicated than that. In my first draft I was much too revealing about myself and too flowery about how great analysis was. And seeing that, I realized that I was doing what I always do: that is, trying too hard to please. So again I had to face the feeling that I wasn't done with analysis and that I was angry that my analyst had let me go too soon. As I said before, I realized as I was doing it that agreeing to be a part of writing about my analysis was a way to come back and see my analyst. I had been sending her a lot of postcards and letters and, I think, kind of asking her to rescue me.

My analyst also asked me how I feel or what I think about the part of this chapter that she wrote. The most significant difference in our two points of view is, as she says, that I feel like she saved my life, in a way, and I don't always understand why she has to insist as much as she does that I saved myself, too. I know I did a lot of work, too, but I do also feel like she handed me a rope and pulled me up or rescued me and I responded. So I'm glad I get to put in my two cents about this.

I guess I should also say that a lot of the other stuff about me is disguised and also that some parts of it (some of her writing and some of mine) were changed after my analyst and I talked about it. A lot of the things I said in the first draft were too private, and so this final version is a lot shorter. I guess I'd feel differently if I thought anyone would recognize me, but even as it is I have to admit it's hard to read. But on the other hand, it makes me feel like I've done something with my life.

What would I be like if I hadn't had an analysis? I think about that question a lot. I did try regular therapy two times. Analysis is something very different from that. Why? Well, I'd really like to explain why to all the people who might be in my shoes. I think it's because you and your analyst become sort of like close friends. Perhaps I shouldn't say that because it's a professional relationship, but my analyst was also a person who really cared about me and sort of like a real friend like I'd never had before. I can barely remember the names of my therapists in the two shorter therapies. They just didn't get that close to me.

I should also say why I came to analysis in the first place. The reason is that I was very depressed. But I was so numb I didn't really know I was depressed. My wife and I had a completely asexual relationship, and I really had no feelings for anyone except my children. I was one of those very agreeable, out-of-touch kinds of people. I related to the world the way I related to my mother. She saw everyone in terms of her needs, and I don't think she ever really noticed me. So I didn't notice me either.

I used to think I had a difficult childhood because my mother had so many men in her life and it was so chaotic. But really it was her personality that made everything so horrible—the fact that she didn't think about other people. It took me years to realize how angry I was about this and at her especially. I was living my life as a shadow of a person. Then I started to feel more feelings about everything because of talking about things like this in analysis. When I felt what I was really feeling, I felt even worse because then I knew I was depressed. I realized I'd never had a life of my own. Suddenly, I saw it. It was so depressing. I could see the walls of my prison. I was in a deep dark hole, like a medieval dungeon. But somehow it was better to reach out and feel the cold, damp walls and know that I was in a prison than to be numb about it. At least I could finally cry. And I had my analyst there, caring enough to listen to me. But it was horrible to be there.

How did I get out of that depression, my dungeon? I don't really know. I think my analyst showed me that it was safer to feel my own feelings. It took a long time, but I woke up. I began to feel that horrible, horrible pain and then, finally, some happiness. After a lot of pain I had enough feelings about everything inside of me that I began to feel more confident that I could get back to the happy feelings eventually.

Suddenly (and slowly) I noticed I could talk to people without boring them. And I really cared about them for the first time. My children and my wife noticed the difference, too, and time with them didn't seem tedious the way it used to. My older daughter actually laughed at my jokes. And I'm getting better at listening to my wife. Just ordinary life, I suppose, but the word "ordinary" means so much more to me than most people.

One of the main reasons that analysis touched me and changed me is that I was really listened to. Deep, deep parts of me, the deepest parts of me, were seen by my analyst. She would say to me something like, "You have a way to tell your story now." I would always argue with her that what we talked about didn't matter as much as that she rescued me or let down that rope that pulled me out of my depression, but then after we terminated and I realized I wasn't completely finished, I realized that I had terminated too soon because a part of me also didn't want to be rescued.

When I think about the idea of having a story, though, I think I understand that one of the most important changes in my life is that I can talk to people about myself now. I know how I feel and who I am much more than ever before. And that also makes it more possible for me to listen to other people. I used to be more of a phony, and I didn't even know it.

I also want to say that I was just hungry to be loved and understood and that it's as simple as that. That would be too simple, though, I guess because it leaves out that it was not easy, that we argued and that she was firm with me, too. She insisted that we talk about and think about things that I didn't want to think or talk about. I went through a lot of painful times with her. I acted in some ways I'm embarrassed about now, but even the worst times ended up being something to think about later.

I think another one of the main feelings I have about my analysis is that now I'm not as scared of myself. I think you should try analysis only if you really aren't afraid to know your pain and feel things, no matter how bad it is. But also don't be scared about the idea of exploring things. It really makes you stronger to face things, like in my case facing that I was still angry and going back after my termination and talking about it some more. It's probably not for everyone, but I hope all you readers can see that some people really can change even if they think they can't. You'd probably be surprised.

CHAPTER 8

Andrew: Insecurity, Inferiority, Social Anxiety, and Submissiveness

While there are many aspects of classical psychoanalysis technique that are reassuring to psychoanalysts in training and hence of persistent presence in most training programs, it remains for graduate psychoanalysts to determine which aspects of the technique they have learned are most effective for the patients they actually treat. Many accounts of psychoanalysis further an image of the analyst as a silent being whose personality and input are kept to an absolute minimum in the service of uncovering wishes and patterns from the patient's infancy and childhood. To have it otherwise would, in many analysts' opinion, reduce psychoanalysis to a treatment of influence. In truth, however, the subjectivity (read as *personality*) of the analyst cannot be avoided. There is no such thing as a "pure" or objective way to investigate a patient's unconscious.

It is with this reality in mind that I will describe the treatment of Andrew, a twenty-eight-year-old man when he began his analysis, which is now in its fourth year. I believe that this report demonstrates how psychoanalysis has changed the life of an individual once locked into a lifelong pattern of insecurity and submissiveness. My own personality was a primary tool in our work to help Andrew expand his perspective on his life and experience. Given his original passivity, we were alert to the danger that my influence as his analyst might lead Andrew to change out of compliance. I would stress, however, that as we worked together, we took every opportunity we could to explore his compliant tendencies, which were a very important aspect of his personality and in need of analytic attention. Far from encouraging Andrew's compliance, our persistent exploration eventually began to clarify it and to enable him to integrate less submissive ways of perceiving and acting.

Andrew presented his problems in a tentative fashion that was typical of him. He had been referred to me by a colleague in the city of his college days with whom he had been in treatment during most of his undergraduate years and intermittently since then. He had been on Prozac for about six years, and he was reluctant even to consider the possibility that it might ever be stopped; he felt dependent on it to keep him going. His appearance belied his uncertain demeanor and his insecure self-image. Tall, blond, and athletic, Andrew had the kind of striking good looks that seem to demand an equally striking self-assurance. His dress, mostly black and casual, reflected an artistic style that blended surprisingly well with his athletic body; he had been a serious competitive tennis player throughout his high school years. But this confident-looking young man had spent six years after college in a series of negligible jobs, and despite his looks, the dominant aspects of his sense of self were insecurity, social anxiety, and feelings of inferiority.

Andrew reported two immediate problems: work and his love life. For years his father had preached that Andrew must find work that really interested him because to do any other kind was the equivalent of soul murder—the destruction of a meaningful life. This theme and the discouraging sense that he could never find that just-right work or career overshadowed everything that Andrew had ever done or thought of doing. Highest on his priority list was art; at various times he had studied painting, film, and furniture design and construction. But all had left him feeling that he simply couldn't produce enough of quality, that he lacked motivation and perseverance. He had come to my town to study architecture, which at first he had considered a choice worth pursuing vigorously because it incorporated his artistic interests. Characteristically, however, shortly after school began he found himself tormented by the fear that in going to architecture school he had sacrificed his true calling: painting. He hoped that therapy might help him persist in his attempt to become an architect. But considering his proven history of abandoning career projects once he decided that they weren't representative of his "true self," he had little idea of how that might happen.

Andrew's other problem was his relationship with a woman whom he met as a freshman at his Ivy League college and who took over his life there. Many years later, Cathy was still dominating Andrew's existence and eventually his analysis. Their initial friendship became a consuming romantic relationship during his junior year. From that time on, Cathy assumed a kind of ownership both of Andrew and of their future. She conveyed to him her conviction that they were fated to be together and that nothing could ever separate them permanently. She wanted an exclusive relationship with him, resisting even his wish to socialize with his friends. Andrew had moments of awareness that Cathy was unreasonable in her demands, but he nonetheless tried to see her point of view. He felt responsible for her well-being and accepted her assumption that he was ultimately responsible for curing her despair and giving her the life she felt she deserved.

They lived together for several years, and then Cathy decided that she needed to live in Paris. Andrew knew that finding work in France would be impossible for him, but he agreed to move there with her. In that setting, however, she became increasingly difficult. She would spend days in bed, crying and insisting that her life would be hopeless unless he pledged himself to making it better. She resisted leaving their apartment and insisted that he stay in with her, living the life of a shut-in or recluse. She began to reject the sexual aspect of their relationship, and this became an issue between them. Ultimately Andrew discovered that she was having an affair. He tried to reason with her about stopping it, but Cathy insisted that it was meaningless—she was in love with *him*, not the other man. Andrew was upset and humiliated by her actions (both the affair and her continued refusal to have sex with him), but he stayed with her in Paris for a while, trying to persuade himself that her affair had nothing to do with their relationship.

But it did. Finally, when it became clear that Cathy would not change her behavior, he managed to convince himself that he had to return to the United States, although he did so without breaking off the relationship. Even as he was leaving, she insisted that the relationship was still ongoing and that he could never leave her. If he did, she said, her life "would be over." She e-mailed him constantly to remind him of his continuing obligation to her and to inform him of her suffering and thoughts about suicide. During the first two years of the analysis she visited Andrew four times from France, each time enacting terrifying scenes of threatened suicide and blaming him for her despair. At each of those visits she renewed her insistence that he was "pledged" to the permanence of their relationship; she also attempted to convince him that the analysis (which she understood was supporting his desire to be free of her) was fraudulent and needed to end for the sake of their "love." She was successful enough in this effort that at times it really looked as though the Andrew might disrupt the analysis or bring it to a halt.

Andrew's denial of Cathy's destructiveness was a major initial issue in his relationship with me. He refused to put together the data he presented about her. This was at first hard to understand, and it grew progressively more frustrating. He was so blind in his concern for her safety and future (despite her horrendous behavior and her attacks on his character) that he sometimes appeared almost mentally deficient. I couldn't help getting irritated at him sometimes, and on the occasions that this showed, he was able to recognize a bit more clearly for a while that maybe there was something worth paying attention to in his unswerving devotion to this hellion. What I tried to do most steadily, however, was to let him see how angry I was at *Cathy*—I let him know clearly that if it had been me in that situation, I wouldn't have been concerned. I'd have been furious. Andrew was so oblivious to his own anger—as we were to learn, he had grown up with no help at all in making sense out of what he felt and had been sharply discouraged when he even noticed his feelings—that it was an eye-opener to him to see another person handling annoyance openly and without anxiety. Still, Andrew was paralyzed by her threats of suicide and his images of her all alone in her room crying. I patiently explained the need for limit setting with a person like Cathy, but although he knew that her behavior was manipulative for a long time, he continued to be disarmed and disorganized by the very thought of her suffering.

We had a long period of struggle while Andrew worked through the conflicting demands of his wish to be free of Cathy and his old tendency to put himself at her disposal without any regard for what his own needs might be or how to get them met. This habitual stance was a problem for Andrew in many aspects of his life, and we gave a lot of attention to exploring it.

Although at first sight Andrew's family appeared to be quite ordinary, this comfortable vision did not hold up for long. Early on, the family had led a conventional suburban life while the father commuted to a banking job that he hated. When Andrew was in his teens, his father quit the bank and entered his own father's business, a manufacturing empire with holdings around the world. Andrew's father and grandfather had a turbulent work relationship that ended after several years; they eventually mended their personal fences and so apparently preserved the line of future inheritance, but Andrew's father never worked again. Instead, he moved the family to a large ranch in a very remote area of Montana. By this time Andrew was already in college. He was aware that the ranch was extensive and that the house his parents had built was huge and elaborate, but he had no idea about what it cost or, more tellingly, where the money came from to support this extravagant lifestyle. He had learned by then not to ask questions, and mostly he didn't. When he did, no answers were forthcoming.

It appeared that Andrew's mother had not been consulted in any of these momentous decisions. Her husband did what he wanted, and she did what he wanted too, without question, even when it meant leaving her community for deep rural isolation. She seemed to consider any act of aggression or even assertion extremely dangerous, and she did not challenge him on her children's behalf either; she did nothing to contain his despotic use of them for his own needs. Her no-questions policy was enforced on Andrew as well by her and by his father. He was told nothing of his parents' reasons or motives for anything they did. When he asked, he received no answer. When he tried to figure things out for himself, he was stymied by the peculiarities of their behavior. Eventually he gave up in defeat.

The classic example of this was the family conundrum about money and work. The perfect job or none, Andrew's father preached, and indeed he seemed to model this philosophy. Yet the question of how one supports oneself on those terms was never discussed. Andrew's father had plenty of money, but it certainly didn't work out that way for Andrew. He had inherited a sum of money that kept the wolf from the door, but it wasn't enough to live on. His father spent his mysterious income freely on his own behalf, but he doled it out to Andrew in arbitrary dribs and drabs that left Andrew feeling humiliated, dependent, and guilty about breaking the bank. And confused. If Andrew took a temporary job to bring in some money, he was a sellout and a loser; but when he had to ask his father for money, he ended up feeling like a kid who doesn't even have the security of an allowance. He had to account for every cent he spent, and there was no rhyme or reason to what expenditures were okay and which weren't. His father would finance extravagant Asian vacations, and he refused to give Andrew the money he needed for a job-interview suit.

By the time he came to analysis, Andrew was firmly identified with his mother's utterly passive approach to life; it was not his to reason why. This solidarity was in part a common bond forged by Andrew's own sufferings at his father's tyrannical hands and in part a function of his despair at ever being able to make any sense out of what was going on.

I felt that it was imperative that Andrew come to understand just how unreasonable Cathy's claims on his life were. He found my firmness reassuring, perhaps because it was the first time anyone had ever acknowledged to him that one could notice unreasonableness and challenge it. It was a struggle for him to accept the implications of her manipulative destructiveness, but he did attempt to limit her access to him. Still, it was hard for both of us. He felt guilty about revealing his phone or e-mail contacts with her because he knew I disapproved, and I felt guilty about causing him such conflict. But the more Andrew tried on this strange new attitude toward life, the more he began to see its merits and the possibility that *some* things, at least, can be expected to make sense. Eventually, while Cathy was still living in France and seeing her boyfriend there, Andrew did assert his right to date other women despite her efforts to guilt him out. My impatience with his inability to get angry at her controlling manipulativeness made him feel defensive in the way that he always did when he was confronted with his inability to achieve the magical effortless grasshopper life that his invulnerable father seemed to exemplify, but it also had a role in helping him change his position toward her.

We tried to apply the same kind of thinking to his work concerns. Andrew's indifference toward earning a living was extremely frustrating to me, and he presented no plan for an economically viable future. He persistently devalued any work that wasn't in the area of art. Yet soon after he began architecture school, his satisfaction with architecture as a form of artistic expression was replaced by an obsession over whether he should return to painting. This was characteristic of Andrew. He wanted to be the kind of painter who formulated unusual ideas about the visual world. But as soon as he began to suspect that he might not be sufficiently gifted to achieve this, he would give up painting in despair. He would turn to something else, only to resume his obsessive preoccupation with painting as soon as the "imperfections" of the new work became intolerable. Neither of Andrew's parents had ever helped him observe, let alone tolerate, the divide between our dreams and our capacities. Nor had they taught him anything about how he might fit himself and his unique assortment of strengths and weaknesses into the world in a way that, compromise though it might be, could feel good to him.

My approach to this problem was quite a contrast to the vision that Andrew's had adapted from his father. It was something of a bitter pill because it rejected the possibility of a life of pure pleasure. Yet it was a relief as well. It acknowledged that Andrew's father's demands that he somehow manage to design such a life—and Andrew's own assumption that he was a failure for not being able to do this—was unreasonable. This acknowledgment of reality increased Andrew's budding hope that perhaps some sense could be made out of life after all. If so, he might be able to allow himself some purpose.

I pointed out to him, for example, that in his struggle to find work that he really loved, he seemed to be confusing work with recreation. He was surprised by my definition of work as something that required effort against the desire for pleasurable activity but also that it was something that brought in adequate financial compensation—that is, it wasn't incumbent on him to work for other people for a pittance. Once we clarified this confusion, the possibility of making sense arose again. The disclosure of my attitude toward work and my belief that mature individuals must harness their energies into structuring a work life *that could support their goals* challenged his father's grasshopper/ant dichotomy and gave work a new value that allowed him to persist with his architectural studies. The idea that earning a living was part of what work was about was entirely new to him.

Andrew was more surprised at our discussions of work than he was resistant, and I went on to clarify some other very confusing messages about money that his parents had inculcated in him. When Andrew asked for money, his father implied that he didn't have enough to give, leaving Andrew feeling needy and guilty and once again humiliated for his dependency and his failure to find that perfect job. But the reality of how the parents lived indicated that this wasn't the truth. Furthermore, if Andrew remained firm about what he was asking for in the way of financial assistance, his father *did* eventually come through—although always slightly on the short side. He funded elaborate trips, however, without any question, especially when these were timed to interrupt continuity in Andrew's work life or in his analysis.

Andrew's architecture program contained elements that were particularly difficult for him to manage and endure. Periodically, his work was reviewed with that of his fellow students in "pinups"—very painful public critiques in which instructors criticized the students' work after their drawings had been posted and examined. Again, Andrew's model allowed for only two views of people—the monied and successful and important ones and the working stiffs who wasted their lives doing the menial jobs that their betters rejected but that they couldn't avoid. It was an "I'm Chevy Chase and you're not" view of the world. The "Chases" were the only ones who mattered, and the "nots" were beneath contempt. Andrew was not, by his lights, eligible for group one, and he saw only one alternative, which was excruciatingly painful to him. He was so devastated by his feeling—of being absolutely helpless in the face of a dismissive and sadistic abuse of power—that during those reviews he often lost his ability to defend his work against his critics, who indeed seemed to have little regard for tact or for minimizing injury. I pointed out to him that his reviewers were not necessarily better equipped than he was to make judgments as to the creative merits of his work. To the extent that they indulged in gratuitous cruelty, they were not functioning as teachers and so not fulfilling their obligations to him; they forfeited the position that entitled them and their opinions to respect. With my direct assistance he became able to fend off his tendency to attack himself in response to unfair criticism. I explained to him the idea that we all entertain negative self-images that have to be neutralized if they are not to destroy our capacity for creative work. Our work on the ability to accept one's failings and go on from there—indeed, on the recognition that we all have failings, however disguised these may be—injected another element of comprehensibility into the world. By sharing some of my struggles with this issue, I was able to demonstrate to Andrew some ways to avoid a downward spiraling of affects as a result of cruel criticism. In discussing his wish to be his own style of architect, for example, I was able to draw on parallels in my own training, where it was important to be able to withstand the pressure of supervisors when you believe that their view is not in the best interest of your patient. We talked about the importance of standing up for what one believes. His view of the world as a place where one is helpless, passive, and clueless once more yielded slightly to the possibility that one could keep one's own counsel in the face of "authority" and stick up for oneself.

The craziness of the world of architecture school, like the craziness of his girlfriend's demands and his father's ideas about jobs, had eluded Andrew. So monolithic and closely held were his convictions that questions were forbidden and anger prohibited that without my forceful input he had not allowed himself to see these things. Now, however, although the pain of the pinups continued, he began to be able to tolerate it. He neither broke down nor gave up as he once had when his creative work was criticized. He began to develop the capacity to see the shortcomings of his instructors and critics and so to continue to value the originality in his own work even when other people for their own reasons put him down or otherwise sought to constrain him.

Now we looked back in more detail about how Andrew's relationships with women and his neurotic guilt about his wish to have his own opinions could be traced to his earlier relationships with his parents. He recalled a period in his life at about age nine when he began to be more independent and actually "talk back to his mother." But she became so upset with him that she sat on him and cried about his rebellious behavior until he agreed that he would stop it. (He did.) His father was so overinvested in Andrew's tennis that he insisted that Andrew play despite injuries that required continuous physical therapy. In fact, the young Andrew thought that his father often seemed nearly crazed in his insistence that Andrew compete in one tournament after another. Although he had initially loved tennis, he eventually came to feel that this activity had become his father's rather than his own. Yet he could neither reclaim it as his nor reject it. He recalled, too, that although he had always done extremely well in school and especially in math and science, no one ever suggested to him that he might enjoy a career as a physician, for instance, or a biochemist. No one saw Andrew, and he never learned how to see himself.

The course of Andrew's analysis was not perfectly smooth, of course. Despite his acknowledged attachment to it, he often felt drawn to movements and activities that interrupted or even threatened to end it. Perhaps to some degree this reflected discomfort with the work we were doing, but Andrew did not ordinarily seem very uncomfortable. He was, however, profoundly unperceptive at first and completely unreflective about the grasshopper philosophy by which school and work appeared as unwelcome intrusions on a life of excursions to Aspen and Hong Kong. The need for regularity escaped him. He was only slightly aware of his parents' dislike of the gains he was making and the increasing autonomy that he displayed. The elaborate vacations that he planned during school breaks, for instance, he did not at first even consider relevant. Over time, however, he began to see that progress in the treatment required his presence and some sacrifice of his self-indulgent travel to exotic places—and that that sacrifice, rather than proving him a contemptible "not," was giving him something that mattered to him very much.

In exploring this, we learned that his travel was an attempt in part to identify himself as an interesting person who had gone to interesting places; he was driven to try to acquire by absorption the feeling of worth that he couldn't claim naturally. True to his dichotomous view of life, he sought value by association. He wanted to work with certain distinguished architects who were known for their intellectual positions, believing that contact with such people would transform him into one of them and protect him from contemptuous dismissal. Yet the cost of this route to architectural respect was very high. To work as an intern in their firms would mean going without salary and interrupting the analysis. I stressed these points in our work together, and again my parallel psychoanalytic fantasy of becoming an exalted supervisor or a famous theorist was helpful to me in understanding—and conveying to him—why he might be so willing to impoverish himself in another person's interest. It was useful for me to share with him both my own insights about fame by association and the source of them in my own experience training as a psychoanalyst.

For a long time Andrew experienced any acknowledgment of a failure of judgment as very injurious to his feelings. While he took valuable things in from me, the very fact that he needed my help made him feel painfully inferior. He could learn from my example and from what I conveyed to him, but he still felt that this was humiliating and that it would be better if he were completely in control of his life. He began a relationship with a new woman despite Cathy's continuing bombardment from France of his in-box. At first, Mary appeared to be a good choice. Involved in a similar line of work, she came from an accomplished family, had graduated from a prestigious university, and initially seemed very interested in Andrew. But she had problems that gradually emerged in the relationship—a prodigious capacity and need for alcohol, an inability to work, and a history of chronic unemployment. Like Cathy, she insisted on her love for Andrew, but her behavior was not consistent with her words. She seemed mainly dedicated to a group of friends with whom she had gone to college and who provided a network of parties that she liked to attend with or without Andrew. But much of this material was uncovered in the analysis around the patient's report of feelings about Mary that weren't directly linked to her behavior at all. Andrew appeared to blame *himself* for a lack of strong feelings for Mary; in fact, he blamed his own inability to feel as the source of difficulty between them.

I felt that this was certainly not the case. I demonstrated to him repeatedly that Mary's claims about her feelings for him weren't substantiated by her actions. His lack of feeling seemed to me to be a response to her indifference to him and her desire to live a life in which work existed only as a potential, not requiring from her the actual possession of a job. More and more it seemed to us that in his relationship with Mary he was taking his mother's position of the downtrodden wife of a selfish and sybaritic husband. Eventually he was able to extract himself from his relationship with Mary. And he was able this time, as he had never been with Cathy, to understand that her insistence that they talk over what had happened (which they had already done) would be an act of surrender on his part.

As Andrew approached graduation, his problem with completing tasks he had undertaken reared its head again. The challenge of completing his final project thesis occupied months of the analysis. Again, he required and made use of my confidence in his ability to design his project. His thesis advisers were inconsistent and self-centered in their demands of him; they provided him with little useful help and left him struggling again with his feeling about being one of the worthless hoi polloi in the presence of contemptuous celebrity. At that time too, Andrew had to choose between moving to another city to take an entry-level position in a highly prestigious firm or remaining where he was in a city with few very well-known architects so he could continue his analysis. He chose the latter. It was hard for him to give up the fantasy of establishing himself right away in a celebrated firm. But Andrew recognized clearly that while his journey to reasonable self-sufficiency and self-confidence was well on its way, it was not yet time to give up the analytic work. That awareness made the decision easier. It also signaled the solidity of his relationship with me and the progress he had made toward a personal life in which he could make his own decisions and establish his own priorities about what mattered to him.

This growth became more apparent as money questions came up again in his family. Andrew's father had been paying for Andrew's analysis, but he discontinued his support as soon as Andrew got a job. Yet now he was repeatedly urging Andrew to cut back his sessions if not end his treatment entirely. The peculiarities in his father's attitudes toward money remain an issue for Andrew. I had to point out that his parents travel widely and put large sums of money into home improvements before he could see that there was no actual shortage of money. His father lives as though his funds were inexhaustible, but Andrew's analysis is always presented as a threat to the family's finances—even now that Andrew is paying for it himself and even though the advances that Andrew has made are so striking that no one can deny them. Perhaps his father kept Andrew on a short leash because he feared that if money were plentiful, Andrew would never work, never get and hold a job. Yet he himself discouraged a reasonable attitude toward work, and now that Andrew *has* a profession, he continues to plead poverty. Either Andrew's father is penny-wise and pound-foolish to an extraordinary degree, or he is having trouble with his son's increasing independence and success—a new confusion that Andrew now has to begin sorting out.

As we explored this struggle it became clear that Andrew's father had never been able to acknowledge that his son had any emotional problems. Both parents had supported his relationship with Cathy, never acknowledging the danger that she represented to him even long after he had been able to understand and describe her destructiveness. When Andrew became able to stay at work, they were distressed that he no longer dropped everything to visit them in Montana whenever summoned. His achievements were viewed by them as negative developments rather than indications of maturity.

But as this shift in core values and the accompanying increase in functionality accrued gradually over the course of the analysis, it became possible to look in new ways at Andrew's vulnerability to "guilting out" and to attacks on his self-esteem. Now we were able to consider why he felt so extremely fearful of others. We could also begin to consider his avoidance of any aggressive feelings of his own. He was now actively examining and addressing his experience and relationships with others. He continued to neutralize his paralyzing perfectionism by adhering to some ideas expressed by me about the need for creative work to proceed free from criticism, either from others or from oneself.

I had shared with Andrew my humorous conclusion that we all need to accept our "fundamental worthlessness" as the essential beginning of creative freedom. This was an insight I had gained while negotiating the perils of psychoanalytic supervision, during which I found solace in the idea that no matter how much my supervisor might disapprove of what I said to my patient, I was, nonetheless, the only analyst working with this particular patient. What I said and thought would have to be good enough. My judgment on the matter was the only one that counted, and however imperfect I might be, the task had to remain in my hands, where indeed it belonged. Similar approaches were useful to Andrew as he dealt with discouraging self-appraisals and those of his architectural "supervisors," and we worked our way slowly to a meeting of the minds. For a long time "fundamental worthlessness" had meant something very different to Andrew. But now it became for him, rather than a condemnation and a judgment, a condition in which there could be no demands and so no failure.

Progress in Andrew's analysis has always been slow, and although he has not always shared my opinion about this, it has also been steady. Even when he could not resist his girlfriend's demands or produce the required number of architectural drawings, I always believed that he could overcome his self-doubts and his paralysis about acting on his own behalf. He still struggles with the need to be "perfect"—that is, not ask any questions, not bug anybody, not have any wishes of his own, and go along with the game plan—and so not to evoke the contemptuous and sadistic dismissal of those whose respect and appreciation he wishes to earn. As I have said, this seems to have been his mother's approach to his father, and Andrew adapted it very early to his own situation. Still, he was managing to resist efforts by his parents to force him to the ranch at times when work required his presence. He was able, with help, to understand that his guilt, while the "perfect" response to their pressure, is really not justified by any real injury to them, whatever sense of injury they may convey. In fact, he has noticed that since his parents are retired, they are free to travel to see him if their wish for contact is great enough. Andrew is beginning to catch up with my faith in him. And I have little doubt that my positive opinion about his basic character and abilities, which I have shared liberally with him, have been important in achieving both a therapeutic alliance and a therapeutic outcome.

There is little question in either Andrew's mind or my own that he is a vastly changed individual. While he still tends at first to accept domination by those around him who would enslave him, he now can reappraise his too-quick willingness to go along. He is aware of normal aggressiveness in himself now when he encounters hostility at work or in other aspects of his life, although he still seldom expresses this anger directly. I have been for him a continuous model of adult functioning, an alternative to the ones embodied by his parents. Andrew's view of life seems to have been established by identification with his mother, but while Andrew's use of me may have something to do with his views of masculinity, more often it is linked less to gender than to the ability to approach life in a reasonably assertive fashion. My clear preference for calling it as I see it and accepting the presence of hostility and destructiveness in my interpersonal environment when I encounter it has been, in my estimation, a crucial determinant of Andrew's ability to change.

Presenting a treatment that neither has been terminated nor allows for a follow-up glimpse at the patient five, ten, or twenty years after termination is certainly not an ideal way to demonstrate the effectiveness of treatment. The dramatic nature of the change in Andrew's life and character, however, do illustrate essential aspects of the impact that psychoanalytic treatment can achieve in a relatively short period of time. By eliminating the requirement of anonymity on the analyst's part and giving myself over to the open use of my own life experiences and characteristic modes of approaching interpersonal and emotional issues, I became a person that Andrew could use to help himself grow. I have come to view psychoanalysis as a deeply personal experience in which a kind of "exchange transfusion" occurs—the analyst may give more than he receives, but he does so in a fashion that benefits both parties in the treatment dyad.

Andrew's fears of damaging anyone he relates to is still a problem for him. He is now aware of things that bother him in his relationship with his new girlfriend—a big improvement over her predecessors—but his fear of hurting her feelings leaves him unable to be direct with her. It is easier for him to see his father's "bullshit" than to confront him about it. At work, he has finally asked to be paid for the many extra hours he spends at work. But although the senior architect with whom he works is understood by everyone to be supercilious, Andrew still finds it hard to stand up to him as much as he clearly could without any risk to his job. Getting directly angry at anyone, under any circumstances, is still very hard for him. His history of having been controlled and manipulated by the significant figures in his environment sometimes makes me wonder if he will ever be able to do differently. But in moments of discouragement, I remind myself of the changes he already *has* made and that his fundamental decency and desire to live a full life will motivate him to do the work that remains.

This will focus on the irrational fears that keep him from being able to feel and express anger appropriately. Even now, while his recognition of the destructiveness of others has greatly increased, his access to his own anger lags behind. I don't find this particularly alarming, however, because the ability to extricate himself from damaging relationships and situations is now firmly established and reliably observable. With this new capacity he can survive and live a full life both in the present and in the future. After four years, whether we'll be able to anticipate when termination will naturally seem right to both of us is a question that is "in the air." My sense is that in another year or so of active, uninterrupted psychoanalytic work, Andrew will be ready to terminate and move on in his life. His new girlfriend lives in another city that offers better work opportunities for him than exist here. Parting will be difficult for both of us. But I suspect that in some ways it may be harder for me. He will be moving on to an exciting life, and I will be left behind, deprived of the pleasure of his analytic company and the chance to watch how our work together has transformed him and the life he is leading.

Andrew's Commentary

One of the concerns I have in writing this piece is that my story is incredibly boring. I did not come to analysis because of a long history of sexual abuse. My parents did not die in my arms at the age of eight. I am not now considering, nor have I ever considered, a sex change. I am neither an alcoholic nor a drug addict. I am not suicidal, manic depressive, a genius, an idiot, an autistic outsider artist. I'm not even that terrific with numbers. My anxiety and my neuroses revolve around banal everyday existence and are suffered by so many people that I have known in my life that I assume that they are commonplace worldwide. Television commercials for Paxil or Zoloft or Prozac embarrass me because they make my problems seem all the more quotidian and trivial. Yet I went to see my analyst four years ago because my boring problems were strangling my ability to lead a productive and fulfilling life. They prevented me from working effectively, from maintaining relationships that were satisfying and supportive, and from seeing any way that my life would move forward in the field that I had chosen.

I have been seeing my analyst for the past four years. Looking over the process, I am somewhat in awe of the changes that have occurred. In fact, perhaps it is only in this last year that I can fully appreciate the transformation that has taken place in my life. Having said that, the process has been less an explosive, groundbreaking metamorphosis, the likes of which I imagined Prozac might bring about when I began taking it ten years ago, but a slow, laborious and subtle change in the way I treat my life and the decisions I make in this world on a daily basis. Yet the significance of the change cannot be overstated. Given where

I was when I first began treatment, I have often wondered what would have become of me if had forgone it. Would I have stayed in graduate school? Would I have retreated to the same relationship that had bled me dry of self-esteem, a healthy sex life, and any drive to make a productive and happy life for myself? Would I be living at home? Would I be sucking down Prozac in hopes that it would treat any and all unhappiness in my life related to love and work and money? I can't really answer these questions with any certainty, but I can say that while the effects have been subtle, they have in fact been monumental.

When I began treatment, I was not new to the process. As an undergraduate, I had been in and out of a once-a-week treatment with a social worker; this seemed to have some positive results but was never able to truly take hold of my life. Afterward, I tried taking Prozac for about five years without being in therapy. Initially I sought the drug's supposed power to transform one's life, to revolutionize one's personality and make everything that I detested about myself go away. I had the fantasy of a total metamorphosis, the likes of which I had read about some patients experiencing in *Listening to Prozac*. But instead, after an initial change in my level of anxiety, all I was really left with was a dependence on something that was costly and ultimately ineffective for my purposes. When I began analysis, I still desired something of a miracle cure and was disappointed to find out that the process would be slow and require a lot of work not just from my analyst but from me, the patient, in order for the analysis to work.

IN THE BEGINNING (APRIL 1999)

When I first came to analysis in the spring of 1999, I was in my first year of architecture school, struggling to get the work done and struggling to decide whether to maintain a relationship I had been entrenched in for the past six years. That relationship, which I had followed to an eastern city, then to Paris, and had somehow been able to leave for grad school, was one that I had been desperate to extricate myself from. But I could not muster the wherewithal to act on that desire out of a fear of not having anything else in my life to ground me. Work had been a problem since I left college not because there were no jobs but because work itself was something that my girlfriend and I had no real desire to engage in. While I did have certain ambitions, such as painting and architecture, I made no connection between my desire to accomplish and the need to actually engage in the tedium of work in order to reach those accomplishments. I was stuck in several ways. I was stuck in the relationship and unable to act firmly one way or the other, and I was stuck in school, not able to get the work done that was necessary. I had known that in terms of the work, I would run into problems in architecture school and that therapy would be something I would try again.

Looking back on that time, what strikes me most is how hostile I was toward therapy and my analyst specifically for trying to, as I feared then, take over my life, debunking certain preconceptions that I had developed to justify my position. It took maybe a year and a half before I felt that that period had passed and a reconstructive period had begun. But I felt as if parts of me were being destroyed. Certain fantasies I had about myself that were perhaps in place to mask other things were taken away from me, leaving me to feel raw and exposed, without my old security blanket to comfort me. In architecture school, I was wracked by self-doubt and a trust only in my absolute inferiority and inability to do the work. I was obsessed with how good I was or was not. One way that I had been able to bandage that problem throughout my life was by fantasizing about my ultimate superiority, my innate mastery of architecture—if I could only just allow it to come out, everyone would see that I was in fact the best architect. This is a fantasy that can be sustained only by doing exactly what I was not doing—producing a finished design. I imagined that somehow I was sabotaging myself and therefore unable to express my earthmoving greatness. But the process of therapy eventually and almost completely destroyed that fantasy. At first I was left with nothing to protect me from the bitterness of my incessant thoughts of inferiority, and things seemed to worsen. But gradually, a new understanding of myself and of what I needed to do emerged.

Most of my sessions with my analyst are discussions of one sort or another. They transition from talking about my weekend, to talking about discussions with my parents, friends, or lovers, to reminiscing about specific moments in my past that may or may not be relevant to what is going on right now in my life, to chats about movies, restaurants, or the news. Anything is relevant. But while we sometimes try to understand certain motivations I may have that relate to the narrative of my life, the end goal is not merely that understanding but how to deal with the current day-to-day struggles of relationships, work, and money. And this is important to me because more than understanding my motives and perhaps even the origins of the ways I think and act is to acquire the tools necessary to use that understanding in order to change the way I am in the present in certain ways. This is probably contrary to a popularized view of psychotherapy that posits the process as an old academic mining for unconscious motives and primal scenes in an orgy of self-congratulatory nonsense that gets the patient nowhere.

I have gotten to the point in therapy that I can sense a process of rebuilding—reconstructing my life in such a way that I am able to live fully. My problems have always been that I am afraid of life, of people, of people who may be better than me, of people criticizing me and realizing my weaknesses, my inferiority. I am afraid of women, of exhibiting sexual desire to them, of making an idiot out of myself, of taking risks that may make me vulnerable in any way to criticism. To a certain extent I have taken paths around these fears instead of confronting them. And what I have done about these fears in the past is to feel sorry for myself that I had them and assume no one else has had them. Now I realize that I, like everyone else, just have to accept that those fears exist and confront them as best as possible.

What I think has facilitated the process is my analyst's extremely active engagement in each session. He does not play the passive analyst, allowing me to simply talk and offering no direct commentary. Because the point of the treatment is to figure out how to change the way I deal with situations that occur on a daily basis, it has been extremely helpful to me that my analyst shares with me his own life experiences and how he has dealt with them.

I remember talking to a friend of mine who was also in analysis. She was once enraged because her analyst wrote a letter to her alumni magazine. My friend thought this was an intrusion into her nontherapeutic life that was absolutely unwarranted, disruptive, and counter to her treatment. I asked her whether she knew anything about her therapist's life, and she said absolutely not and furthermore that she wanted no knowledge of it. That attitude stands in stark contrast to my own experience with my analyst. Furthermore, what he shares with me of his own life has been an integral part of the treatment. Our sessions take the form of a dialogue. Because I know more about him, I have a better understanding of where his input is coming from, and thus I understand it as emanating from a person with certain characteristics and life experience, not merely from the body of psychoanalytic knowledge. I am dealing less with someone who represents an ideology that posits itself as truth and more with a person who can critically relate his own experiences to my own.

In this way, I have sometimes thought of my analyst as a surrogate parent not because he has actually taken on a parental role but because his own experience has in certain instances acted as a model for my own in a constructive way. Because he shares with me his own views about particular issues that affect my life, I am able to engage these topics more effectively as they relate to me. For most of the treatment, I have had to deal with basic issues that affected my ability to initiate and complete projects successfully in graduate school. Architecture school demanded that I produce quickly and efficiently, something that I always had a hard time accomplishing. I was riddled with thoughts of my own inferiority with respect to other students and to the criticism that was liberally dealt out by critics, alleged teachers of architecture. Architecture school eats people like me alive in that it is an academic training that has no objective criteria with which to rank its students and at the same time is obsessed with criticism. Its teachers are therefore more than willing to critique someone into a paste, and if you don't have the means by which to protect yourself (namely, enough of a feeling about your own self-worth to disregard academic critique), to a paste you shall be reduced, as was I. In the beginning, in fact for the first two years of school, these thoughts were so debilitating that I could not always follow through with studio work, which at times put me in academic jeopardy. My own obsessive thoughts of my lacks, my own inferiority, in fact my total inability to do the work, would haunt me. As I was making models, I would be going over the various criticisms that would be dealt to me in the pinup the following week. Of course, these criticisms never materialized. They were in my own head. My own ability to evaluate my work was lacking. But through the analysis, by the time I was in my thesis semester I was able to give my own design work enough legitimacy to carry it out effectively. From the beginning, my analyst was convinced that the system by which we were evaluated, a series of desk criticisms and reviews, was not only absurd but destructive. And at first I was not really able to see that. His first advice to me in developing a strategy for managing the reviews was blunt. He would say, "If they start criticizing, tell them, 'Look, if you don't shut up, I'm going to have to fucking kill you.'" The fact that he saw that I was clearly not standing up for myself compelled him to instill in me a more aggressive attitude in defending my own work. Clearly the message was not to murder faculty members but to offer me the possibility that I could become stronger in defending my own right to produce the work that I produced, especially given the fact that evaluation of creative work is, for the most part, arbitrary and driven by the narcissism of those who do the critiquing. This one small comment, which he repeated over and over, was part of a larger project of getting me to believe in the value of my own work and to silence not only the inner critic but those external critics that life boundlessly provides for us all. Of course, this extends well beyond the realm of creative work into other facets of daily life.

Furthermore, my analyst would also use his own experience of writing as an equivalent task. We talked about his own doubts, which he would experience every time he set out to write an article or book review or prepare a presentation. He would overcome the self-doubt only by beginning to write. This was directly parallel to my own experience in school and now at work, in which any design task is daunting until work is put on paper. I used to stare at the blank page for days, fearing that anything that was committed to paper would be disgusting, all the while being ravaged by my own running commentary on my own lack of talent. I think that analysis has quite effectively dealt with those inhibitions. Now that I am working, staring at blank paper and waiting for the perfect idea is not possible, and I am finally able to get it out quickly and with little self-critique.

In considering his proactive role in the treatment, I have worried in the past that this kind of relationship with my analyst could have the effect of having undue influence over me, acting less as a model and more as a prescription. When I recently decided to continue treatment instead of going to a city where I was more inclined to be, certain friends reacted strongly. They said, "You're staying

there for your analyst? That's crazy! He's sucking you dry! He owns you!" My father's reaction was more indicative of his own feeling that I didn't really need to
be seeing an analyst. He told me, "Well, you didn't really stay for your analysis,
it was a practical decision. It was easier to get a job there, you had a reasonably
affordable apartment, and you didn't have to pay for a move." In fact, I stayed
first and foremost to continue my analysis. In deciding what would be most beneficial to my career, my romantic life, and my overall contentment, staying in
treatment until I felt I was reasonably able to effectively lead the life I wanted
was the best thing for me to do. And yes, my analyst has had a very strong influence in my life. If he didn't, I would be throwing a lot of money into the chip-
per. He has influenced me in ways that have allowed me to get out of the influence of others who don't have my interest in mind. He has influenced me
strongly, and at times against my own bad judgment, not to indulge Cathy and
go back to France to lead the pathetic life of a castrated and bedridden caretaker.
He influenced me to get away from the influence of a subsequent relationship
that was, although less suffocating, equally debilitating in many ways. He has influenced me to actually work for a living and hopefully make a career out of my
present occupation. And he has influenced me to seek out a new relationship
that is currently allowing me to see how easy a relationship can be.

The fact that he becomes an active participant in each session has been most
effective in the parts of my life that have needed help the most. In the area of
work and my related fear of production, his own attitude toward work has
helped me redirect how I deal with work in my own life. When I first came to
analysis, my resume was spotty at best. For five years I had held some jobs but
also spent some of that time unemployed; and I had not pursued work as if I
were trying to earn money or find a career. I found myself working for free sometimes or working in jobs that were going to get me nowhere. The idea of making a living was not as apparent as it might have been if I had not had a chunk
of money after college on which to live. This kind of lifestyle did not make my
parents happy, but they were unable to do anything about it, perhaps not wanting to interfere with their grown-up child's mistakes. My analyst made it clear
that this attitude toward work was going to get me nowhere and was especially
inconsistent with my newer desires to pursue a career in architecture. The fact
that his life and his attitude toward work were presented to me as an available
option helped me focus on tangible ways that I needed to change my own habits.
I was essentially able to replace the dominant model for a working adult, my parents, with my analyst. This made a lot more sense and was much more conducive
to an active and aggressive work life.

If my analyst had taken a more passive role with me and allowed me to simply speak through my thoughts, relying primarily on the premise that I would
eventually gain a certain understanding of my unconscious motives, I don't think

that I would have been able to progress as I have in the analysis. If I understood my actions to be the product of past experiences and neurotic thoughts, I think I would be more inclined than ever to think that I was trapped by those past experiences, doomed to repeat them, no matter how well I understood what was motivating me. His feedback and active engagement helped me not only to give meaning to those unconscious motives but also to figure out how to use that understanding throughout the day to actually change my responses to them. In fact, it was when I started to see my own problems as surmountable that I was able to fully realize how effective the treatment had become. That moment came gradually. As I said earlier, this process has required patience and a lot of repetition, and I could feel its full impact only after the third year of analysis, when it all started to really take hold.

Perhaps the hardest part of analysis has been in the area of my past relationship with Cathy. When I moved back from Paris to attend graduate school, my relationship with her was not yet over, but it had gone through some turmoil. It had lasted six years. We had lived together for most of it, and for a long time I had wanted to leave it but found myself totally unable and unwilling to make the break. I was completely emotionally dependent on this woman and imagined that she was just as dependent on me—in fact she insisted that that was true. For someone outside the relationship, that would have been an easy assertion to debunk since Cathy had been having an affair with someone else for six months, a fact that made me somewhat uncomfortable but one that I was willing to accept. She insisted that it had no impact on our relationship because she still loved me and that that would never change. And because she said so, I believed it.

Nevertheless, during the first three months of grad school, I very tentatively began a new relationship with someone else. But for Christmas I returned to Paris to see Cathy, who was still involved with the other guy. We both insisted that we were together, yet during the week I informed her that I was beginning to date someone else, which she met with several fits of crying and punching that usually became mutual fits of crying and my telling her that I wanted her to come back to the States to live with me and try to make things work. As I said this to her, I remember feeling the weight of fifteen Germans coming down on my head, suffocating me, yet I promised her that she could come, partially knowing that she wouldn't but partially thinking that if I didn't say it, she would either kill me or kill herself.

I saw her four times over the course of the next year, each time more strained and each time making it more clear that we were separating for good, but to this day, I do not know when we actually formally split, and in her mind, I am not quite sure that it is clearly over. For two and a half years we didn't see each other. I became involved with someone else for a year, and our phone calls and e-mails became less frequent, except for an occasional barrage of heavy insulting e-mails painting a picture of me as a callous, betraying, and careless boy with not a care in the world for her, as she sank slowly into depression, poverty, and suicidality. I was not at all callous to these characterizations of either of us and was on the contrary quite moved by them. I was always afraid of her, always trying to manage her. I believed her that her life was terrible, and I worried constantly that I would get a call from a mutual friend that she had just killed herself. I imagined pledging myself to her, agreeing to stay with her in the belief that this would keep her alive. Not for one second did I believe that I was being played. And though I knew that I did not want to be with this woman anymore, I forwent that possibly self-preserving knowledge and became easily caught up in trying to, transatlantically, resuscitate her, motivate her to get her life on track.

How did my analyst help me through this experience? With extreme difficulty. I think that he was often frustrated by my undying allegiance to her. My inability to see her as a truly destructive force that was not supportive of my best interests, and my own willingness to forgo my own best interests was baffling to him. He often felt like he was doing battle with Cathy. As long as we were on different continents, things were in his favor. But then, after two and a half years of not seeing her, I invited her to come to my apartment to clear out all her belongings that I had been storing for four years. She was in the United States for a month, and we arranged for her to come and gather her things, a task that I imagined would take about three or four days if done efficiently. The experience wound up taking about ten days, during which time my life was turned upside down, and it became clear to me that for her the purpose of her trip had not been to safeguard a few valuable belongings and her boxes and boxes of worthless papers and books but to try to coax me back into a relationship of some sort.

I suppose I have decided to trust this process more than I have ever trusted anything else—more than school, more than a relationship, more than a job. I have chosen to stay in analysis. While some friends think that is crazy and my father simply tries to convince me that I am wrong, I trust that that is what is necessary. Because therapy is something I do not do as an extracurricular activity, because it is interesting, but because I have to do it in order to have a happy and productive life. I am currently dating a woman in a different city with whom things are going brilliantly. I don't exactly like where I'm living, and I plan to move to this other city as soon as possible. And everything in my life would dictate to me that I should go there, except the therapy, and I need to weigh the things that are really going to improve my life and make me happy in the long run, and it is clear beyond any doubt that what I need to do in order to achieve that is stay here in therapy until I can reasonably say that I am ready to part with therapy. There is no question in my mind that this is the right decision. I have indeed decided to trust this process.

Up to the fall of 2002, I had been in school for the entire time that I was in psychotherapy. I have decided to stay here in order to continue treatment while I enter the next phase of my life, that of beginning a career in architecture. It is important to me that I stay with therapy during at least the beginning of this phase so that I can work through the problems that I know I will encounter in the working world and indeed have already begun to encounter. For me, living life vigorously and aggressively has not come naturally, and I am in the process of trying to become more vigorous and aggressive not only in work but in love and other personal relationships. My relationships with bosses during my spottily employed past was often just like those with my professors at school. I was way too easily swayed toward merely trying to meet their expectations rather than working hard and trying to get the most out of my job. I think this led to a certain resentment of my bosses, which in turn would lead to a slack day at work. I have never met the challenges of work or school well when motivated by fear, and that has been the condition under which I have worked. Working through the daily churn with my analyst is one significant facet of the therapy that benefits from repetition.

At this point, at the end of four years, I have begun to experience the benefits of psychotherapy. Simply put, I actually believe that change is possible in my life. That is not something I could have said four years ago or three years ago. It has taken that long for the benefits of therapy to truly take hold.

One of the most satisfying moments that I have had, and there have been several at this point, is when I realize that what we talk about in therapy becomes conscious thought throughout the day, in the midst of particular situations. At that moment I realize that this is not some magical transformative drug that will automatically change who I am and how I interface with the world; it is slow and takes effort on my part to actually integrate what we have talked about in my analyst's office. There is a point at which I can use what I have learned or I cannot. It comes down to whether I am willing to take the risks necessary to change.

The realization of transformation comes in very small doses. Sometimes I realize that I am overriding certain feelings (that I will call pretherapeutic) with conscious thoughts that result in actions that I have learned in therapy. Those moments happen from time to time. And it is in those moments that there is progress. Therapy is a long and somewhat painful experience that has required repetition, going over experiences many times with my analyst, receiving the same feedback over and over again so that at some point it may actually occur to me out in the field, and my actions may be affected by it.

There have been times throughout the process that I have suddenly begun to question the therapy and its effectiveness, and this sometimes manifests itself as a fear of having been, once again, taken over by a dominant force in my life. At these moments, a flood of questions enter my mind. Was Cathy so bad?

Should I have pursued painting as a career? Has my analyst steamrolled me into a life that I do not want for myself, robbed me of certain aspects of myself that I should have cherished? Was I too willing to take on his idea about which direction my life should be taking, about what I should deem important? After all, this is one tendency that I am actually in therapy to control. My analyst takes a very proactive role in his work with patients. One of my central problems has been that I have had a soft sense of who I am and difficulty in maintaining a belief in myself when faced with strong, perhaps overly narcissistic personalities, friends, bosses, teachers, girlfriends, authority figures. I have struggled to give value to my own thoughts, ideas, and wishes, to engage with an analyst whose job it is to at once direct and enable is sometimes a balancing act. The difference in analysis is that my analyst's position as a critical force in my life is geared toward enabling me to give value to my own thoughts and experiences in the face of others.

CHAPTER 9

Strengthening Analysis, Protecting Patients

Zenobia Grusky

> Observation of structural change [in the patient] comes
> down to the analyst's inferences, while observation of ther-
> apeutic benefit comes down to the patient's self-report. At
> the end of the day, either the analyst's inferences or the pa-
> tient's self-report takes precedence. The question of which
> to prioritize comprises a crucial controversy in our field.
> (Owen Renik, American Psychoanalytic Association Ple-
> nary Address, 2003)

Embedded in the structure of this book is a question, or a conflict, about how
we can know whether an analysis has been successful or understand what has
made it so. Whom do we ask? The patient? The analyst? If we ask only the analyst, we lose a vital 50 percent of the analytic equation. And yet there are many
good reasons why analysts have, historically, been hesitant to seek out or rely too
heavily on patient reports. These provide very important subjective information,
but patients (understandably) do not focus their thinking on the long-term technical or theoretical goals that have been defined by experts in the field. And their
qualitative assessments are necessarily influenced to some degree by their feelings
about the analyst and the analysis. To further complicate matters, asking both
patient and analyst raises questions of its own; Owen Renik suggested in his
2003 plenary address to the American Psychoanalytic Association that one or the
other view must take precedence. But why must we choose?

This abstract question encompasses a more concrete but equally important
one about how to share the answers we get, whether from analyst or from patient, without endangering either the confidentiality of the patient or the analytic process itself. All of us, both analysts and patients, want analysis to be a ro-
bust science and useful therapeutic art informed by clinical practice. If analysts

cannot draw adequate conclusions about the usefulness of analysis or even construct analytic theories without greater reference to the patient's experience, then they need access to this experience. But how can the material necessary for learning be safely shared?

Concerns like these become even more acute when the patient's appraisal takes the form of a public document. There are many patients who would never agree to write openly about their analyses, and there are many analysts who would never consider asking their patients to do so. And yet, if we do not attempt to deal with the tensions between openness and confidentiality, how will patients ever be able to make known what *they* actually think about how their analyses turn out? How can the detail necessary to appraise and assess a process as immensely complicated as psychoanalysis be accumulated and organized? How can patients make clear where analysis succeeds and where it fails them, and how can clinicians hear their patients' and their colleagues' appraisals—not only the intellectual and public ideas but also the deeper and more personal thoughts that people share with their analysts—about what really worked or didn't in their treatments? If psychoanalysis is to use feedback from patients as well as from analysts, we must keep track of the price of this information and never stop asking if the benefits are worth the cost.

In preparing this book, the authors paid very careful attention to questions like these, both the ones that are salient in the psychoanalytic literature (which I will summarize here) and some new ones raised by this book project. Clearly this is a topic that demands very careful investigation, and one of our hopes in offering this volume is that it may ultimately contribute to a better understanding of the risks, rewards, and implications of the kind of case study we present here.

All the analysts who contributed to this book discussed extensively among themselves their general thinking on the permission/privacy issue as well as such specific matters as how they chose which patient to discuss, how they weighed the pros and cons of asking for permission to write up the analysis, and, finally, how they made the decision to ask—or not ask—the patient to contribute a written perspective of his or her own. Two of the contributing analysts chose not to tell their patients about this project, disguising them with great care instead. One analyst's patient consented to be included when asked but declined to write a discussion. The other four analysts' patients agreed to be included and also to contribute their own views of their analyses. Some of the background of these decisions and the negotiations that informed them are detailed in the remainder of this chapter. Those analysts who did not ask their patients to contribute recount their reasons for this decision. Those who did ask offer their thoughts about the effects of their request on the analytic process, for example, what impact the task of writing and the extra contact with the analyst had on the patient and his or her feeling about the analysis or, if the analysis was still in progress, how the writing process influenced it.

Current Questions about the Use of Case Material

There is a wide and widening literature on the confidentiality issues involved in the sharing of analytic material. It addresses such matters as the advantages and disadvantages to the patient of being asked for permission before being written up as a case, the pros and cons of showing the patient the actual manuscript, and the relative risks and benefits of the various techniques of disguising patient material so that it is unrecognizable. The literature stresses repeatedly that it is the *patient's* advantage or disadvantage that must remain uppermost in analysts' minds in these considerations. In this country, individual states establish the legal guidelines that guarantee patients and therapists/analysts a carefully protected confidential relationship. There are a few exceptions to this guarantee, the most common of which are the requirement that threats of harm be reported to the authorities and the right of clinicians to write about and discuss therapies and analyses for the purpose of training and educating other clinicians. In training situations, for example, a trainee's supervisor has the same legal rights and responsibilities as he or she would have as the analyst.

In professional publications written for the advancement of the field and the continuing education of psychotherapists, careful disguise rather than consent has been until recently the most common method of handling clinical writing. (In research studies, of course, it is expected that permission will be asked and granted.) Lately, however, potential problems of this time-honored tradition have received increasing attention. Even a most careful disguise may sometimes be penetrated; as one of our analysts pointed out, occasionally a patient has stumbled on a published study, recognized him- or herself through (what the analyst considered) a good-enough disguise, and was left feeling exposed and vulnerable. The Internet has made the professional psychoanalytic literature far more accessible than it has ever been before and the likelihood of patients' reading it far greater. Finally, even (or perhaps especially) when disguises *are* successful, they may depend on such extensive manipulation of the analytic circumstances that they invalidate the conclusions drawn in the actual clinical situation. Extreme or so-called overly distorted disguises change the meaning and significance of a case report, diminishing its worth as a source of valid data or even as a relatively realistic account of what happened. These are inescapable concerns; even when a patient does consent to being written about, a great deal of disguise is always involved.

Another, third technique is to limit clinical studies to short vignettes. But this raises the familiar question about how much such brief illustrations are organized, trimmed, or taken out of context to fit the theoretical or technical needs of the analyst. Clearly, detailed and extensive case writing can give a more accurate picture of the complexities and nuances of the unique particularities of analyst–patient dynamics.

Specialized and technical issues complicate these fundamental questions of patient privacy. Most of these are probably of greater interest to analysts than to their patients or to the public at large; a number of these are compiled in an appendix at the end of this book. But some inquiries are particularly relevant to this book, and these investigate the technical, theoretical, and, above all, personal implications of collaboration between patient and analyst in writing up an analysis (Aron 2000; Gabbard 2000; Hoffman 1994; Pizer 2000; Reiser 2000; Slochower 1998; Stein 1988a, 1988b).

What the Analysts Had to Say

We began by asking the contributing analysts for their initial responses to the idea of asking a patient to write about his or her analysis and about how their feelings developed as the project proceeded. George's analyst commented drily, "First of all, there's no way to do it right!" This sentiment was echoed by all the authors of this book.

When an analyst asks a patient for permission to write about an analysis, the patient knows that the analyst has a personal or professional investment in the outcome and a point of view about the case. Furthermore, the patient's permission may require reading or actively giving feedback about a specific article or book. This raises still other questions. What is the impact on the patient of reading what the analyst has written? The written analytic case report does not offer the kind of control and responsiveness that in the analytic hour permit the analyst to convey complicated thoughts to the patient with tact and sensitivity. In an analytic session, a patient may disagree with the analyst's position and at the very least work through the feelings that come up about what the analyst has said. But once the analysis has been terminated, the patient has no venue for this work unless contact with the analyst is resumed. If the patient takes issue with what the analyst has written, how should it be decided what should be changed? When patients are asked to contribute their own views, the situation becomes still more complicated.

George's analyst addressed the dark side of these dilemmas. "You can't get a real consent before or after with anyone; . . . it could be that it only *appears* as if they are agreeing. A patient could agree, but unconsciously disagree. You don't know how people feel for a long time."

Caroline's analyst saw the matter differently. "It's good that we're concerned about compliance and what's best for our patients, but there are other important issues, too. For one thing, I think that many of my patients could, and would, tell me if they didn't want me to write about them. . . . It depends on how one sees one's authority as an analyst. In addition, psychoanalysis also has the problems of its lack of data, and its lack of good public relations. . . . . How can people know that we can really help if we don't show them what we do?"

Jacob's analyst added, "Some patients are more comfortable than others about disagreeing with their analysts, or arguing, or saying no. Are the ones who are agreeing to write simply complying? . . . I know that transference is ubiquitous, and in thinking about this I thought, 'Just as some people say no to their mothers more than others, some people say no to their analysts more than others. And it's a question of personal style and degree. How can we say in general who have the better relationships with their mothers, or are being more true to themselves?'"

This debate led many of our analysts to the following question: Does showing a patient the analyst's view of the analysis (or asking the patient to write about it) interfere with or intrude on the patient? Or is it "grist for the mill" and a chance for deepening and consolidating the analytic work?

In response to this question, all the analysts in this book raised concerns similar to the one voiced previously by George's analyst. Their concern is that to write about a patient, even with an "informed consent," can be an act of self-interest or exploitation by the analyst. At the same time, however, all the analysts acknowledged that in many situations seeing what the analyst writes can be potentially beneficial for the patient or helpful to both (Pizer 2000). How can both of these positions coexist?

"It's important to approach it in a thoughtful, individual way," Caroline's analyst said. "It wouldn't be helpful to ask . . . people who are extremely disturbed or paranoid. There are a lot of considerations. We are probably selecting patients who are somewhat compliant and eager to please. However, if the writing means that this is talked about even more, then it [the writing] is a slice of the transference/countertransference like everything else. It's more material to be analyzed."

"I also know that it was tricky with my patient," this analyst went on. "But what I'm saying is that we can't ever keep our hands clean anyway. However you cut the pie, you're giving something up. There is always some other way to cut it. And you only get one piece."

Watt's analyst expressed a similar point of view: "It's a huge request to ask a patient. I agree it's not possible for a patient to be completely honest about something so complicated. But it is possible for us to be thoughtful about it, I think. I thought with my patient that there was a good chance it would be helpful to him in a self-affirming way and useful. It felt like more a part of his particular process than an intrusion. . . . If it's analyzable, it could be good. . . . Sometimes the messy [feelings] can be the best ones for learning."

Andrew's analyst took the issue further: "Usually I don't write about my own patients. . . . But I would not consider doing a long, extended case write-up like the ones in this book without getting permission. Why? Because I feel there is a kind of trust with my patient and I don't want to use my experience with my patient without letting him or her know about it."

Here I took an opportunity to review with Andrew's analyst some of the differences among the participating analysts. "Some of the other analysts have shared your view that no matter how well disguised the case report may be, to discuss patient material without patient permission is a breach of patient/analyst trust. However, it's interesting to notice that while all of the analysts approach this question in terms of how best to protect their patients, some analysts feel that disguise is more protective, and some analysts feel that permission is more protective. How do you think about that?"

Andrew's analyst responded, "I think the acknowledgement of a real relationship is avoided by analysts because we haven't really defined how 'realness' in the analytic relationship is real in a different way than other relationships are real. Someone who comes over for dinner [may] know the analyst in a less real way, in a way, than the patient knows his analyst. We're all nice in a simpler way in our social lives. Analytic relationships are much deeper. And so more real, in a way. We don't think about this enough."

"So," I said, "you're saying that it's like *any* relationship, where if you did something that mattered to someone, you'd just assume that you'd want to tell them about it." "Right," said Andrew's analyst, "and I'm saying even more than that. I'm saying that maybe there's something wrong with the concept of anonymity. . . . Even my grocer knows the obvious things I'm doing. . . . But to get back to the idea of whether the writing is grist for the mill. I think the idea of writing about an analysis, at least with my case—and my case was one where I felt like it could really be helpful—the writing definitely added a thrust to what he'd already gotten from me. When we talk about things deeply, of course it brings up hurt feelings—and all kinds of feelings—but that's the way it should be. It reintroduces all of the most important issues in a helpful way. The areas where he's not living his life as fully as he could get dealt with even more. Grist for the mill, for sure."

Two of the other analysts also had things to say about the process of dealing with the written material with their patients and the implications of learning what one's analyst thought about one's analysis. "My patient responded to me after two months by mail," George's analyst said. "He granted me permission to publish my understanding of our work, but he expressed reluctance to read what I wrote. How was I to understand this? I thought, without any confirmation from him, that he wished to preserve *his* understanding of what had occurred. . . . Later he read my draft and said he agreed with it. . . . He commented on minor points, which I corrected. . . . I feel that there is relative consensus about what went on in the analysis. I am quite certain, however, that if we met face to face for several hours this consensus would be compromised. . . . If another analyst were to interview him, that consensus might be even more questionable."

Jacob's analyst addressed related issues. "I think it is true what George's analyst says, that you don't know what people think for a long time. . . . However, because of this process, Jacob has had a lot of chances to tell me to take out parts and rewrite parts of my writing and to write and rewrite the parts that he wrote. It's been such a good chance for him, too, to define what *he* thinks, by disagreeing with me and then seeing that we are able to arrive at a mutual decision. Also, sometimes it was a chance for the two of us to negotiate and go back and forth and find a middle ground. This is really good ego-building experience for someone with a shaky ego or a shaky sense of self."

Since George's analyst seemed to represent most clearly the other end of the spectrum from the "grist for the mill" argument, I summarized the previously mentioned comments for him and then asked him again, "Is this such valuable data that we should take these risks anyway?" George's analyst replied, "Maybe. You'd only know later on. But you never completely analyze the transference. Just like people never 'get over' hearing gossip about their analysts. It's always unfolding, unknown. So should you try? If you want to, but you're not a coward if you don't. It's important to think about the implications of it, but if you do that I think it's worthwhile to try this experiment and see."

Sarah's analyst, who chose not to discuss the project with the patient, expanded on some similar ideas in a useful way. "Inspecting all my present and past patients, I found only a few I could have asked to write about their treatments. My chief concern in thinking about it was the degree of their psychopathology: the worse it was, the less I could imagine asking them to write. . . . Patients' accounts would certainly be a good way to get raw data, but I wonder if the problem of asking them could be bypassed if a third person—another analyst—were to ask them and help them write their views about their treatment. . . . Of course that would be similar to the classical follow-up."

But, I asked, do we want to bypass the messy part and, with it, the opportunity for deep discussion with the patient about what the patient thinks worked?

"You're right," said Sarah's analyst. "So in general, . . . I hope that this practice [of analysts asking their patients to write] spreads throughout the psychoanalytic community. I think it is worth getting accounts from patients, providing that analysts pay careful attention to any kind of risk. In order to help them maybe we should have . . . a sort of peer supervision about selecting suitable cases . . . in order to manage possible side effects while the process of writing is going on."

All the participating analysts agreed that that the peer supervision concept was an excellent idea. In fact, one by-product of this chapter is that for this group of analysts, there was a kind of peer supervision in the process of our discussions about these issues.

Laila's analyst, who also decided on disguise rather than involving the patient in the writing process, extended the debate even further: "At first I worried that if I asked my patient to read what I wrote, her parents might read it. And that their feelings about it might not help my patient in her relationship with them. . . . And as I said in my case report, maybe I didn't contact Liala about the writing because I thought I had made the wrong decision in deciding not to see her just one time a week. . . . I guess my feeling about it is that it would have been too painful for us to confront this failure. . . . This is a patient who needed to have me stay an idealized person for her. She couldn't have tolerated that I missed the boat on that, I think."

"Are you saying that this was your assessment of this patient's limits?" I asked. "I'm interested in this point because it fits in with what so many of us are thinking about: that each patient probably requires a different kind of thoughtfulness."

"Exactly," said Laila's analyst. "This particular patient needed to have a happy ending."

"That's an important point," I said. "I wonder if you'd also agree, at the same time, that other patients who were less fragile could grow from a confrontation with that kind of failure or disappointment in the analyst."

"I agree with the 'grist for the mill' argument absolutely, but not for this patient," said Laila's analyst. "I believe she achieved the optimal outcome for her. My patient couldn't be too angry at me or her parents because it was life and death for her. The thoughtfulness about the patient is the issue. So, the thoughtfulness could fall on either side of the debate."

So, I suggested, perhaps the book project illustrated how writing could be good for the analyst as a kind of growth-producing self-supervision of our own strengths and weaknesses. "And sometimes our patients grow from seeing the reality of that messiness and sometimes they don't." "Yes," said Laila's analyst. "If she and I were in a position to resume treatment for at least a year, then I'd feel comfortable about it, maybe, but only in that context."

Pre- or Posttermination Patient Contact/Writing about Analysis

This project also made us wonder whether and how asking a patient's permission to write (or asking the patient to write about an analysis) opens up the question of more treatment in terminated cases. Is this a good thing? Or is a request to write better raised *during* the analysis so that the patient's feelings about it can be analyzed?

Jacob was one patient who decided to come back to treatment after his termination; the idea of writing enabled him to ask for more time in analysis. His analyst said about this: "For a while I wondered if there was a way I could have handled it that would have been more helpful. On the other hand, he may have just had to leave and come back the way he did before he could feel more comfortable taking up space and expressing anger. So, is it better to ask a patient to write after termination or during the analysis? I'm not sure about the answer to that either. . . . Perhaps like many patients without very much good mothering this man wasn't able to know [certain things] unless I said them first, or did them first, or invited him back to treatment first. So, in Jacob's case . . . although at first I approached him to write posttermination, the way that the writing facilitated the second part of his treatment probably does illustrate the way that writing can be grist for the mill."

Watt's analyst said, "My patient had terminated a few years before, but I thought there was a good chance it would be useful to him to do it at that point after termination. . . . It felt like a part of his process more than like an enormous intrusion."

This was similar to the view of Caroline's analyst: "My patient was on my mind to ask because we were in the termination phase. I wouldn't assume that's always the best way for all patients, but I tried to think about it in a thoughtful individual way with her. She wasn't obviously very disturbed or paranoid. She had changed . . . in significant ways. . . . I felt as though she identified with my successes, and that it would probably help her feel more OK about pursuing her career. There are risks in any intrusion, but analysts get pregnant, have careers . . . and some people do have less transference over time. Some people grow up more than others."

Andrew was the only one among our patients who was in the middle of his analysis. "He is four years into treatment," his analyst said. "Not at all near termination. . . . But my selection of him was pretty uncomplicated. He immediately came to mind as someone whose view it would be possible to get and someone to whom the effort would be useful. My main concern was whether he'd complete the task because he has a work inhibition."

Specialness Issue

What is the impact on the patient of the fantasy or the reality of being special to the analyst? Since the analyst's choice of one patient and not another for a project like this is a piece of undeniable reality, how did our analysts understand this dimension—both in their own minds and with their patients? In this context it seems appropriate for the editor of this volume, Dr. Schachter, who developed the idea of the project, to express his opinion: "I think it is important for analysts to keep in mind that the patient, in addition to being the patient of an analyst, is also a person in their own right. Analysts are trained to look for pathology, not health, and to search for potential problems, even in a situation where a patient could feel pleased at being the successful, special one. Why shouldn't that be gratifying? The patient publishing his or her ideas about the treatment, just like a dissertation or sixteen other things, is in and of itself something that has great potential as an expression of achievement. Presumably the analysts publishing case reports in this book are gratified at this success and such gratification is widely regarded as healthy. Publishing is a success to be proud of, both for patient and for analyst. In addition, if a patient is grateful to the analyst for therapeutic benefits, why shouldn't he or she be pleased to give something to the analyst in return? It can be very valuable for a patient not only to be the recipient of giving but to also be able to give something back. I think we need some fresh ways of looking at this kind of experience, and I think the analysts and the patients in this book should be applauded for giving us that."

A central point that all our analysts came back to repeatedly was that any piece of reality—pregnancy, a wedding ring, a meeting on the street, being asked to write, and the sense of specialness or intrusion that these situations may bring with them—needs to be thoughtfully analyzed. At the same time, however, a contemporary viewpoint consistently voiced by many of our analysts and articulated in some detail by Dr. Schachter is a receptive attitude toward exploration and experimentation in general. If analysts are trying to be thoughtful about the possibility that a feeling of specialness could be an idealization or a compliance, why may they not give equal weight to the idea that that feeling could also be something positive?

"If there is one thing that we know as analysts, it's that transference trumps everything," Caroline's analyst said. "My patient did feel that I wrote about her because she was special. And she was right. We shouldn't try to deny it. It's a fruitful area of exploration. But transference trumps everything in the end. Some people think I was thinking about them in something I write when I wasn't. Some people don't recognize their own dreams but see themselves in someone else's material. Transference, or one's own subjective take on things, does trump everything else. Often it's something you never thought of that the patient picks up on."

Conclusion

The last question we asked our analysts was a more philosophical one, intended to speak to general readers as well as analysts: Is material of this kind so valuable that more analysts and patients should take the risks of providing it? Is it a meaningful consultation for the analyst, one that allows an especially open, honest, and real dialogue about what makes analysis work? As George's analyst said at the very beginning, all options are imperfect. But after considering this controversy from many angles, the analysts in this book concluded that patients' writings about their experiences in analysis are valuable and that continued exploration is in order. We have tried to give our readers the wherewithal to think about these issues themselves.

CHAPTER 10

Discussion and Conclusion: Seven Analyses

Joseph Schachter

Freud's Original Concept of Psychoanalytic Treatment

Let me introduce my discussion of these seven cases with a brief review of Freud's original conception of psychoanalytic treatment. Trained as a scientific researcher, Freud adopted a scientific model shaped by the experimental philosophy and theory of his time. He tried to examine the patient's mind, as reflected in his or her "free associations," from a presumably neutral and objective point of view—like a scientist examining a specimen. He believed that for psychoanalysis to remain scientific, identical conditions should be established and maintained for all patients. Personally, Freud was neither cold nor aloof, but he regarded his friendly human relatedness as something separate from and outside the boundary of analytic technique.

Freud originally supposed that childhood sexual traumas caused adult psychopathology, but he later came to believe that childhood sexual *fantasies* were the root cause of adult neurosis. The constellation of sexual fantasies that he held responsible reminded him of Sophocles' dramatization of the Oedipus story: Oedipus unwittingly murdered his father and married his mother; later, overcome with guilt when he realized what he had done, he plucked out his own eyes. Freud named the constellation of related fantasies that he observed in his patients the *Oedipus complex*.

The etiological Oedipus complex referred to powerful, innate drives, thought by Freud to be phylogenetically inherited, that urge every child to wish to possess the parent of the opposite sex and to destroy the rival same-sex parent—drives that necessarily engender guilt and rage. In his clinical work, Freud focused on exploring memories of these childhood fantasies; he thought that once they had been reconstructed, acknowledged, and accepted, along with their associated guilt and rage, resolution and cure of the patient's adult neurosis were possible.

As it turned out, however, it was not that easy. Even when the patient relived these childhood fantasies and attempted to resolve them—with the analyst experienced as a substitute parental figure—improvement was often less than desired. Freud later realized that insights about childhood fantasies have to be applied to the patient's current emotional life; he called this process "working through." Still, the proportion of analytic patients who achieved substantial or dramatic therapeutic benefit was not large.

Some psychoanalysts, undoubtedly, would characterize this description of Freud as flat and insufficiently qualified and nuanced. But I am delineating very briefly here only his earliest conceptions; there were many changes later. In fact, there are almost as many versions of Freud's texts as there are of the Bible, but no canonical version of either exists. Just how treacherous interpreting a famous text can be is cogently illustrated by the fact that in the 1631 edition of the Bible, the Book of Exodus contained an admonition that "Thou *shall* commit adultery." Was the "not" omitted in the printing (a Freudian slip), or was this God's intent on Mount Sinai? (Hitchens 2003, 7).

It was thought at first that analysts rarely had personal feelings toward their patients and that such feelings, when they existed, were a neurotic problem of the analyst's that interfered with analytic work. However, Heimann (1950) asserted what experience was slowly making clear—that analysts *do* have personal feelings, unconscious as well as conscious, about their patients. Further, these personal feelings and responses to the patient could *help* the analyst understand the patient. The emotional quality of the patient's interactions with others could be clearly seen in analysis of the patient–analyst interaction. Freud's earlier scientific model of the objective, neutral analyst as only an "analyzing instrument" was no longer applicable and could no longer be sustained.

This was the beginning of the relinquishment of the early "scientific model" of psychoanalysis. With it, clinical exploration for presumed pathogenic Oedipal childhood fantasies began to diminish. Instead, patient and analyst searched for and created plausible narratives that could make the patient's emotional development comprehensible and meaningful and so, it is hoped, foster further growth.

Can Psychoanalysis Be Distinguished from Other Therapies?

This is a period of burgeoning diversity in analytic theories of technique. Attempts to define a basis that is common to all psychoanalytic treatments have so far foundered for lack of consensus. Can psychoanalysis be distinguished from other psychotherapies? Are these seven treatments, for example, so obviously different from each other, all examples of psychoanalysis? I think that the answer is yes, but it is not easy to go beyond the trite and unsatisfactory response that these are analytic treatments because they were all conducted by trained psychoanalysts. Concrete determinants—such as the patient's use of the couch or the frequency of the sessions—do not in themselves make a treatment a psychoanalysis.

I suggest that the seven treatments outlined in this volume all qualify as psychoanalytic because they make use of derivatives of Freud's fundamental contribution: a new conception of human nature that delineated the complex, powerful, dynamic, *unconscious* forces of the human mind. What may distinguish psychoanalysis from other psychotherapies is "the intensive examination of conscious and unconscious feelings and fantasies of *both* patient and analyst that underlie their habitual relationship patterns" (Schachter 2002, 229). For example, Laila's analyst's access to her own unconscious feelings enabled her to realize that she had to deal with her own envy of her patient's financial freedom. Another example is Laila's analyst's recognition that a fantasy of her own—that charging high fees was unfeminine, unmaternal, and not nurturing—was interfering with her work with Laila around her fee.

The goal is to delineate these underlying feelings and fantasies—to discern and confront them accurately, honestly, and directly—and to help the patient develop the freedom to reshape previously automatic responses into more appropriate, adaptive, and satisfying ones. The seven analysts in this book all worked, implicitly or explicitly, toward this goal. They also all shared a conviction, a passionate belief, in a theory of technique and in a meaning system that gives them confidence in their ability to help their patients. That confidence is communicated to the patient and helps empower the patient's belief that they are capable of therapeutic change.

The Effectiveness of Psychotherapeutic Treatment

The following brief review of work on treatment effectiveness starts not with studies of psychoanalysis proper but with the broader range of psychotherapies that have been derived mostly from psychoanalysis. Psychotherapy studies are more numerous, include larger numbers of patients, and have the advantages (as well as the disadvantages) of greater objectivity than pure psychoanalytic studies.

An overwhelming number of controlled studies of psychotherapy reveal a positive outcome compared with no treatment. Psychotherapy patients also show gains that surpass those resulting from placebo controls and pseudotherapies (that is, "therapies" not actually expected to be effective by the therapist) (Lambert and Bergin 1994). However, although there are many psychotherapies, each with its own rationale and specific techniques, there is only modest evidence to suggest superiority of one school or technique over another. Since differences in effectiveness among different schools are small, it seems likely that effectiveness is largely a function of factors common to all the schools (such as the therapist's concern for and interest in the patient as expressed in the ambience of warmth, trust, and acceptance within the human encounter). In addition, despite careful selection, training, and supervision, therapists offering the same treatment have highly divergent results; the individual therapist's personality and skill make a difference.

In one large-scale study of the psychotherapies conducted by *Consumer Reports* (Seligman 1995), 2,100 subscribers treated by mental health professionals reported greater improvement than 3,000 other subscribers who spoke to no one about their problems or confided in friends. However, in seeking help, those 2,100 exhibited greater initiative in dealing with their problems, which itself may have had positive prognostic implications separate from the particulars of the professional help received. People in long-term treatment fared better than those in short-term treatment, but the former were more severely disturbed (for example, more seriously depressed or living more chaotic lives), and that may have allowed more room for perceived improvement.

A study (Freedman et al. 1999) of patients who had completed psychoanalytic psychotherapy in a clinic indicated that patient satisfaction was positively correlated with both session frequency and treatment duration. We don't know if the patients with more frequent sessions and longer durations were more troubled initially and so more likely to experience improvement. Therefore, we cannot with certainty attribute the greater therapeutic improvement to these factors. Luborsky (2001) reviewed the question of whether long-term psychotherapy is more effective than short term and concluded that the question cannot yet be answered definitively. The cumulative impact of a positive relationship with the therapist and session frequency was a powerful predictor of treatment outcome.

The Effectiveness of Psychoanalytic Treatment

Surprisingly, it is still not clear how effective psychoanalytic treatment is, and because of this, analysis has been subjected to bitter criticism. However, there are formidable difficulties in constructing straightforward empirical assessments of psychoanalytic effectiveness, and in this psychoanalysis is little different from many other professions, such as law and teaching, where circumstances are complex and results multidetermined. While many patients who participate in psychoanalytic treatment report improvement, this reflects only an *association* between treatment and benefit. It is difficult to prove definitely that improvement was *caused* by the treatment—that is, that improvement might not have occurred with some other treatment or even without any specific treatment at all.

What do studies of psychoanalysis reveal? In one uniquely intensive and comprehensive study (Wallerstein 1986), forty-two seriously disturbed patients were treated with psychoanalysis; in some cases supportive techniques predominated, and in others traditional interpretations were paramount. The therapeutic changes associated with supportive techniques were found to be just as extensive and long lasting as those associated with traditional interpretive techniques. However, the forty-two patients studied were not representative of most analytic patients in that they were more seriously troubled than is common and more frequently required hospitalization. A later critical review of studies of analytic treatment (which encompassed a total of approximately 1,800 patients treated by approximately 475 students and graduate analysts) succinctly concluded, "The majority of patients selected as suitable for psychoanalysis derive substantial therapeutic benefit from it" (Galatzer-Levy et al. 2000, 123). Here too, however, it cannot be concluded that the treatment *caused* the improvement since it was not possible to rule out improvement resulting either from a spontaneous remission, another relationship, or some chance occurrence. There was some tendency for better pretreatment functioning to be associated with greater improvement. Similarly, Blatt and Shahar (2004) reanalyzed the data from Wallerstein's (1986) study and found that more mature interpersonal relationships before treatment were positively associated with improvement in both psychoanalysis and psychotherapy. We know that some well-functioning patients, presumably good candidates for analytic treatment, fail to improve and that some may even get worse. An impressive negative finding by Craige (2002) reveals that 28 percent of a highly motivated and psychologically minded group of psychoanalytic candidates described themselves as "highly disappointed" with the degree of improvement they derived from their training analyses, which were conducted by very experienced analysts.

How Does Psychoanalysis Effect Therapeutic Change?

Having read the case reports here, you may have some ideas of your own. But it is widely acknowledged that even after a hundred years of psychoanalytic treatment, we still don't know with any certainty what the transformative elements are. We have ideas, of course, but they are only ideas, not reasonable certainties. Certainly change can take place without the person's being able to specify how or why. Caroline confronts this straightforwardly and courageously: "I do know that analysis has changed all that, but I honestly don't know how." Jacob commented similarly, "How did I get out of that depression, my dungeon? I don't really know."

Some of the mutative elements in psychoanalytic treatment are interpretation, construction of a personal narrative, and modification of the patient's habitual relationship patterns.

INTERPRETATION

Analytic interpretation can be helpful in a variety of ways: it may enable a patient to formulate a more adaptive way of dealing with a troublesome problem, the insight produced by an interpretation may reduce the anxiety associated with a conflict, and just the feeling of being understood may increase the patient's feeling of security. Many analysts regard interpretation, or the closely related *analytic listening*, as the primary mechanism of therapeutic benefit. However, a patient may hear an interpretation very differently from the way the analyst intended it; this is just one example of the many problems in determining what generates change in psychoanalysis. An interpretation may be experienced instead as an explanation, as an expression of support and reassurance. Conversely, a comment intended by the analyst to be supportive rather than interpretive may be experienced instead as an illuminating interpretation—or as a criticism by the patient.

CONSTRUCTION OF A PERSONAL NARRATIVE

Construction of a personal narrative is another element widely regarded as therapeutic; it gives the patient a coherent and meaningful explanation of his or her past development and present affective experiences. To some degree, the creation of such narratives has replaced the reconstruction of those childhood Oedipal experiences and fantasies that were once presumed to be pathogenic. Although a constructed narrative may be helpful, it must be acknowledged that the actual accuracy—the veridicality—of the story is uncertain. Even several hundred hours of participatory observation of a patient cannot remove all uncertainty from the effort to describe accurately relationships that occurred decades earlier. Still, many analysts believe that construction of such a narrative is beneficial, and this conviction may in itself constitute a subtle, inadvertent suggestion to the patient. The ever-presence of suggestion is yet another reason that it is so hard to determine the mutative effects of psychoanalysis.

On the other hand, many people—especially but not exclusively Buddhists—consider the self to be an artificial construct, elusive, unstable, and incoherent. Their belief is that the self's drives and desires contribute to frustration and unhappiness. They would shun any narrative of the development of the self as an exercise in illusion—yet another challenge to a potential explanation of how psychoanalysis works.

MODIFICATION OF HABITUAL RELATIONSHIP PATTERNS

People come to treatment with fixed patterns of feelings and attitudes that determine how they regard themselves and how they respond to others. Developed over years, these patterns allow their owners to limit the anxieties and difficulties that unconscious feelings and fantasies lead them to anticipate in their relations with others and within themselves. They are protective, although at a cost; they are rigid, and they do their work by limiting the patient's repertoire of feelings and responses to what are considered safer choices. Andrew's malignant compliance is one example of such a pattern; George's intense competitiveness with and mistrust of authority figures is another. Caroline's pattern defined her as a destructive person whose drive for independence and success would inevitably damage those she cared about. Sarah displayed a similar pattern in the sexual domain; she feared that acting on her sexual desires would ultimately hurt the other person. Jacob kept himself isolated or withdrawn; when he had to engage with others, he resorted to a chameleon-like effort to blend in.

Restrictive patterns like these protect by avoiding actualization of unconscious fears—for instance, compliance may be an effort to avoid unconsciously feared punishment for assertiveness. Thus, they provide some emotional security. But repeated use makes them almost automatic; they stop being a matter of choice. No option is available for appropriate assertiveness. There is no room for flexibility of response. The patient no longer notices the specific context of an experience that might otherwise alter its perception; the experience is shaped to conform to the patient's familiar expectation. It is these *habitual relationship patterns*, as I have called them (Schachter 2002), that are modified in successful treatment. Fonagy (1998) and others have described them as sets of implicit (nonverbal, often nonconscious) mental procedures for regulating emotional relations with others and with the self. Treatment works by modifying these procedures, Fonagy has suggested, rather than by creating ideas learned in treatment.

Two technical factors are associated with positive outcome: patient–analyst compatibility and treatment duration.

Patient–Analyst Compatibility

One element that is increasingly being singled out is patient–analyst compatibility, that mesh of the personal qualities of analyst and patient (Kantrowitz et al. 1989, 1995). One review of many studies of psychotherapy (not psychoanalysis) concluded, "Clearly the person of the therapist is a critical factor in the success of therapy" (Wampold 2001, 202). We know that across many treatments the *therapeutic alliance*, a concept closely related to patient–analyst compatibility, is the best predictor of therapeutic improvement (Luborsky 2000; Novick and Novick 1998). Therapeutic alliance refers to the patient's positive feelings toward the analyst based on the conviction that patient and analyst are working together on the patient's behalf. In addition, the better the alliance, the more intense the attachment to the therapist (Eagle 2003).

There are several examples illustrating the importance of patient–analyst compatibility in these seven case reports. For example, Caroline's analyst knew that Caroline had long felt that her mother was damaged by her wishes to separate from her. With this context in mind, she could sense Caroline's intense anxiety and concern when she was away from her analysis for a time. The analyst adopted the reassuring custom of shaking hands with Caroline and wishing her well at the beginning of any interruption in the analysis. Jacob's analyst was comfortable about acknowledging mistakes and did not get defensive about them. Watt's analyst was comfortable about departing from traditional analytic anonymity by disclosing his personal interest in sports. Andrew's analyst, to help Andrew deal with criticism in his training program, departed even further from traditional anonymity and analytic neutrality by sharing with him both his personal insight and the sources of it in his own experience in psychoanalytic training. A patient like Sarah who felt secure with her analyst's neutrality and anonymity may not have felt comfortable with Andrew's analyst actively providing advice. Similarly, Andrew may have felt insecure and anxious with an analyst who adopted neutrality and anonymity. Patient–analyst compatibility can be critical.

Treatment Duration

Many analysts now believe that Freud did not allow sufficient time for most of his patients to achieve optimal benefits (Thompson 1994). There has been a gradual and continuous increase in analytic treatment duration over the past eighty years as analysts and their patients have recognized the association of duration and benefit and striven to enhance therapeutic results. Galatzer-Levy et al. (2000) found in their critical review of psychoanalytic outcome studies that treatment duration is another element that has been found to be associated with positive outcome. As we have said, because association doesn't provide proof of causation, longer duration cannot be said with certainty to *cause* better outcome. Erle and Goldberg (2003) also found that the longer the treatment duration, the better the outcome, and they noted that four years seemed to mark the minimum duration of analysis before much significant benefit appears.

Psychoanalytic Treatment and Brain Changes

Recent neuroscience investigation (Kandel 1983) offers a speculative answer as to why it might be that longer treatments are associated with greater improvement, namely, that psychotherapy is a form of learning. All learning involves modifications in the patterns of neuronal synaptic transmission in the brain, and this process takes time (Kandel, Schwartz, and Jessel 1991). Learning to ride a bike, for example, involves developing new neural networks in the brain. Brain synapses—the gaps between neurons over which electric impulse propagation takes place through the mediation of active chemical transmitters and receivers— are ultimately the key to the brain's many functions (Le Doux 2002). Synaptic patterns are stabilized by the fact that neural activity keeps synapses alive and active, while unused synapses tend to become less responsive and the chemical transmitters and receivers they need to function less active. Neural activity in a set of synapses prevents synapse decline and thereby stabilizes synaptic patterns.

This is why long-established, repetitive maladaptive defensive patterns are likely to be associated with well-defined synaptic patterns. Habitual use of maladaptive patterns increasingly stabilizes them and their associated neural patterns. Psychotherapy helps the patient switch to a more adaptive pattern; hypothetically, this involves switching to a different, less used synaptic pattern. Metaphorically, it is like abandoning a well-worn, familiar, and therefore safe-feeling toll road in favor of a less costly and faster new route that seems riskier— if only because it is strange. Developing new synaptic patterns takes time (Brickman 2000), and analytic treatment needs to both be intense enough to initiate the process and last long enough to allow it to become firmly established.

Furthermore, unless newly developed synaptic patterns are used frequently, they begin to deteriorate, and the well-established old patterns may reassert themselves as a form of default setting, displacing the newly acquired patterns and reactivating the prior maladaptive ones (Schachter 2002). After termination, actual contact with the analyst or repeated activation in the patient's mind of representations of the analyst may provide reinforcement for the new, more adaptive patterns and prevent the old patterns from reasserting themselves. Patients who had posttermination meetings with their former therapists did not show the diminution in therapeutic improvement over time that was found in patients who had no such meetings (Luborsky 1989). There may be former patients who never think about or communicate with their analysts but whose benefits persist, perhaps because of reinforcement from other relationships.

To date, this intriguing neuroscientific model of analytic therapeutic benefit must be considered highly speculative.

The Seven Cases:
Differences in Analytic Technique

How do considerations like these apply in the real world? The seven people reported here showed marked therapeutic gains. This is not unexpected, as they were selected to demonstrate successful psychoanalytic outcomes. They achieved these gains with seven very different analysts. This is not surprising either. As we have seen, studies suggest that technical variations do not greatly influence outcome. These analysts were chosen to illustrate a spectrum of analytic techniques; they work in styles ranging from the "traditional" to the "relational"—not necessarily in pure culture but in proportions and admixtures that reflect the individual analysts' theoretical convictions, clinical experience, and personalities. ("Traditional" technique emphasizes personal anonymity, a neutral stance toward the patient's conflicts and decisions, and the use of interpretation of the patient's past to increase the patient's self-understanding; the "relational" view holds that a certain amount of self-disclosure by the analyst is inevitable, countenances occasional suggestion and advice, and examines interactions between the patient and analyst in the here and now to provide new experiences and reshape the patient's customary maladaptive ways of relating.)

Sarah's analyst illustrates the traditional viewpoint. She adhered strictly to analytic anonymity: "I told her nothing about my private life. . . . I would not express opinions about social, cultural, or political events." The theoretical rationale for analytic anonymity is to allow the patient's thoughts and fantasies to reflect the patient's own concerns, as accurately as possible, presumably free from the analyst's influence. Minimizing the patient's access to the personal attributes of the analyst is supposed to allow the analyst to function as a "blank screen"— that is, to mirror accurately the patient's own projected feelings. The patient's distortions are highlighted since there is no "reality" to obfuscate the picture the patient paints. These ideas are residues of Freud's earlier one-person model of analytic treatment, in which the analyst strives to be an objective, neutral observer and to use a single, standard, scientific technique with all patients. This analyst felt that her neutral, anonymous attitude, which did not interfere with her empathy and concern for her patient, contributed importantly to Sarah's becoming secure in the relationship.

Other analysts adopted a more "relational" point of view. They used a "two-person" model in which the analyst's influence on the patient–analyst interaction, including the flow of the patient's associations, is taken to be not only unavoidable but also desirable and a central focus of analytic work. Clearly, the degree to which these seven analysts believe it is useful to contribute their own attitudes and values varied widely. Watt's analyst, for example, was more open than some about his personal characteristics and communicated his interest in basketball to his patient, consciously or unconsciously, feeling this would strengthen his bond with Watt. Andrew's analyst was even more markedly relational in his view of treatment and felt that it was important to share with Andrew his own views of issues in the patient's life. He told Andrew that he believed a particular girlfriend was unreasonable in her demands on him, and on another occasion he offered Andrew quite emphatically his own definition of "work."

Although all analysts use both one-person and two-person models to varying degrees, the exaggerated dichotomy helps make clear the characteristics of each position. Wherever the analyst lies on this spectrum, he or she strives to understand any interactions that take place, including the contribution of the analyst's influence.

As we have said, so far no studies have demonstrated that differences in analytic technique affect therapeutic outcome. That is, whatever convictions analysts may feel about the superiority of their own particular techniques, no one technique has been shown to be more effective than others. This has been called the "Dodo effect," a term from *Alice in Wonderland* that refers to the Dodo Bird's announcement that all the entrants in a race have won and all must have prizes. The fact that all seven patients showed marked improvement despite significant differences in technique among their seven analysts further supports the supposition that differences in technique do not determine outcome.

One set of studies (Blatt and Shahar 2004) reported not that differences in analytic technique effected outcome but that psychoanalysis is best suited for introjective patients, those primarily concerned with self-definition or identity, whereas psychotherapy works most effectively with patients concerned with interpersonal relatedness.

The Seven Cases: Common Elements

Underneath the differences, though, lie elements common to all analyses. As we have seen, it is the presence of these in the analytic process, rather than technical differences, that appear to account for psychoanalytic success. Some of these common elements are the growth of mutual fond feelings between patient and analyst, the experience of moments of mutual intense feelings, and the development in the patient of a capacity to express anger at the analyst.

MUTUAL FONDNESS BETWEEN PATIENT AND ANALYST

Mutual development of fond feelings seems to be a regular function of the effort between two people to communicate in such intimate, genuine detail and to forge a trusting relationship. When the analyst communicates (not necessarily directly or verbally) his or her sense that the patient is a worthwhile and lovable person, I think that makes an important contribution to the patient's therapeutic improvement. If an analyst does not experience a genuine fondness for the patient, this should be explored and an attempt made to elucidate both parties' contributions. If the analyst is unable to resolve his or her own contribution to the difficulty in creating such feelings, transfer of the patient to another analyst should be considered. The patient's own loving feelings for the analyst, which also arise in the intimate, caring privacy of the analytic setting, may generate mutative effects as well because recognizing the capacity to be loving can greatly enhance the patient's self-esteem. When these feelings develop in the patient, they offer the opportunity to explore ways of dealing with impossible wishes that may arise, such as the wish to be the analyst's lover or child. Understanding these feelings can help the patient resolve them.

MOMENTS OF MUTUAL INTENSE FEELING

Many analysts believe that "something more" than interpretation is necessary to account for change in psychoanalytic treatment. Stern and colleagues (1998) found that when former patients recall their analyses, they usually remember not interpretations but salient emotional experiences with their analysts. In the same vein, Eagle (2003) suggests "that procedural knowledge and 'rules' [in my terminology *habitual relationship patterns*] . . . require noninterpretive, interactional, and strong emotional experiences in order for them to change" (50). Caroline's experience argues for this view. She thought that her analyst valued pattern recognition and insight (narrative development?) more than she did; what stood out to *her* were moments of mutual intense feeling.

My personal inclination is also to privilege these moments of mutual intense feeling that are common elements in analytic treatment. Caroline herself cites an instance in which her analyst was moved by her story and became teary-eyed. Jacob was moved by his analyst's concerned listening, her toughness, and especially her reaching out to him. When George's analyst departed from his customary analytic stance and told him that he thought it would be a mistake to leave treatment at that point, the experience was critical. Watt's experience of talking about sports with his analyst drove home important realizations, as even more powerfully, did his panic attack after he got openly angry with his analyst for the first time.

EXPRESSING ANGER TOWARD THE ANALYST

One other characteristic common to the six patients who have completed their analyses (Andrew has not yet finished) is that, in one form or another, all were able eventually to experience and express hostility and anger toward their analysts. Whether this is a necessary prerequisite for substantial gain in analytic treatment for all patients is not clear. However, some patients have created unconscious fantasies that their anger has enormous destructive power. If expressed, they fear, it could hurt the person—often a loved person—against whom it is directed, resulting in either terrible loss or an equally terrible retaliatory punishment. When the patient can take the risk of expressing angry feelings toward the analyst, he or she has a chance to see that angry feelings do not destroy the analyst, that the analyst does not retaliate with abandonment or a dreadful revenge, and that the fantasies responsible for these beliefs can be explored and understood. In the exploratory process, the patient can revise the frightening fantasies, allowing the possibility of direct, appropriate, and constructive anger with others to become feasible.

Selecting a Psychoanalyst

If the transformations described in this book move you to seek psychoanalysis, you may be wondering how to choose an analyst. This is a challenging task, and different analysts, surely, would suggest different approaches to the process of selection. My own view is that the patient–analyst relationship is critical to therapeutic outcome and that personality compatibility between patient and analyst should be accorded the greatest weight. So the first step in the process is to understand what makes a good match.

The patient and the analyst need not be alike, but they should like and respect each other, and the patient should be able to feel, even within the constraints of the therapeutic relationship, that the analyst is an authentic person. Patient and analyst need to be able to work together in a spirit of mutuality rather than in an authoritarian or hierarchical way. That is, while the analyst must take a guiding role in the analytic situation, this is because he or she is trained to take this role, to make use of an acquired expertise; it is not because he or she is intrinsically the patient's superior. The analyst should be empathic, a good listener, and above all safe and trustworthy. The patient should feel that this analyst has the capacity to understand what he or she has to say. The analyst should be reasonably self-confident but not arrogant and able to acknowledge a mistake when necessary. To some patients an analyst's capacity for warmth matters a great deal, but that is not universal. However, if the patient actually dislikes the analyst or does not feel valued and respected by the analyst, too heavy a burden is placed on the treatment.

The analyst's gender will probably influence the patient's experience of treatment, so the patient should certainly take any preferences into account. Does race or religious affiliation matter? These are critical for some patients but of little import to others; if critical, the patient should include them among the required characteristics. Does it matter what the analyst's academic degree is? As long as the analyst is well trained, I think that the discipline is of relatively little relevance (as did Freud). A nonphysician analyst can easily refer the patient to a medical consultant for medication if needed, and a patient with an ongoing illness would need to provide a liaison with his or her physicians no matter what the analyst's degree.

Some analysts feel that a patient's preferences are neurotically determined and that rather than choosing for him- or herself, the patient should go to a psychoanalytic consultant and rely on the consultant's recommendations. I believe, however, that although a patient's preferences may be *influenced* by neurotic elements, it is unlikely they are completely a function of those elements or even primarily a function of them. Even patients struggling with very troublesome conflicts have many healthy strengths and can make informed choices. When the patient honors his or her preferences, optimum conditions are established for starting the analytic work. Later in the treatment, if the patient or the analyst decides that change is advisable, this can be arranged. But if the patient's preferences are not met at the outset, work will begin under uncomfortable conditions, and treatment may flounder at its inception. The experience of a failed treatment is very painful. It may also be destructive to the patient, diminishing his or her hope for change and discouraging a second try.

Since there is a good deal at stake financially and emotionally, I urge that prospective patients shop for an analyst the way they might shop for a new home, perhaps meeting with two or three and seeing each at least twice. On the other hand, there are plenty of instances in which a patient impulsively decides to work with the first analyst consulted and ends up with a very satisfying treatment. Patients who have trouble making decisions sometimes get bogged down consulting one analyst after another, and intuition may be more important than method in these cases.

Where are good analysts to be found? I think that the people who know analysts best are their colleagues—other analysts who know them personally as well as professionally. Talk to several analysts, informally if possible. Give them some idea of the kind of analyst you would like and ask for several referrals. If you don't know any analysts, most physicians, psychologists, or social workers can give you some names. You can then set up meetings with these analysts and decide which ones you feel comfortable with. Psychoanalytic organizations have websites that list analysts. Another source of information about an analyst is his or her patients. But no one can refer you to an analyst's patients, and knowing the patients of any particular analyst is a matter of happenstance. Moreover, some analysts object that patients may be too irrational about their analysts to make appropriate judgments. However you do the initial exploration, you can always feel free to question a prospective analyst about his or her training and experience.

Does it matter whether the analyst is a member of the American Psychoanalytic Association (APsaA) or is a training and supervising analyst? If the analyst *is* a member of the APsaA, does it matter whether he or she is "certified"? The APsaA is the oldest psychoanalytic organization in the United States. It is also the most traditional and the most conservative, and not all analysts (or patients) consider this is an advantage. There are excellent psychoanalytic institutes and organizations that are more flexible in their collective viewpoints and their psychoanalytic politics. Although the members of these may not be members of APsaA, this is not a reflection on their dedication and clinical skills, which may be excellent.

Analysts who *have* trained at APsaA-accredited institutes can apply to be certified. An applicant for certification submits for review case reports of several analyses that he or she has conducted and then is extensively interviewed about the analytic work in those cases. This is a *postgraduate* procedure; an analyst need not be certified to be fully trained and experienced. Certification was conceived as a way of identifying analysts of the very highest levels of analytic competence on the belief that only these analysts should be permitted to analyze and supervise other analysts or to make analytic policy.

However, many supremely competent analytic clinicians have no interest in such pursuits and so have no reason to seek certification. Similarly, an analyst who *is* certified may for personal or practical reasons not be motivated to seek appointment as training or supervising analyst; this says nothing about that analyst's therapeutic competence or effectiveness. I myself do not think that certification or training-analyst status is an accurate reflection of therapeutic skill. The motivation to seek them may be as much political as clinical; furthermore, I have some question about the reliability and validity of the certification process. (There are analysts who disagree; they consider the assessment process to be valid and reasonable and to constitute further assurance of the analyst's competence.) All in all, I consider the match between patient and analyst far more important than these professional markers.

If the cost of private analytic treatment is prohibitive, almost every analytic training institute administers a treatment center, and a prospective patient can apply to one of these for analysis. Fees are much lower and take into account the patient's ability to pay. Treatment is conducted by an analyst-in-training and is reviewed regularly by a senior analyst.

This is an excellent resource for many prospective analytic patients, but it raises another question: Is an experienced analyst a better choice than an inexperienced one? Not necessarily. Experience is useful, but newer analysts are building their practices. They are enthusiastic and adventurous, and they are likely to be especially motivated to ensure that a treatment is successful. Interestingly, of the seven markedly successful treatments reported here, two were conducted by inexperienced analysts during their analytic training—this is how George and Watt were able to manage their analyses.

Should a very well-known or famous analyst be given preference? Again, not automatically. Some famous analysts are superb therapists, but some achieve fame for reasons other than their clinical work. They may publish widely or have a particular interest in psychoanalytic politics and administration. But these attributes are not particularly relevant to their devotion to psychoanalytic practice or their effectiveness as therapists.

In summary, given that the analyst is well trained, I believe that it is the quality of the ambience that the patient experiences with the analyst that should be given the greatest weight. A satisfactory patient–analyst relationship and hard work are the two most important ingredients for a successful therapeutic outcome.

Conclusion

Controlled empirical evidence is still lacking that psychoanalysis is more beneficial, on the average, than other forms of psychotherapy. This is perhaps because of how extremely difficult it is to design meaningful studies of such a subjective and complicated undertaking. Clearly, not all analytic treatments produce markedly favorable outcomes. However, the seven analytic patients presented here demonstrate that when analytic treatment *is* effective, a life can be dramatically transformed.

In these reports, both the patients and the analysts elucidate in striking and convincing detail the elements that we believe to be mutative in psychoanalytic treatment—the analyst's confidence that he or she can be helpful; mutual fond feelings between patient and analyst; moments of mutual, intense feeling; and the patient's newly developed capability for appropriately expressing anger. In that same elucidation, they describe—from their differing points of view—the transformation of a life.

These problems of these seven patients had existed for a very long time. The purpose of a controlled empirical study is to rule out all explanations but one; that is the essence of the scientific method as we understand it today. Even in the absence of a controlled study, we can ask ourselves, What else could have accounted for such intensive and extensive changes? What evidence can we find in these seven case reports for an alternative explanation? Could the changes these patients accomplished have been wrought by something other than psychoanalysis—another relationship? another experience? chance?

In relation to these seven treatments, at least, it seems to me plausible to rule out the likelihood that some other relationship or experience—or chance—produced these transformations. Whether or not another psychotherapeutic treatment could effect comparable life transformations awaits comparable documentation. I think that the conclusion that these transformations *were actually produced by psychoanalysis*, although not certain, is the reasonable one and one that may be considered "scientific" insofar as that concept applies to phenomena as subjective and complex as psychoanalysis. As Aristotle (quoted in Franklin 2001, 64–65) observed, "The same degree of precision is not to be sought for all subjects. . . . It is the mark of an educated man to look for precision in each class of things just so far as the subject admits."

Appendix: Current Concerns about Confidentiality and Permission

These are the concerns about confidentiality and permission that were discussed among the contributing analysts as we prepared this book. They reflect familiar issues reviewed over many years in the analytic literature as well as some new ones raised by this project:

What was your initial response to the idea of asking a patient to write about his or her analysis?

How did your feelings develop as the project proceeded?

How did your patient see your request for the written piece?

What impact did the interchange about writing have on the therapeutic alliance? (Aron 2000; Gabbard 2000)

How did you understand your patient's agreement to the request? How did the patient feel about being asked—pleased, flattered, burdened, exploited? (Aron 2000; Pizer 2000)

To what extent is it desirable or undesirable that a patient feel that he or she could be helpful to the analyst? (Pizer 2000)

Does the patient feel that he or she is making a contribution in increasing knowledge about analysis for others? (Reiser 2000; Slochower 1998)

How can we increase the likelihood that that is true?

What kind of knowledge or understanding does an extended piece of writing by a patient about his or her analysis bring to the patient?

What does it bring to the analyst?

What impact does such writing have on terminated cases or future posttermination patient–analyst contact?

If it opens up the question of more treatment, does that seem like a desirable development or a contrived one? (Pizer 2000)

How does the patient's perspective influence the analyst?

What is the impact on the patient of reading what the analyst has written? (Hoffman 1994)

What is the impact on the patient of being "the one" chosen to write?

How does the writing influence the patient's realistic view of the analyst?

How does it influence the patient's fantasies?

What is the impact on the patient of "only relative" confidentiality—since there is always some risk of recognition, no matter how careful the disguise?

Is material of this kind so valuable that more analysts and patients should take these risks? (Stein 1988a, 1988b)

If it is, how can the process be made less risky?

How can we best explore questions like these with our patients and within ourselves?

Bibliography and Suggested Reading

Alvarez, A. 1992. *Live Company: Psychoanalytic Psychotherapy with Autistic, Borderline, Deprived and Abused Children*. London: Routledge.

Arlow, J. 1969. Unconscious fantasy and disturbances of conscious experience. *Psychoanalytic Quarterly* 38: 45–58.

Aron, L. 2000. Ethical considerations in the writing of psychoanalytic case histories. *Psychoanalytic Dialogues* 10: 231–45.

Bader, M. 1996. Altruistic love in psychoanalysis: Opportunity and resistance. *Psychoanalytic Dialogues* 61: 741–64.

Balint, E. 1993. *Before I Was I: Psychoanalysis and the Imagination*. Edited by J. Mitchell and M. Parsons. New York: Guilford.

Baumeister, R. F. 2000. Gender differences in erotic plasticity: The female sex drive as socially flexible and responsive. *Psychological Bulletin* 126: 375–80.

Beebe, B., and F. M. Lachmann. 1988. Mother-infant mutual influence and precursors of psychic structure. In *Frontiers in Self-Psychology*, vol. 3, edited by A. Goldberg. Hillsdale, N.J.: Analytic Press, 3–26.

Beigler, J. S. 1975. A commentary on Freud's treatment of the rat man. *Annual of Psychoanalysis* 3: 271–86.

———. 2002. Personal communication.

Bernstein, J. W. 2001. The trials and tribulations of psychoanalytic writing. Paper presented at Division 39 Spring Meeting, Santa Fe, New Mexico.

Bion, W. 1967. *Second Thoughts*. Reprint, London: Karnac, 1984.

Blatt, S. J., and K. N. Levy. 2003. Attachment theory, psychoanalysis, personality development and psychopathology. *Psychoanalytic Inquiry* 23: 102–50.

Blatt, S. J., and G. Shahar. 2004. Psychoanalysis—With whom, for what, and how? Comparisons with psychotherapy. *Journal of the American Psychoanalytic Association* 52: 393–447.

Brenner, C. 1982. *The Mind in Conflict*. New York: International Universities Press.

Breuer, J., and S. Freud. 1893–1895. *Studies in Hysteria.* Standard ed., 2: 3–181. London: Hogarth Press, 1955.

Brickman, H. R. 2000. Revisiting Freud's "Bedrock": Evolution and the neurobiological turn in psychoanalysis. Paper presented at the meeting of the American Psychoanalytic Association, New York, December 15.

Britton, R. L. 1994. Publication anxiety: Conflict between communication and affiliation. *International Journal of Psychoanalysis* 75: 1213–24.

Cardinal, M. 1983. *The Words to Say It.* Cambridge, Mass.: VanVacter & Goodheart.

Craige, H. 2002. Mourning analysis: The post-termination phase. *Journal of the American Psychoanalytic Association* 50: 507–50.

Daniels, L. 2002. *With a Woman's Voice: A Writer's Struggle for Emotional Freedom.* Lanham, Md.: Madison Books.

Eagle, M. 2003. Clinical implications of attachment theory. *Psychoanalytic Inquiry* 23: 27–53.

Erle, J. B., and D. A. Goldberg. 2003. The course of 253 analyses from selection to outcome. *Journal of the American Psychoanalytic Association* 51: 257–94.

Fonagy, P. 1998. Dual aspects of therapeutic action: Learning from cognitive science. Paper presented at the annual meeting of the American Psychoanalytic Association, Toronto.

Fonagy, P., M. Steele, H. Steele, T. Leigh, R. Kennedy, G. Mattoon, and M. Target. 1995. Attachment, the reflective self, and borderline states. In *Attachment Theory*, edited by S. Goldberg, R. Muir, and J. Kerr. Hillsdale, N.J.: Analytic Press.

Fonagy P., M. Target, and G. Gergely. 2000. Attachment and borderline personality disorder. *Psychiatric Clinics of North America* 23: 103–22.

Franklin, J. 2001. *The Science of Conjecture.* Baltimore: Johns Hopkins University Press.

Freedman, N., J. D. Hoffenberg, N. Vorus, and A. Frosch. 1999. The effectiveness of psychoanalytic psychotherapy: The role of treatment duration, frequency of sessions, and the therapeutic relationship. *Journal of the American Psychoanalytic Association* 47: 741–72.

Freud, S. 1896. *Heredity and the Aetiology of the Neuroses.* Standard ed., 3: 143–56. London: Hogarth Press, 1972.

———. 1900. *The Interpretation of Dreams.* New York: Avon Books.

———. 1909. *Notes upon a case of obsessional neurosis.* Standard ed., 10: 153–318. Reprint, London: Hogarth Press, 1962.

Gabbard, G. O. 2000. Disguise or consent: Problems and recommendations concerning publication and presentation. *International Journal of Psychoanalysis* 81: 1071–86.

Galatzer-Levy, R. M., H. Bachrach, A. Skolnikoff, and S. Waldron Jr. 2000. *Does Psychoanalysis Work?* New Haven, Conn.: Yale University Press.

Goldberg, A. 1995. Homosexuality as compensatory structure. In *The Problem of Perversion: The View from Self Psychology.* New Haven, Conn.: Yale University Press.

———. 2001. Depathologizing homosexuality. *Journal of the American Psychoanalytic Association* 49: 1109–14.

Gottlieb, R. 1989. Technique and countertransference in Freud's analysis of the Rat Man. *Psychoanalytic Quarterly* 58: 29–62.

Greenblatt, S. 1980. *Renaissance Self-Fashioning.* Chicago: University of Chicago Press.

Grünbaum, A. 1993. *Validation of the Clinical Theory of Psychoanalysis: A Study in the Philosophy of Psychoanalysis.* Psychological Issues, Monograph 61. Madison, Conn.: International Universities Press.

Grusky, Z. 1999. Conviction and conversion: The role of shared fantasies about analysis. *Psychoanalytic Quarterly* 68: 401–30.

———. 2002. Conviction and interpretation: Hiding and seeking with words. *Psychoanalytic Quarterly* 71: 81–112.

Gunn, D. 2002. *Woolgathering, Or How I Ended Analysis.* London: Brunner-Routledge.

Heimann, P. 1950. On counter-transference. *International Journal of Psychoanalysis* 31: 81–84.

Hitchens, C. 2003. Blessed are the phrasemakers. Review of *God's Secretaries* by A. Nicolson. *New York Times Book Review,* May 18, 7.

Hoffman, I. Z. 1994. Dialectical thinking and therapeutic action in the psychoanalytic process. *Psychoanalytic Quarterly* 63: 187–218.

———. 1998. Ritual and spontaneity. In *Psychoanalytic Process: A Dialectical and Constructivist View.* Hillsdale, N.J.: Analytic Press.

Isay, R. 1989. *Being Homosexual.* 3rd ed. New York: Farrar, Straus & Giroux.

Kandel, E. R. 1983. From metapsychology to molecular biology: Explorations in the nature of anxiety. *American Journal of Psychiatry* 140: 1277–93.

Kandel, E. R., A. H. Schwartz, and T. M. Jessel. 1991. *Principles of Neural Science.* 3rd ed. New York: Elsevier.

Kantrowitz, J. L., A. J. Katz, D. A. Greenman, M. Humphrey, F. Paolitto, J. Sashin, and L. Solomon. 1989. The patient-analyst match and the outcome of psychoanalysis. *Journal of the American Psychoanalytic Association* 37: 893–919.

———. 1995. The beneficial aspects of the patient-analyst match: Factors in addition to clinical acumen and therapeutic skill that contribute to psychological change. *International Journal of Psychoanalysis* 76: 299–313.

Kardiner, A. 1957. Freud—The man I knew, the scientist, and his influence. In *Freud and the 20th Century,* edited by B. Nelson. New York: Jason Aronson.

Kitto, H. D. F. 1954. *Greek Tragedy: A Literary Study.* Garden City, N.Y.: Doubleday.

———. 1959. *The Complete Greek Tragedies. Vol. II, Sophocles.* Edited by D. Grene and R. Lattimore. Chicago: University of Chicago Press.

Kohut, H. 1971. *The Analysis of the Self.* New York: International Universities Press.

———. 1978. *"Forms and Transformations of Narcissism": The Search for the Self.* New York: International Universities Press.

———. 1984. *How Does Analysis Cure?* Edited by A. Goldberg. Chicago: University of Chicago Press.

———. 1991. *"The Two Analyses of Mr. Z": The Search for the Self.* New York: International Universities Press.

Kolodny, S. 1999. *The Captive Muse: On Creativity and Its Inhibition.* Madison, Conn.: International Universities Press.

Kris, E. 1951. Ego psychology and interpretation in psychoanalytic therapy. *Psychoanalytic Quarterly* 20: 15–30.

Lacan, J. 1977. *Ecrits.* New York: Norton.

Lambert, M., and A. E. Bergin. 1994. The effectiveness of psychotherapy. In *Handbook of Psychotherapy and Behavior Change,* 4th ed., edited by A. E Bergin and S. L. Garfield. New York: Wiley.

Lamot, A. 1994. *Bird by Bird: Some Instructions on Writing and Life.* New York: Knopf.

Le Doux, J. 2002. *Synaptic Self: How Our Brains Become Who We Are.* New York: Viking.

Lipton, S. 1977. The advantages of Freud's technique as shown in his analysis of the Rat Man. *International Journal of Psychoanalysis* 58: 255–74.

Litowitz, B. 2001. Sexuality and textuality. *Journal of the American Psychoanalytic Association* 50: 171–98.

Luborsky, L. 1989. Panel: Evaluation of outcome of psychoanalytic treatment. Should follow-up by the analyst be part of the post-termination phase of analytic treatment? *Journal of the American Psychoanalytic Association* 37: 813–22.

———. 2000. Psychoanalysis and empirical research: A reconciliation. In *Changing Ideas in a Changing World: The Revolution in Psychoanalysis. Essays in Honor of Arnold Cooper,* edited by J. Sandler, R. Michels, and P. Fonagy. London: Karnac.

———. 2001. The meaning of empirically supported treatment research for psychoanalytic and other long-term therapies. *Psychoanalytic Dialogues* 11: 583–604.

Mahony, P. J. 1986. *Freud and the Rat Man.* New Haven, Conn.: Yale University Press.

Marmor, J. 1986. The question of causality. Commentary/Grunbaum: Foundations of psychoanalysis. *Behavioral and Brain Sciences* 9: 249.

McGuire, W. 1974. *The Freud/Jung Letters.* Translated by R. Mannheim and R. F. C. Hull. Princeton, N.J.: Princeton University Press.

Novick, K., and J. Novick. 1998. An application of the concept of therapeutic alliance to sadomasochistic pathology. *Journal of the American Psychoanalytic Association* 46: 813–46.

Ogden, T. H. 1999. *Reverie and Interpretation: Sensing Something Human.* Northvale, N.J.: Jason Aronson.

Pizer, S. A. 2000. A gift in return: The clinical use of writing about a patient. *Psychoanalytic Dialogues* 10: 247–60.

Reiser, L. W. 2000. The write stuff. *Journal of the American Psychoanalytic Association* 42: 351–54.

Schachter, J. 2002. *Transference: Shibboleth or Albatross?* Hillsdale, N.J.: Analytic Press.

Seligman, M. E. P. 1995. The effectiveness of psychotherapy: The Consumer Reports Study. *American Psychologist* 50: 1072–79.

Slochower, J. 1998. Illusion and uncertainty in psychoanalytic writing. *International Journal of Psychoanalysis* 79: 333–45.

Stein, M. 1988a. Writing about psychoanalysis: I. Analysts who write and those who don't. *Journal of the American Psychoanalytic Association* 36: 393–408.

———. 1988b. Writing about psychoanalysis: II. Analysts who write, patients who read. *Journal of the American Psychoanalytic Association* 36: 393–408.

Stern, D. N., L. W. Sander, J. P. Nahum, A. M. Harrison, K. Lyons-Ruth, A. C. Morgan, N. Bruschweiler-Stern, and E. Z. Tronick. 1998. Non-interpretive mechanisms in psychoanalytic therapy: The "something more" than interpretation. *International Journal of Psychoanalysis* 79: 903–21.

Tessman, L. H. 2003. *The Analyst's Analyst Within*. Hillsdale, N.J.: Analytic Press.

Thompson, M. G. 1994. *The Truth about Freud's Technique: The Encounter with the Real*. New York: New York University Press.

Ticho, E. 1972. Termination of psychoanalysis. *Psychoanalytic Quarterly* 41: 325–33.

Wallerstein, R. 1986. *Forty-Two Lives in Treatment: A Study of Psychoanalysis and Psychotherapy*. New York: Guilford.

Wampold, B. E. 2001. *The Great Psychotherapy Debate: Models, Methods and Findings*. Mahwah, N.J.: Lawrence Erlbaum Associates.

Williams, T. 1947. *A Streetcar Named Desire*. Reprint, New York: New Directions, 1980.

Winnicott, D. W. 1971. *Playing and Reality*. New York: Basic Books.

———. 1986. *Home Is Where We Start From*. New York: Norton.

Index

money, emotions around, 36–41, 43–44,
54, 92, 130–40
mothers, issues with, 18–19, 22, 24, 28,
54–55, 59, 76, 84, 85. *See also specific
cases*
mutative factors, in patient
improvements, 15

obsessional neurosis, 10, 11, 13–14
Oedipus complex, 161
Ordinary People (1980), 72

panic attacks, 54, 55, 60, 64–65
parents, issues with, 34–51, 54–55, 63,
76. *See also specific cases*
passivity, 127–48
Paxil, 139
personal narratives, 166–67
play, 86
Portnoy's Complaint (Roth), 57
The Prince of Tides (1991), 88
projection, 109
Prozac, 139–40
psychic dungeon, 113–25
psychoanalysis: analytic interpretation in,
166; brain changes and, 169–70;
common elements in analytic
processes, 171–73; completion of,
24–25; confidentiality of, 5–7,
149–59, 179–80; constructing a
personal narrative in, 166–67; cost
and expense of, 1, 2, 18; decision to
access, 1–2; history of, 1–2; holding
function of, 98–111; low-cost analysis
in, 18; measuring treatment outcomes
of, 2, 6–7; modification of habitual
relationship patterns in, 167–69;
patient-analyst compatibility in, 3, 6,
168; patients' personal experiences of,
5–7, 72–74, 89–93, 122–35, 139–48,
149–59; process and goals of, 1, 3–7;
qualitative characteristics of, 3–5;
silence/talking gaps in, 33–51;
sociopolitical changes and, 1–2;
stabilizing effect of, 98; symptom relief

of, 2; techniques of, 170–71;
termination of, 24–25, 48–50, 68–69,
86–87, 168–69; therapeutic alliances
in, 13–14; therapeutic changes with,
163–69. *See also specific cases*
psychoanalysts: active engagement in
therapy by, 127–48; age/youth of, 18;
here-and-now interpretations of, 12;
measuring effectiveness of therapy,
149–59; patients disappointed by,
20–21, 61, 63–64, 70; patients keeping
in touch with, 17–31; resources for
finding and selecting, 173–77; theory
of technique and personal qualities of,
4–5; training of, 3
psychotherapy, measuring effectiveness of,
163–64, 168

Rat Man, case of, 6–15
receptivity, 109
reflection, 98
rejection, fear of, 23, 57, 66
relationships: brain maps of, 79–81;
prototype of, 80–81, 83. *See also
specific cases*
Renik, Owen, 149
repression, as cause of hysteria, 9

Schachter, J., 80
seducer-seduced relationships, 1–5
self-esteem, 50, 83
self-reflective function, 95–111
self-regulation, 80
Sendak, Maurice, 64
sexual abuse, childhood, 103–11
sexual feelings: as cause of neurotic
symptoms, 9–10, 11; fear of
intercourse, 19; sexual orientation,
case report of, 53–74; toward
psychoanalyst, 42–43; trust and,
91–92
sexual trauma, feelings about, 9, 103–11
Shahar, G., 165
siblings, issues with, 18–19
sleep, 61

About the Contributors

Henry J. Friedman, M.D., is associate clinical professor of psychiatry, Harvard Medical School, and teaching and supervising psychoanalyst, Massachusetts Institute for Psychoanalysis.

Zenobia Grusky, Ph.D., is faculty at the San Francisco Psychiatric Institute Faculty and the Psychiatric Institute of Northern California Clinical Faculty, UCSF.

Maria Ponsi, M.D., is full member of the Italian Psychoanalytical Society (Società Psicoanalitica Italiana) and of the International Psychoanalytical Association.

Arlene Kramer Richards, Ed.D., is IPTAR Fellow, New York Freudian Society Training Analyst, faculty at the Psychoanalytic Association of New York, and member of the American Psychoanalytic Association and the International Psychoanalytic Association.

Joseph Schachter was trained as a clinical psychologist in the Department of Social Relations at Harvard University, obtained his medical degree from New York University-Bellevue Medical School, and received his psychoanalytic training at the Columbia University Center for Psychoanalytic Training and Research. In mid-career he spent a number of years in full-time physiological/developmental research with infants and children. He subsequently returned to psychoanalytic practice and was a training and supervising analyst at the Pittsburgh Psychoanalytic Institute. He is the author of *Transference. Shibboleth or Albatross?* published by Analytic Press (2002). Recently retired, Dr. Schachter now resides in New York City.

Alan Skolnikoff, M.D., is training and supervising analyst at the San Francisco Psychoanalytic Institute, associate clinical professor in the Department of Psychiatry, University of California, San Francisco, and contributing editor to the *Journal of the American Psychoanalytic Association.*

Jeffrey Stern, Ph.D., is lecturer in psychiatry at the University of Chicago Pritzker School of Medicine and Rush University and on faculty at the Chicago Institute for Psychoanalysis.

Susan C. Vaughan, M.D., is assistant professor of clinical psychiatry, Columbia University College of Physicians and Surgeons and faculty at Columbia University Center for Psychoanalytic Training and Research.